French Cultural Debates

Edited by
John Marks and Enda McCaffrey

Monash Romance Studies

Newark: University of Delaware Press

Monash Romance Studies is a series of scholarly publications
devoted to the study of any aspect of French, Italian and
Spanish literature, language, culture and civilization.
It will publish books and collections of essays on specific themes,
and is open to scholars associated with academic institutions
other than Monash.

Proposals for the series should be addressed to the general editor, from whom
details of volumes previously published in the series are available:

Professor Brian Nelson
School of Languages, Cultures and Linguistics
PO Box 11A
Monash University
Melbourne Vic. 3800
Australia.

Fax (+61 3) 9905 2137
Email: brian.nelson@arts.monash.edu.au

First American edition published 2001

Associated University Presses
440 Forsgate Drive
Cranbury, NJ 08512

ISBN 0-87413-780-2

Cataloging-in-Publication Data is on file with the Library of Congress

The cover illustration reproduces, with permission from Rex Features,
a photograph from *Le Nouvel Observateur*, no. 1819, 16-22, septembre 1999

Monash Romance Studies

General Editor: Brian Nelson

MONASH UNIVERSITY
in association with
UNIVERSITY OF DELAWARE PRESS

We would like to thank the
Department of Modern Languages at the
Nottingham Trent University for its generous support
in the production of this volume.

We would also like to thank Trevor Pull
for his invaluable technical assistance.

Contents

Introduction

John Marks and Enda McCaffrey

The contributions to this collection, which deal with a variety of contemporary French cultural debates, can frequently be read as continuations of the broad debate set in motion by Régis Debray when he posed the question, 'êtes-vous démocrate ou républicain?' (Debray 1989). In this seminal article Debray highlights a particular point of confusion in France as it is about to enter the 1990s. The confusion is between 'l'idée de *république* issue de la Révolution française' and 'l'idée de *démocratie*' which is essentially an Anglo-Saxon model (p. 50). Debray suggests that the confusion needs to be cleared up, that the two traditions need to be distinguished, and that it is necessary to make a choice, to be either 'republican' or 'democrat'. His own position is clear. He comes down on the side of the republic: 'La république, c'est la liberté, *plus* la raison. L'Etat de droit, *plus* la justice. La tolérance *plus* la volonté. La démocratie, dirons-nous, c'est ce qui reste d'une république quand on éteint les Lumières' (p. 50). Debray acknowledges that the French Republic[1] can always become more 'democratic', but only by becoming more thoroughly republican, and not by *confusing* the Republic with the idea of democracy:

> Nous le savons bien: il faut mettre plus de démocratie dans notre République. Lui enlever cette mauvaise graisse napoléonienne, autoritaire et verticale; cette surcharge de notables, cet héritage monarchique, cette noblesse d'Etat qui l'empâtent. La République française ne deviendra pas plus démocratique en devenant moins républicaine. Mais en allant jusqu'au bout de son concept, sans confusion. (p. 50)

The series of distinctions that Debray draws between the republican and democratic traditions have been at the very heart of much debate in France from the late 1980s onwards. For Debray, a republic conceives of individuals as free 'citizens' who together compose a nation, whereas democracy conceives of the individual as belonging to a community, a 'tribu'. What is more – and here Debray appears to define the French republican tradition against Anglo-American neo-liberalism – democratic government conceives of the individual as in essence a *productive* animal, born to manufacture and exchange (p. 51). A republic achieves liberty through reason, and is governed by the notion of the 'universal', 'les droits de l'homme universel', whereas democracy functions according to the principle of the local, the 'constituency'. Democracy confuses the public and the private, whereas a republic scrupulously separates the private and the public for the same reasons that it separates the spiritual and the temporal.

---

1. Debray distinguishes in his text between 'notre République' (i.e. the French Republic) and 'la république' as a general concept. We have followed this convention for the Introduction, but elsewhere in the collection we have capitalised the noun 'Republic' (taking this to stand for the French Republic).

The 'nerve centres' of each village in a republic are 'la mairie' and 'l'école'; in other words 'l'Assemblée nationale et la Sorbonne', whereas democracy looks to 'le temple et le drugstore, ou encore la cathédrale et la Bourse' (p. 52). In general terms, a republic places great importance on the notion of society as a form of school, which educates citizens so that they are able to form their own judgements. For democracy, on the other hand, the school must resemble society, and must have as its primary function the creation of a workforce. A republic seeks the adult in the child by means of education, and holds the institution of the school in high esteem, whereas democracy 'panders to' the child in the adult, and neglects the school. A republic respects above all the teaching of philosophy:

En république, la philosophie est une matière obligatoire, qui n'a pas pour fin d'exposer des doctrines mais de faire naître des problèmes. C'est l'école et notamment le cours de philosophie qui, en république, relie d'un lien organique les intellectuels au peuple, quelle que soit l'origine sociale des élèves. (p. 52)

A republic does not confuse education with information, and it favours the *institution* rather than democracy's preference for *communication*. In this way, democracy confers prestige upon journalists, advertising executives, singers, actors, and business people, whereas the republic prefers to elevate teachers, writers and academics. The republic is a 'library', conscious of the debt to the past and of memory which must be preserved, whilst democracy is preoccupied with the immediacy of television (p. 53). A republic prefers considered reflection to the 'vacarme ambiant' of popular culture in a democracy (p. 52).

Democracy is concerned with consensus, using discussion to harmonise differences between individuals. Since consensus can all too easily shade into conformism, democracy needs scandals and 'revelations' in order to confirm who or what is 'in'. The republic, however, is not afraid to acknowledge acute differences of opinion. Whilst it is the case that 'une république malade' runs the risk of becoming authoritarian, democracies are threatened by demagogic tendencies. The republican ideal might seem old-fashioned, and it has certainly fallen out of favour, particularly in an era of global neo-liberalism. However, its values are still worth fighting for as far as Debray is concerned. At a point in time when the free-market policies – the 'rolling-back' of the State – introduced by Thatcher and Reagan in the early 1980s had become firmly established as a new sort of global economic-democratic motor, Debray sought to make the case for the republican State:

Le recul du service public sous couvert de la lutte contre les monopoles d'Etat. Le salut par la privatisation, le mécénat et la sponsorisation, l'alignement des chaînes publiques sur les chaînes privées, et tant de reconversions amplement décrites. La République ne veut pas un Etat fort mais un Etat digne. (pp. 54-5)

The readers of Le Nouvel Observateur, in which Debray's article appeared, were invited to apply their own classification – democrat or republican – to a list of celebrities and politicians, and readers of this collection might do the same. Michel Maffesoli, for example, whose work is discussed in some detail in Max Silverman's chapter, is undoubtedly a 'democrat', or rather a proponent of 'new democracy', as Silverman puts it. As Silverman shows, Maffesoli seeks to emphasise the importance of the 'affective' – that which is spontaneous, ambiguous and life-affirming – in favour of the 'cognitive'. Maffesoli claims that the rediscovery of the playful, affective and the aesthetic has become an *everyday* activity. His celebratory vision of the new freedoms on offer today, of this 'new democracy', which replaces the cognitive constraints of modernity, is essentially post-modern. Silverman shows that Maffesoli's celebratory tone sometimes runs the risk of ignoring problems which might accompany such a post-modern, polymorphous 'socialité'. However, he feels that Maffesoli's work is important and necessary precisely because French intellectual life is still, to a large extent, governed by 'republican dogma'. The crucial point, for Silverman, would be whether Maffesoli's re-enchantment of everyday life could also entail a new ethical dimension to social life.

As for republicans, they are – and perhaps this confirms Silverman's views on the continuing prominence of the republican model – present throughout the collection. David Looseley, for example, in his article on youth music, discusses the way in which Alain Finkielkraut and Marc Fumaroli sought, in the late 1980s, to defend republicanism against the 'democratic' populism of *le tout culturel*, and the cultural democracy of Jack Lang. Similarly, John Marks, in his chapter on *l'affaire Sokal*, draws in some detail on Jacques Bouveresse's intervention in the debate. Bouveresse pours scorn on those French intellectuals who have used scientific material erroneously in order to 'seduce' – a journalistic tendency – readers rather than present rational arguments. 'La République des Lettres' has, in their hands, abandoned its properly republican function of creating, as Debray puts it, an 'organic' link between intellectuals and 'le peuple'. Bouveresse is not suggesting that intellectuals renounce their republican heritage, but, rather, echoing Debray's desire that the Republic goes 'jusqu'au bout de son concept', that intellectuals re-examine the integrity of their republican credentials.

Martin O'Shaughnessy, in his chapter on the 'cinéastes' debate, picks out Frodon's position on cinema and criticism as essentially republican. Frodon argues that all films emerge into the public sphere on an equal footing, regardless of production or advertising budget, and will be judged by critics within this neutral public space. In other words, as Debray argues, the republic is not afraid to judge, since critical judgement will be applied rigorously and fairly. A 'democratic' approach, on the other hand, would, whilst being concerned with consensus and a populist urge not to offend, have no mechanism for equalling-out economic imbalances which exist prior to entry into the public sphere. Ultimately, however, O'Shaughnessy argues that Frodon's republican vision for cinema looks suspiciously like the imposition of the taste of an elite group. He sets up, as an alternative, a vision of 'plural cinemas in collision' as characterised by Comolli.

Finally, José Bové has, as Ben Taylor points out in his chapter on food in France, become nothing less than a symbol of republican values. Jean Viard, writing in *Libération*, sees Bové and Marianne as 'un couple superbe', and Bové's critique of *la malbouffe* is situated firmly within the republican resistance to global neo-liberalism. McDonald's is, for Bové, a key symbol of globalisation, 'la mondialisation anonyme'.

However, such clear-cut categorisations do not tell the whole story. Firstly, the definition of a particular individual as either democratic or republican is, to some extent, a matter of perspective. Régis Debray, for example, is roundly criticised by Jacques Bouveresse for tendencies towards intellectual 'seduction' in his work, which are somewhat un-republican. In other words, the republican-democrat opposition can be seen as a rhetorical device, the genuinely descriptive value of which is rather limited. This brings us to the second point: looked at from a different perspective, republicans often become a little more democratic, and vice versa. José Bové, for example, argues that modern food practices have lost the festive symbolism they once enjoyed, and explicitly criticises the industrialisation of agriculture that was part of *les Trente glorieuses*, surely one of the major achievements of modernising republicanism. Bové's call for a return to the pre-modern significance of food might appear close in tone to Maffesoli's 'democratic'/ post-modern attachment to the affectivities of everyday life.

There also seem to be a number of voices emerging in this collection which are situated, consciously or not, within some sort of middle ground that rejects, or reinterprets Debray's original opposition in new ways. For example, Brian Rigby, in his chapter on Paul Yonnet, a crucial presence in this collection, emphasises that Yonnet has evinced a desire to bring France into the mainstream of mass and popular culture whilst remaining true to republican roots. Rigby suggests that Yonnet's interests – particularly his passion for sport and rock music – and his attitudes mean that, although he is a regular contributor to *Le Débat*, he may not quite fit in with the modernising 'elitist' stance of someone like Alain Finkielkraut. Yonnet is undoubtedly a liberal republican, but, unlike Finkielkraut, he is preoccupied with the dilemma of how to create a modern French Republicanism which acknowledges the everyday cultural and leisure experiences of the French. Again, Yonnet's celebration of popular sociability – the carnivalesque ridicule of politically correct values in *Les Grosses Têtes* would be an example – seems not so far away from Maffesoli's celebration of the everyday. Both Maffesoli and Yonnet invoke, for instance, a sort of Bergsonian vitalism which offers possibilities for a broader, more affective or immediate sociability.

In his chapter on the reception of the PaCS legislation, Enda McCaffrey widens the net of Yonnet's liberal republicanism to include a discussion of his position on sexual difference and particularly on the status of same-sex relations within the Republic. Yonnet accepts that the republican model of a neutral, non-judgemental equality is a properly French way of proceeding, but also recognises that a space needs to be found for difference and identity. Similarly, Gill Allwood, in her chapter on the parity debate, accepts what she sees as the laudable defence of equality and an inclusive universal which pertain to republicanism, but emphasises that parity, like the PaCS, has provided a site in which a radical questioning of universalism and radicalism can take place. Allwood highlights the importance of Wieviorka's work in suggesting ways in which the recognition of cultural diversity might provide a way of articulating universal inclusion with a respect for cultural particularism.

Several broad themes emerge, then, from the collection. The position of intellectuals within the Republic is, for example, an issue which arises at several points. Michael Kelly, in his chapter on the transformations of the French intellectual, illustrates how French intellectuals were effectively 'nationalised' in the immediate post-war period. This 'nationalisation' meant that they enjoyed unprecedented prominence and influence, but also meant that they have found it difficult to adapt to a changing world of global capital and communication. The notion of an 'organic' link between the intellectual and 'le peuple' has perhaps been replaced by more 'democratic' and pluralistic ideals.

In a general sense, several of these essays touch upon the ways in which the links between the Republic and nation are problematised and challenged in an era of globalisation. Georges Salemohamed, in his chapter on *l'exception française*, examines the tension between the exceptionalist republican model, as culturally rooted in work and management practices, and the neo-liberal 'network firm and market philosophy' of globalising capitalism. One tendency which emerges from this tension is characterised by Bové who, like Bourdieu, invokes the construction of an internationalist republicanism as an alternative to older models of protectionism. For Bové, as Taylor points out, the problems of globalisation cannot be resolved simply by a defiant appeal to French patriotism: 'l'agriculture et l'alimentation ne seront pas sauvées dans le cadre de l'Etat-nation contre le reste du monde'.

Finally, the issue of culture itself runs through several of the contributions. Opposing the republican cultural model, as espoused by Finkielkraut and Fumaroli, are the positions of Maffesoli and Teillet. The key issue here is the struggle over what actually constitutes culture and where it is located. As Silverman shows, Maffesoli 'challenges the classic Enlightenment distinction between culture and everyday life; culture is that which is lived in a concrete way, the "habitus of society"'. Teillet, on the other hand, as Looseley shows, calls for 'the popularisation of the "popular": that is, for the traditional principles of *action culturelle* laid down by Malraux to be applied to pop.' Teillet's position is perhaps analogous to Bourdieu's call to universalise the means of access to the universal. In these ways, what it means to be 'républicain ou démocrate' continues to be challenged and redefined.

Bibliography
Debray, R. (1989) 'Etes-vous démocrate ou républicain?', *Le Nouvel Observateur*, 30 novembre – 6 décembre, pp. 49-55.

Popular Conceptions of Gender and the Parity Debate

Gill Allwood

Current controversies around parity were triggered by a simple demand for the equal representation of women and men in political institutions, yet quickly became the site for the continuation of a number of long-running debates. The first of these is the gender debate which has recently been played out in questions concerning the family, the PaCS, bioethics, new reproductive techniques, violence and equality at work. Secondly, parity became a focus for debates about the crisis of representative democracy. Some argued that the exclusion of women was the cause of this crisis; others that it is a symptom of it. In either case, many claimed that parity would resolve the crisis and bring about the 'democratisation of democracy'. Thirdly, at the centre of the parity debate was the question of universalism and particularism, and specifically, how to deal with differences. Finally, French exceptionalism featured in the parity debate. Both the problem of women's under-representation and the proposed solution of parity are portrayed as specifically French and opposed in particular to all that is American.

The pressure of the vociferous and organised campaign for parity and the increasingly clear political interest in supporting it culminated in an amendment of the Constitution.[1] This event, although not unique, is nevertheless institutionally and symbolically significant. It required the agreement on a single text of the right-dominated Senate, the left-dominated National Assembly, the socialist Prime Minister and the conservative President. The Act was passed by a special congress of the two houses which met at Versailles to carry out this exceptional procedure. However, the occasion was somewhat overshadowed by the public debate which surrounded the issue and escalated around the time of the second parliamentary reading of the Bill in February 1999. It took the form of an acrimonious exchange of articles between women, and mostly feminist, intellectuals in the national newspapers and weekly news magazines.[2] The media, rarely admitting the existence of feminism in France, preferring to portray it as an American evil, delighted in the spectacle of feminists divided amongst themselves.

---

1. A special congress of both houses of Parliament met at Versailles on 28 June 1999 and voted 741–42 in favour of inserting in Article 3 of the Constitution: 'La loi "favorise" et non "détermine" l'égal accès des hommes et des femmes aux mandats électoraux et aux fonctions électives' (*Le Monde*, 30 juin 1999, p. 6).

2. See, for example, Agacinski (1999); Perrot (1999); Mossuz-Lavau (1999); Pisier (1999); Roudinesco (1999); Sallenave (1999); Badinter (1999).

Feminists have indeed been deeply divided on parity, as can be seen in the books, articles, conference proceedings and special issues of journals which have appeared on this theme since 1992.[1] The debate which has been conducted in the media does not reflect the diversity of feminist theory on this subject, tending instead to condense the arguments into two opposing poles. This article analyses the popular version of the debate, focusing on the construction of French exceptionalism, sexual difference and universalism, and the struggle over meanings which is a central characteristic of this, as of other, gender debates.

The term 'parity' has acquired a multitude of meanings. At the outset, parity was a relatively straightforward concept, deliberately kept as simple as possible by its advocates, who recognised that the simpler the slogan, the broader the support which could be attracted. And support for the idea that there should be more women in politics was indeed readily available.[2] There are very few who would publicly argue against this principle, although rather more who implicitly oppose it through arguments about women's inferior competence. The underlying disagreements around parity were not so much polarised around pro- and anti-parity arguments (although this format appealed to the weekly news magazines, which tended to exaggerate the binary opposition) as focused on the innumerable interpretations of the term, possible ways of achieving (or, for the less committed, 'working towards') parity, and the implications of these methods for the collective understanding of the republican ideals of universalism, liberty and equality. When the idea of parity moved into the public domain, its primary advocates lost control of its definition.[3] The parity which was demanded by Françoise Gaspard, Claude Servan-Schreiber and Anne Le Gall (1992) – an amendment to the Constitution ensuring numerical equality in elected bodies – was transformed by the media and politicians into one or all of the following: an improvement in women's representation; something very similar to, or indistinguishable from, quotas; and later as a 'catch-all' headline for any articles to do with women, feminism or equality.[4] Significantly, the word 'parity' does not appear in the texts which have been added to the Constitution, having been removed at Chirac's request in order to make the reform more acceptable to the opposition (Bacqué 1998).

However, what had been a fluid and complex debate changed in February 1999 into a fixed and antagonistic opposition between those who supported parity on the grounds of sexual difference (arguing for the recognition of the universal duality of humanity) and those who fiercely opposed such a position because of its implications for the much prized universalism at the heart of the French Republic.

---

1. Examples include Martin (1998); *Nouvelles Questions Féministes* (1994; 1995); *Projets féministes* (1996).

2. For an analysis of opinion polls conducted amongst the general public and amongst politicians on questions relating to the role of women in politics see Sineau (1998).

3. Within academic feminist theory, there were also debates about the meaning of parity and attempts to develop the idea of power-sharing to include the social, economic and domestic as well as political spheres.

4. For example, 'Parité' was the headline of a women's history book review in *Libération*, 16 février 1999.

Amongst the consequences of this polarisation was that it placed those opposed to the particular form which parity was by then taking in the same camp as the most reactionary Senators, deputies and politicians of the far right. During the debates in the Senate, opponents of the Bill took great delight in citing left-wing philosopher Elisabeth Badinter as the source for their arguments. Her husband, Socialist Senator and former Minister for Justice Robert Badinter, made a much quoted speech against parity during these debates, stating explicitly that he shared her views (Gauthier 1999).

French exceptionalism

From the outset, both the under-representation of women in politics and the demand for change were presented by parity advocates and by commentators in France as being particularly French.[1] It was stated that France, instigator of the principle of universal rights, was amongst the last to extend these rights to women and still today has one of the lowest levels of political representation of women in Europe. Similarities with countries throughout the world, in terms of women's representation and action to increase this, were underplayed, as were attempts at the European level to fight for parity. However, in 1993, when parity campaigners were stressing the exceptionalism of France's poor performance, women were under-represented in all European countries. Finland, Denmark, Sweden and Norway all had over 30 per cent in the lower or single chamber (Sineau 1994, p. 276), but in seven European countries, including France, women accounted for 10 per cent or fewer elected national representatives. Although France was placed near the bottom of the league table with 6 per cent women deputies, it did not stand out as an exception (Allwood and Wadia 2000, p. 192).

The claim that the parity campaign was particularly French also needs to be put in perspective. A variety of demands had been made in other European countries, including appeals to the parties to introduce voluntary measures and calls for absolute parity by, for example, the 300 Group in the United Kingdom (*Women of Europe*, 1988, p. 50). Women's place in politics had been on the European agenda since the early 1980s, and the idea of a *démocratie paritaire* was introduced by the Council of Europe in 1989. In France, the origins of the demand are often traced back only as far as the publication in 1992 of *Au pouvoir citoyennes!*, in which Françoise Gaspard, Claude Servan-Schreiber and Anne Le Gall (1992) made the case for constitutional reform, but in the international, and particularly European, context, this was not the revolutionary idea it was often claimed to be.

An aspect of the French campaign which is exceptional, however, is its narrow focus on constitutional reform. European initiatives have encouraged a broad range of measures intended to address the problem of women's under-representation at the individual and structural level and to engage governments and parties in processes of change. These include training, childcare provision, data bases of potential women candidates, funding for women's groups in parties,

---

1. See, for example, Gaspard, Servan-Schreiber, and Le Gall (1992).

quotas for public appointments and the revision of candidate selection procedures (Leijenaar 1996, p. 30). Many of these measures have been discussed in France, but the idea of changing the Constitution fired the imagination of the original campaigners and of key political figures, who recognised parity's potential at a time when public confidence in the political elite was low. Lionel Jospin and Jacques Chirac became involved in a contest to appear more 'modern' than the other, and parity became a symbol of the modernisation of political life.[1] At this level it was argued that women are closer to everyday concerns than men.[2] Their greater participation in decision-making would bridge the gap between the political elite and the people and restore public confidence in the system of representation. As political rhetoric, this line of argument is unsurprising. When it is taken up in the public arena by philosophers and political scientists, however, it tells us much about current ideas of representation and gender. These are discussed in detail later in this chapter.

The narrow focus of the French campaign has had its advantages: it mobilised support across a broad spectrum and, in combination with fortuitous political circumstances, achieved constitutional reform. It is, however, neither the only, nor arguably, the best way to bring about the equal presence of men and women in politics. The amendment to the Constitution only reiterates the principle of equality which is already in the preamble and does not explicitly require equality of outcome. It remains to be seen what concrete effects it will have, especially in single-candidate constituency elections.

The portrayal of gender relations in France as specifically French has been evident throughout the post-68 period. From its baptism by the press in 1970, the *mouvement de libération des femmes* was compared with the American women's liberation movement, usually in tones which suggested how fortunate French men and women were not to be American and therefore immersed in a war of the sexes. The French, with their gift for seduction and with the special understanding or complicity between the sexes are portrayed as superior to Americans, who are at the mercy of feminists and unable to speak or act freely because of the tyranny of political correctness. Feminism, in this popular representation, is typically American. If mention is made of French feminists, it is brief and dismissive, and usually refers only to a historical aberration of the 1970s (Allwood 1998, pp. 38-41).

This popular representation of national gender relations has provided one of the contexts in which the parity debate has been conducted. The representation of minorities or group interests is portrayed as American and as a threat to republican universalism which is valued by almost all participants in the debate.

---

1. Jospin's election platform included a commitment to increasing women's representation, and Chirac, in a speech at Rennes, 4 December 1998, underlined the importance of opening up political life which would allow for constitutional reform favouring the access of women to posts of political responsibility (*Le Monde*, 6-7 décembre 1998, p. 5).

2. Lionel Jospin, in the speech he gave at the special congress of the National Assembly and the Senate at Versailles in June 1999 (http://www.premier-ministre.gouv.fr/PM/D280699A.HTM, accessed 9 October 1999).

Similarly, the threat of the disappearance of sexual difference is invoked as something against which France must be protected.

Sexual difference

Sexual difference – its origins and implications – occupies a central position in many French cultural debates, and has become one of the key points of contention in relation to parity. French feminists, perhaps more than their counterparts elsewhere, have always been divided around difference. A very crude opposition can be identified between, on the one hand, those who believe that women and men are intrinsically different, but that this should not be the basis for inequalities between them and, on the other hand, those who believe that, in all important respects, men and women are the same, and there are no grounds for differentiating between them. In Britain and the United States, this opposition divided the women's movements in the 1970s, but became less pronounced in the 1980s, as Black and lesbian feminists criticised the false homogeneity of the category 'women', and poststructuralist theory challenged the notion of the unified subject. Equivalent French debates remained far more polarised, however, with the 'sameness' position dominating (Allwood 1998, pp. 63-9). The parity debate has witnessed an upsurge in 'difference' arguments, which emphasise sexual difference and insist on its recognition in, and relevance to, the law and politics.

The starting position for arguments in favour of improving women's political representation is that they are excluded from politics *as women*, and it is unlikely that this discrimination will be overcome without reference to gender (Gaspard 1994). Neither the equal right of all citizens – men and women – to be elected, nor the 'natural evolution of society' have succeeded in producing political institutions with anywhere near equal numbers of men and women. But once sexual difference is named, other questions are thrown up: will women find a place in politics *only* because they are women? Will their difference be used to other – less positive – ends? And why *sexual* difference – what about other differences? Feminists are once again caught in the paradox of having to draw attention to difference in order to fight for its eradication as a reason for inequality.

Some parity supporters (including, for example, Gaspard 1999, p. 20; Viennot 1994) have worked within this paradox. They argue that the aim of parity is to reach a point at which sexual difference will be socially, politically and culturally irrelevant, but that, in order to do this, it is necessary to pass through a phase in which difference is named, otherwise it will remain invisible.

This argument runs into most difficulties when it is confronted with the question of why parity applies only to women and not to other under-represented or excluded groups. In other words, why is sexual difference different from other differences? It is easy to understand why this single-issue campaign is so insistent on maintaining the focus on its objective, especially given the panic which the mention of claims for the recognition of identities can induce in France and the way in which this panic is used explicitly to oppose parity. However, the sometimes violent denial of parallels between inequalities based on gender and those based on other differences can shock outside observers.

Many parity supporters are reluctant to justify their call for the recognition of sexual difference on the grounds of natural or biological difference, but it is difficult to sustain opposition to claims from other social groups unless it can be argued that sexual difference is somehow different from other differences. There are several ways in which this is done. The specificity of sexual difference is said to reside firstly in the fact that women are present in all social categories and therefore do not form a category of their own (Gaspard 1997, p. 123; 1999, p. 20). Gender theorists brought up on the idea of intersections will find this unconvincing. Black, disabled and homosexual people are also present in other social categories, including the category 'women'. Individuals are situated in numerous social categories at any one time, the complex interactions between them contributing to the construction, and reconstruction, of identity and to the positioning of the individual on numerous axes of power.

Secondly, it is claimed that sex is different from all other categorisations, because it is immutable and is the only one recognised by French law and noted on the birth certificate (Gaspard 1997, p. 123). This, too, is highly contentious. Firstly, the fact that the law has chosen to emphasise this difference above all others tells us nothing about the difference itself. The law constructs social reality and social categories just as other institutions do and, if feminist critiques are to be believed, is amongst the stalwarts of patriarchy. So to use its construction of gender as justification for an argument in favour of women is somewhat contorted. Gaspard's suggestion (1999, p. 20) that gender is more inescapable than religion, colour or class is also unconvincing, perhaps especially in the case of colour. Gaspard presents 'métissage' as an 'escape route' which is not available in the case of gender. This too depends on social and historical context: the example of South Africa under Apartheid demonstrates the limitations of 'métissage' as a way to 'escape one's identity'. The gender of an individual may be very deeply entrenched and intricately bound up with their subjectivity and their social and cultural experiences, but it is also in constant construction, and is neither fixed nor immutable. Gender theorists in France, as in Britain and the United States, have questioned the binary opposition of masculine and feminine, highlighting the heterogeneity of both terms and the difficulty of establishing a clear division between them. The reluctance in France to use the term gender means that for many theorists it is very closely attached to, if not identical in meaning with, biological sex, which is indeed quite difficult, although not impossible, to change. However, even here, there are suggestions that sex itself is a social construction. Feminist biologists have attempted to demonstrate that even biological sex is not a binary division, but is instead a continuum (Peyre, Wiels and Fonton 1991; Wiels 1999).

There does not seem to be a coherent case for parity which does not lead one to ask why other oppressed groups should continue to be marginalised from politics, but campaigners intent on achieving the single aim of parity have tried to avoid engaging with what they see as a diversion. The odd exasperated comment by an advocate of parity responding once again to this question stresses that the parity campaign cannot do everything, and should not be criticised for failing to achieve what it never set out to achieve. And this seems more honest than the somewhat tangled argument that women do not constitute a category, and that parity would therefore not set a precedent for any other claims for representation. Eliane Viennot (1996, p. 184), for example, states that the aim of the parity campaign is not to correct all the inequalities in contemporary French society, but simply to bring about equality between men and women in elected institutions. She and others argue that the campaign does not have to be opposed to attempts to improve the representation of foreign residents and sexual minorities, for example, and that support for parity does not exclude the possibility of fighting for other transformations in the functioning of representative democracy. Viennot writes:

> Ceci étant, je crois que l'on doit assumer les limites de la parité, en disant clairement qu'elle n'a pas pour objectif de réaliser l'égalité entre les êtres humains, mais entre les hommes et les femmes. Ce qui suffit à légitimer la parité, mais ne suffit pas à satisfaire toutes celles et tous ceux qui ont aussi comme aspiration de changer le monde et dont nous faisons partie. Le combat pour la parité ne prendra pas la place des combats pour la justice et il ne faudrait surtout pas refuser l'un au nom de l'autre. (1996, p. 184)

The differentialist tendencies, which have been present in the parity campaign from the beginning, became more vocal in 1999. One of their most prominent exponents is Sylviane Agacinski, whose views have received wide exposure and authority. Antoinette Fouque and Luce Irigaray may share some of her opinions, but they have not had the same impact. It is difficult to know how pertinent it is that she is married to the Prime Minister, but it is not implausible that this has added credence to her arguments, and that they are having some influence at a policy-making level, if only in shaping the contours of 'scientific opinion' within which policy is formed. Agacinski's articles are polemical and do not engage with gender theory, aspects of which are simply rejected. She states, for example, that 'que l'être humain soit sexué, qu'il naisse garçon ou fille, qu'il puisse devenir père ou mère (mais non les deux à la fois, telle est la contrainte de la dichotomie des sexes), cela n'est pas politique – quoi qu'en disent Judith Butler et quelques autres' (Agacinski 1999). These 'quelques autres' include French and non-French gender theorists who have been working in this area for the last thirty years and have developed complex and contradictory understandings of the meaning of gender which do not easily reduce to a binary opposition between two distinct and homogeneous groups of 'men' and 'women', as Agacinski suggests.

Although she stresses (1998, p. 151) that equality does not necessarily mean sameness and that there is no reason to assume that sexual equality would mean the end of sexual difference, her conception of difference is binary and applies only to the difference (in the singular) between men and women. These two uncomplicated and complementary incarnations of humanity are its essential components – humanity is universally dual. Agacinski believes that this duality does not rule out the possibility of equality between the two. Indeed, once their essential difference is recognised, new and equal gender relations can be constructed. Motherhood is a central component of the femininity which Agacinski reveres and which, in her view, was wrongly rejected by Simone de Beauvoir and her followers. Agacinski wants equality between two categories, but they must remain diametrically opposed. This is because, without sexual difference, everyone would be the same and life would be dull: 'Quoi de plus ennuyeux à imaginer qu'un monde où le masculin et le féminin s'effaceraient au profit d'une uniformité unisexe ou asexuée?' (1998, p. 151) But why should such a world be uniform? Why should it not be infinitely diverse?

As far as women's presence in politics is concerned, one of the consequences of differentialist arguments is that decisions are claimed to be illegitimate unless they are made by equal numbers of men and women. This contradicts traditional republican views of representation, in which the elected representative acts in what he (and less often, but theoretically equally, she) believes to be the best interest of the sovereign people. It also contradicts the view of representation which holds the representative accountable for his/her actions to the voters who elected him/her. Finally, in refusing to admit the legitimacy of claims from other excluded groups, differentialist arguments contradict the model of representation in which representative bodies reflect the composition of the electorate. Interestingly, this was the image of representation chosen by Jospin in the speech he gave at the special congress of the National Assembly and the Senate at Versailles in June 1999:

> Il faut donc agir, afin que notre démocratie représentative soit le reflet aussi fidèle que possible du corps électoral pour que nos concitoyens, ayant des élus qui leur ressemblent davantage, se sentent plus proches d'eux et pour que notre démocratie, profondément renouvelée par la féminisation, gagne en dynamisme, en vitalité, en imagination. (http://www.premier-ministre.gouv.fr/PM/D280699A.HTM, accessed 9 October 1999)

In this view, however, the only way in which elected representatives would resemble their voters is in their sex. No mention is made of other differences between voters and the political elite.

Parity is advocated by those who believe that women should be able to exercise their right to participate in the body which represents the will of 'the people' or 'the nation' and also by those who believe that women should be present in the representative body in order to represent 'women's interest'. This latter position is the most difficult to reconcile with the view of representation outlined above and also raises the question of whether groups can be adequately represented only by their own members. If this is the case, it is difficult to deny the claims to representation of all groups. Unless representatives are accountable to their electorate, however, there is no assurance that a woman, simply because she is biologically female, will represent the interests of other women, and this lack of attention to what women would do once present in decision-making bodies worries left-wing feminist theorists such as Michèle Le Doeuff (1995) and Eleni Varikas (1995). Varikas for example, is particularly critical of the idea that feminists should support parity on the basis that women are best represented by women, regardless of political programme or policy objectives:

> Depuis quand a-t-on transformé le féminisme d'un projet pour l'auto-émancipation des femmes – projet politique à construire – en idéologie qui postule que les femmes ont toujours raison? Depuis quand avons-nous converti la confiance dans la dynamique libératrice d'un tel projet en confiance dans la capacité intrinsèque des femmes (de toute femme) de mener une meilleure politique que les hommes (que tout homme)? (1995, p. 100-1)

Women do not express themselves *as women* on every question, because they never form part of only one group, and their loyalty to a certain group varies according to the question. So do women constitute an interest? Can they be shown to constitute a coherent category whose views differ from those of men? Studies in other countries have revealed that in most areas, including 'women's issues', women's views overlap with men's, and divisions between parties are clearer than those between men and women of different parties (Lovenduski and Norris 1993, p. 6). However, Lovenduski and Norris' study of British politics shows that, although party is the most important factor, gender does make a difference to policy interests, political activity and support for women's rights (Norris 1996, pp. 103-4). There is also some evidence to suggest a gender gap in attitudes towards the environment, welfare and military spending (Sineau 1992, p. 488). So women probably do constitute an interest different from men, even if this is heterogeneous and cut through by many other divisions, but there is little evidence to support the argument that more women in parliament would better represent this interest.

Differentialist arguments suggest that there is an essential difference in men's and women's perspectives which requires both groups to participate in making decisions which affect a nation made up of men and women. This does not fully address the question of *which* women are represented by these women representatives, who are not only women, but are of a particular class, ethnic and political background.

Universalism

Universalism has been the principle on which many of the opponents to constitutionally imposed parity have based their arguments. Most parity supporters have not rejected universalism, however, but have instead argued that it needs to be modified. Three conceptions of universalism dominate the debate, and they are discussed below. They can be referred to crudely as 'traditional republican', 'dual' and 'multiple'.

The first group of universalists, which includes philosopher Elisabeth Badinter (1999) and Socialist Senator Robert Badinter (1999), is firmly attached to this fundamental principle of the French Republic, according to which all citizens are equal, regardless of their differences. Differences are not denied, but are effectively ignored. They are perceived as irrelevant to an individual's public life, belonging in the private sphere.[1] Elisabeth Badinter concedes that the principle of universalism has not yet been fully applied, but argues that this is no reason to abandon it as an ideal.

According to Elisabeth Badinter (1997), the importance of universalism is that it protects against the dangers of communitarianism and the fragmentation of the one and indivisible Republic. Parity contradicts the principle of universalism by making a difference relevant. This reinforces a difference which, as a social construct – and one which causes inequalities – should instead be diminished. It increases the possibility of it being used against women in the future, and it will lead to claims by other communities. In addition, by making sexual difference special, it does not address the issue of discrimination and does not reinforce the principle that *everyone* is equal regardless of their differences.

Badinter opposes measures which draw attention to differences, rather than minimising their relevance. She claims that her ideal is an inclusive universalism. However, she does not suggest how this can be achieved without the explicit recognition of differences and the implementation of corrective measures aimed at bringing it about. Simply ignoring or denying the existence or relevance of these differences in the name of the abstract universal has obscured the way in which women are excluded.

The second vision of universalism examined here coincides with the differentialist position in the gender debate discussed above, and is most clearly defended by Sylviane Agacinski (for example, 1998, p. 15; 1999). In direct conflict with Badinter, Agacinski argues that parity does not endanger universalism, but provides a way of perfecting it. In her view, humanity is universally and intrinsically dual; clearly divided into two – opposite and heterosexual – sexes/genders. She argues that when the 'duality' of humanity is recognised and reflected in sites of decision-making, the universal will become 'concrete', and democracy will become truly democratic. She agrees with Badinter that all citizens are equal regardless of their difference(s), but claims that sexual difference has a separate status.

Parity has a very broad base of support, and it would be wrong to suggest that Agacinski's views are unanimously endorsed. It is significant, however, that few parity supporters have publicly distanced themselves from her arguments,[2] and that these arguments have been so readily and widely accepted. Agacinski's original article in *Le Monde* (1999) provoked far less surprise than the manifesto against parity which was published in response by fourteen women intellectuals, including Elisabeth Badinter and Evelyne Pisier (*L'Express*, 11 février 1999). They argue that parity contradicts the principle of universalism, that it essentialises

---

1. This split between the public and private sphere has been the subject of much criticism by feminists who expose the impact it has had on women's lives and on the issues which are allowed onto the public agenda, hence the slogan of the 1970s women's movements, the private is political. By organising as women, they claimed a group identity and challenged the idea that their membership of this group was irrelevant to their experience as equal citizens.

2. Perrot (1999) is a notable exception. Here she engages with Agacinski, arguing that basing a political claim on a biological difference is a step backwards.

difference, that it makes victims of women and that, given the popularity of the idea, it is unnecessary to change the Constitution in order to achieve something which will happen anyway.

A third interpretation of universalism by participants in this debate, although not those who have the greatest media exposure, is the attempt to construct a vision of the universal which permits the recognition of multiplicity. This has the advantage of not ignoring the differences within the categories 'men' and 'women'. Those who adopt this position (including Pisier and Varikas 1997; Collin 1995; Hirata, Kergoat, Riot-Sarcey and Varikas 1994) argue that replacing a falsely neutral abstract universal with a two-gendered universal is not the solution. Parity would hide the heterogeneity within the categories men and women, legitimise the historically constructed difference between them, and be a representation of *some* women, while claiming to represent them all. Françoise Collin (1995, p. 73) argues that democracy should reintegrate humanity not as an abstract concept, but in all the plurality of its existences, with a migrant and multilingual citizenship.

Proposals for a democracy which would recognise multiple differences are at the centre of many Anglo-American debates on citizenship (for example, Lister 1997; Vogel 1991; Yuval-Davis 1997, pp. 68-92). Feminism and anti-racism have challenged the notion of citizenship and forced an examination of the potential tension between its traditional emphasis on universality and integration and a more pluralist approach, based on a recognition of diversity and difference (Lister 1990, p. 453). A major problem for French theorists arguing for the recognition of multiple group identities and their collective demands, however, is the strength of the republican resistance to communitarianism.

Michel Wieviorka claims that the debate on multiculturalism is practically impossible in France, where it is seen to endanger political life and institutions (1997, pp. 5-6). Particularisms are confined to the private sphere and all identity-based or communitarian demands are rejected and criticised. He describes an unconditional defence of the 'modèle républicain d'intégration', an expression used since the mid-1980s to refer to two distinct logics. The first attempts to eliminate cultural differences, while the second is more tolerant of them. However, both are expected to respect the rules of the Republic, which is seen as the best defence against intercommunity tensions, violence, political and cultural fragmentation and the destruction of democracy. As Danilo Martuccelli writes in the same volume, 'l'appel à la tradition républicaine sert toujours de support à la diabolisation et au refoulement de toute exigence identitaire' (1997, p. 69). Wieviorka claims that this is often accompanied by stereotypical representations of immigrant populations and scorn for American debates around multiculturalism and political correctness (1997, p. 6). The contributors to Wieviorka's edited volume argue that the recognition of cultural diversity does not necessarily weaken democracy, and what is needed is a way of articulating, on the one hand, universal references to the law and to reason and, on the other hand, respect for cultural particularisms, even when they are expressed in the public sphere.

The republican universalists laudably defend the principle of equality between citizens and claim to advocate an inclusive universal. However, in the name of equality, they can ignore discriminations and reject attempts to rectify them. It was this which enabled the Constitutional Council to overturn the law permitting the introduction of quotas in municipal elections which was passed by Parliament in 1982.[1] Similar arguments were the greatest threat to the success of the parity Bill seventeen years later. Had it not been for the insistence by parity campaigners that gender matters, then it is difficult to imagine any change in the gendered composition of elected bodies. Parity campaigners must be given credit for putting the under-representation of women firmly on the political agenda and keeping it there until the reform was achieved.

Conclusion

Parity is a site in which the radical questioning of universalism, exceptionalism and gender can take place. The debate which it has stimulated is rich and diverse. At a time when the gender debate was stuck in the sterile ground of sameness versus difference, parity has offered an arena in which ideas of plurality and multiplicity could be explored. Rather than including women in a citizenship constructed by and for men or conceiving a separate women's citizenship, with the dangers inherent in such essentialist diversions, it has been possible to argue in favour of a plural citizenship, recognising diversity and equality. This continues to develop, although the public debate on parity allows only glimpses of the rich debate which is taking place on this issue amongst feminists, lawyers, political scientists and philosophers. Instead, it focuses on a small number of well-known intellectuals who, if they are women, are referred to as feminists and understood to speak for all women/feminists. While feminist and gender theory has developed increasingly sophisticated visions of gender as a complex, contradictory and changing relation, public debate in France still tends to represent it as a binary opposition and one that must be maintained at all costs.

As with many issues placed on the agenda by women/feminists, parity has undergone radical redefinitions and reinterpretations. The wording of the constitutional reform is far more timid than that which was originally demanded, and the discourse which surrounds it and which could frame its interpretation and implementation has differentialist tendencies. However, the debate is not closed and the definitions are not fixed. Parity has the potential to promote radical change throughout politics and civil society, and some activists and theorists have found in it a framework for thinking about all kinds of equality and power sharing in other spheres. It is true that parity is not a novel idea. It does not radically change feminist thought, parts of which have always striven to achieve equality – with or without the recognition of difference – in politics, society and the family. But for some theorists, parity does act as a coherent framework within which these projects can be pursued.

---

1. For an excellent contemporary critique of this ruling, see Loschak (1983). For recent commentaries, see Martin (1998).

Bibliography

Agacinski, S. (1998) 'L'Universel masculin ou la femme effacée', *Le Débat*, no. 100, mai-août, pp. 149-57.

Agacinski, S. (1999) 'Contre l'effacement des sexes', *Le Monde*, 6 février, p. 1.

Allwood, G. (1998) *French Feminisms*, London: UCL.

Allwood, G. and Khursheed, W. (2000) *Women and Politics in France 1958-2000*, London and New York: Routledge.

Bacqué, R. (1998) 'Egalité ou "parité" entre les hommes et les femmes?', *Le Monde*, 15 décembre, p. 6.

Badinter, E. (1997) 'Nous ne sommes pas une espèce à protéger', *Le Nouvel Observateur*, 23-7 janvier, pp. 38-40.

Badinter, E. (1999) 'La Parité est une régression', *L'Evènement du jeudi*, 4 février, pp. 86-9.

Badinter, R. (1999) 'On ne peut parler de parité qu'au niveau de candidatures', *Le Monde*, 14-15 février, p. 6.

Collin, F. (1995) 'L'Urne est-elle funéraire?', in M. Riot-Sarcey, (ed.) *Démocratie et Représentation*, Paris: Kimé, pp. 45-75.

Fassin, E. (1997) 'L'Epouvantail américain', *Vacarme*, septembre-novembre, nos. 4-5, pp. 66-8.

Fontenay E. de (1999) 'L'Abstraction du calcul contre celle des principes', *Le Monde*, 25 février, p. 16

Gaspard, F. (1994) 'De la parité: genèse d'un concept, naissance d'un mouvement', *Nouvelles questions féministes*, vol. 15, no. 4, pp. 29-44.

Gaspard, F. (1997) 'La Parité: pourquoi pas?', *Pouvoirs*, vol. 82, pp. 115-25.

Gaspard, F. (1998) 'La Parité, principe ou stratégie?', *Le Monde diplomatique*, novembre, pp. 26-7.

Gaspard, F. (1999) 'Ajuster la Constitution à la réalité sociale', *Le Monde des débats*, avril, p. 20.

Gaspard, F., Servan-Schreiber, C. and Le Gall, A. (1992) *Au pouvoir citoyennes!*, Paris: Seuil.

Gauthier, N. (1999) 'Le Sénat braque, les femmes trinquent', *Libération*, 27 janvier, p. 13.

Hirata, H., Kergoat, D., Riot-Sarcey. M. and Varikas, E. (1994) 'Parité ou mixité', *Politis: la revue*, no. 6, février, mars, avril, pp. 117-8.

Le Doeuff, M. (1995) 'Problèmes d'investiture (de la parité, etc.)', *Nouvelles questions féministes*, vol. 16, no. 2, pp. 5-80.

Leijenaar, M. (1996) *Comment créer un équilibre entre les femmes et les hommes dans la prise de décision politique: Guide pour la mise en oeuvre de politiques visant à accroître la participation des femmes à la prise de décision politique*, Commission européenne, Direction générale 'Emploi, relations industrielles et affaires sociales', Unité V/D. 5.

Lister, R. (1990) 'Women, Economic Dependency and Citizenship', *Journal of Social Policy*, vol. 19, no. 4, pp. 445-67.

Lister, R. (1997) *Citizenship: Feminist Perspectives*, Basingstoke and London: Macmillan.

Loschak, D. (1983) 'Les Hommes politiques, les "sages" (?)... et les femmes (à propos de la décision du Conseil constitutionnel du 18 novembre 1982)', *Droit social*, 2, février, pp. 131-7.

Lovenduski, J. and Norris, P. (1993) *Gender and Party Politics*, London, Thousand Oaks and New Delhi: Sage.

Martin, J. (ed.) (1998) *La Parité: Enjeux et mise en oeuvre*, Toulouse: Presses universitaires du Mirail.

Martucelli, D. (1997) 'Les Contradictions politiques du multiculturalisme', in M. Wieviorka (ed.), pp. 61-82.

Mossuz-Lavau, J. (1999) 'Les Antiparitaires se trompent', *Le Monde*, 25 février, p. 17.

Norris, P. (1996) 'Women Politicians: Transforming Westminster?' in J. Lovenduski and P. Norris (eds.)*Women in Politics*, Oxford and New York: Oxford University Press, pp. 91–104.

Nouvelles Questions Féministes (1994) 'La Parité "pour"', vol. 15, no. 4.

Nouvelles Questions Féministes (1995) 'La Parité "contre"', vol. 16, no. 2.

Perrot, M. (1999) 'Oui, tenter cette expérience nouvelle', *Le Monde*, 25 février, p. 17.

Peyre, E., Wiels J. and Fonton, M. (1991) 'Sexe biologique et sexe social', in M.- C. Hurtig, M. Kaïl and H. Rouch (eds.) *Sexe et genre: de la hiérarchie entre les sexes*, Paris: Editions du CNRS, pp. 27-50.

Pisier, E. (1998) 'L'Ombre et ton ombre', *Le Débat*, no. 100, mai–août, pp. 166-73.

Pisier, E. (1999) 'Contre l'enfermement des sexes', *Le Monde*, 11 février, p. 12.

Pisier, E. (2000) 'Sexes et sexualités: bonnes et mauvaises différences', *Les Temps modernes*, no. 609, juin-juillet-août, pp. 156-75.

Pisier, E. and Varikas, E. (1997) 'Femmes, République et démocratie. L'autre dans la paire?', *Pouvoirs*, no. 82, pp. 127–43.

Projets féministes (1996) 'Actualité de la parité', nos. 4-5, février.

Roudinesco, E. (1999) 'Une parité régressive', *Le Monde*, 25 février, p. 12.

Sallenave, D. (1999) 'Manifeste' *Le Monde*, 11 février, p. 12.

Sineau, M. (1992) 'Droit et démocratie', in G. Duby and M. Perrot, (eds.) *L'Histoire des femmes 5*, Paris: Plon, pp. 471-97.

Sineau, M. (1994) 'Femmes en chiffres', in G. Halimi (ed.) *Femmes: Moitié de la terre, moitié du pouvoir*, Paris: Gallimard, pp. 272-83.

Sineau, M. (1998) 'La Féminisation du pouvoir vue par les Français-es et par les hommes politiques', in Martin (1998), pp. 61–81.

Touraine, A. (1999) 'L'Enjeu caché de la parité: unir l'égalité et la différence', *Le Monde des débats*, mai, p. 23.

Viennot, E. (1994) 'Parité: les féministes entre défis politiques et révolution culturelle', *Nouvelles questions féministes*, vol. 15, no. 4, pp. 65-89.

Varikas, E. (1995) 'Une Représentation en tant que femme? Réflexions critiques sur la demande de la parité des sexes', *Nouvelles questions féministes*, vol. 16, no. 2, pp. 81-127.

Viennot, E. (1996) Contribution to seminar 'Actualités de la parité', *Projets féministes*, 4-5, février.

Vogel, U. (1991) 'Is Citizenship Gender-Specific?', in U. Vogel and M. Moran (eds.) *The Frontiers of Citizenship*, Basingstoke and London: MacMillan, pp. 58-85.

Wiels, J. (1999) 'Ne pas confondre sexe et genre', *Le Monde*, 25 février, p. 16.

Wieviorka, M. (1997) (ed.) *Une société fragmentée?: le multiculturalisme en débat*, Paris: La Découverte.

Women of Europe (1988) Brussels: Commission of the European Communities, no. 27, June.

Yuval-Davis, N. (1997) *Gender and Nation*, London, Thousand Oaks, New Delhi: Sage.

The PaCS Debate and the Implications for Universal Equality in France

Enda McCaffrey

Introduction

After years of polemic, a new law was implemented in France on November 15 1999, familiarly known as Le PaCS (Le Pacte Civil de Solidarité). In short, the PaCS is a legally binding contract between two people, regardless of their gender, which enables them to avail of some rights which previously were exclusive to married couples. In effect, the PaCS represents a new and radical piece of legislation. For the first time in French history, an alternative to the institution of marriage has been enshrined in French law; unmarried couples now enjoy a legal status and same-sex couples are legally recognised, putting them on a par with their Danish and Scandinavian counterparts.

The debate in France surrounding the implementation of the PaCS was not only long in duration (at least ten years) and controversial (particularly nearer the time of its final passing), but it also followed the broad traditional contours of the French political establishment, with the Church and the right firmly opposed to it, and the left (including the intellectual left) determined to see its final course through the Senate. Within this overarching division, it will emerge that the real substance of the debate on the PaCS actually takes place on the left, with the right acting as a socio-political and cultural block to debate. This dynamic fits appropriately with the democratic/republican opposition that will underpin the issues for discussion in this chapter. The first aim of the chapter is to cover the main parameters of the PaCS debate, looking at the stances adopted by the political right and left. The chapter then goes on to explore how this new law has served to crystallise cultural responses to the increasingly heated debate on 'l'évolution des moeurs'. Finally, the reception of the law by the intellectual left and the homosexual community is situated in the context of opposing definitions of equality, based on traditional (republican) and modern (democratic) interpretations of universalism.

The Church and the right

The family and marriage have occupied a privileged space in the life of the French. After the Second World War, France was the only European country to have 'une politique familiale' which the government used to encourage couples to have large families. For example, the government introduced very generous family allowances, including bonuses for the birth of a new child, accommodation subsidies and reductions on transport for large families. Behind this policy, however, was the unambiguous message that in order to avail of these 'allocations' it was necessary to get married; and if one lived, for instance, in a rural community, the 'entreprise familiale' was one of the few means by which one advanced in life, firstly by getting married and then continuing the family business in which all members of the family would eventually work. The family, therefore, represented a traditional, state-approved, economic entity.

Of course, in the later decades of the twentieth century in France, chinks have appeared in the armour of this relatively stable notion of the family. The number of marriages has steadily dropped[1] and the birth rate has also declined[2], although the number of children born outside of marriage has increased.[3] In accordance, the drop in marriage rates has been accompanied by a rise in cohabitation[4], and of course, the divorce rate is also on the increase.[5] The statistics point to a growing disaffection for marriage as no longer the most essential union in life, and suggest that attitudes to unmarried couples living together and rearing children have changed. In short, the notion of social and political control over the behaviour of citizens appears to have weakened. This evolution/decline of the family has been accompanied by more social and global transformations such as urbanisation, the 'société de consommation', and the usurpation of the 'entreprise familiale' by the 'grandes entreprises', all of which have deflected attention away from the centrality of the family and from marriage as the 'acte fondateur du couple', towards the creation of 'nouvelles formes de vie' founded more closely on 'les droits de l'homme'. All of this seems to represent a move towards what the sociologist François de Singly has called 'le mouvement d'individualisation' and 'la famille recomposée' (Singly 1999).

In the course of the debate on the PaCS, the Church and the political right have been for the most part united against the new law, but for different reasons. Within the Catholic Church, there has been strong opposition to the PaCS on the basis that it devalued the importance of the traditional family. The Church has couched its rejection in terms of an opposition between the evils of modernity and the natural and uncorrupt innocence of family values. The PaCS has been seen to represent a decline in moral values, attributed by the Church to a 'tyrannie des moeurs' which itself, according to Monsignor Louis-Marie Billé, has led to 'une fragilisation de la société, [à] une confusion de repères essentiels' (quoted in Tincq, 1998). In additon to the critique of these socio-cultural factors, the Church

---

1.   From 1972, the number of marriages in France has dropped (374,000 in 1976, 266,000 in 1986, 282,100 in 1998). For more on this, consult Laudet and Cox (1995).

2.   Birth rates have also dropped (from 768,431 in 1985 to 734,338 in 1996). See www. insee. fr/home-page.

3.   The number of children born outside of marriage has increased from 50,888 in 1965 to 285,914 in 1996. See the above site web site for further details.

4.   In 1994, 'concubins' represented 14% of people living as couples, tantamount to 4.2 million. See Laurence (1998).

5.   Divorce rates have climbed over the last decades, from 44,700 in 1972 to 119,189 in 1995. For more on this issue, consult Borne (1992). See also the above web site.

has also invoked philosophical positions to undermine homosexuality. For example, the views of Thibauld Collin, an editorial advisor to the journal *Liberté politique*, have been exploited by the Church to convey the notion that 'derrière les bons sentiments affichés [dans le projet de loi sur le PaCS], il y a la ferme volonté de changer la société et son fondement anthropologique dans la lignée de la révolution homosexuelle post-1968' (quoted in Weill, 1999). Along with perceptions that homosexuality is a rejection of the heterosexual norm of procreation and that the recognition of any union other than that of marriage would be tantamount to undermining 'l'institution conjugale et familiale', the Church has shown itself to be, at least in public, firmly opposed to the PaCS law.

However, the question obviously arises as to the reasons for this hostility. Why is it that, within the context of the PaCS legislation, homosexuality has become a scapegoat for all other coupling arrangements? It would seem that if homosexuals – and the perceived threat that they are seen to have on the social fabric, coupled with the perception that they are the primary beneficiaries of the PaCS – are to have their 'unions' enshrined in law, this not only signifies in the eyes of the Church a legitimisation of the status of the homosexual relationship, but more significantly it gives legitimacy to the PaCS as a moral discourse which can be seen to compete with that of the Church for acceptability. Part of the strategic thinking of the Church as regards the PaCS has been to placate the homosexual community by underlining, on the one hand, its respect for homosexuals in their search for social integration and rejection of discrimination ('l'orientation particulière de la personne homosexuelle n'est pas une faute morale. L'inclination n'est pas un péché' (Hume 1995)), but, on the other hand, to shy away from any commitment to this respect in terms of legal representation, or equivalence. Monsignor Billé reinforces this point:

> *Certes, dans notre culture égalitariste, il y a des distinctions difficiles à faire percevoir. Pourtant, il faut savoir à la fois qu'on n'ira jamais assez loin dans le respect des personnes homosexuelles, dans la recherche de leur intégration sociale, dans le refus des discriminations, et qu'il n'est pas possible de faire comme si l'hétérosexualité et l'homosexualité étaient équivalentes. (Quoted in Tincq, 1998)*

What comes into question here is not only whether this negative stance on the PaCS is in keeping with Church orthodoxy, but whether in its national representation this position is compatible with *laïcité*.

In a Republic governed by *laïcité*, the role of the Church, on social issues for instance, is often limited to 'neutral' pronouncements. It acts as a noble citizen speaking in the interests of democracy. However, the role of the Church is less clearly defined on issues relating to 'l'ordre moral', where 'comments', like those of Monsignor Billé verge more towards 'recommendations' for political consumption. In a Republic where *laïcité* might be perceived as a constraint on, if not a hindrance to, the influence of the Church on State affairs, the opinions of the Church still command respect, and considerably more respect when those opinions tend to chime with republican values. The issue of convergence between Church and the right on points of common morality is an important one in that this proximity can reflect an impression of collaboration between the Church and the political right in their common defence of, and support for, a republican tradition, expressed in this case in a moral order.

'L'ordre moral' has been traditionally a notion invoked by right-wing politicians in their defence, for instance, of the principles of the Republic. In a recent article in *Le Monde*, the respective President and Secretary General of the *Collectif national pour le PaCS*, Jan-Paul Pouliquen and Denis Quinqueton, highlight the concerns of conservative Republicans who see it as 'un peu dérisoire de baser une politique sur une sexualité', or who, out of *mauvaise foi*, defer to the principle of *laïcité* or play on the fears of the electorate, as a means of rejecting the PaCS law. However, Pouliquen and Quinqueton go on to suggest that the PaCS debate has complicated the nature of the moral order in contemporary France, and focused attention on the need to modernise the relationship between the *laïque* tradition and a new moral order. In other words, they claim that there is a need for a clear and balanced case to be made for a democratic revaluation of the Republic along the lines of difference:

> Parce qu'à force de discuter d'une loi pour toutes et tous, nous avons amené nos con-
> citoyens, nos voisins, nos collègues de travail, nos amis, à considérer – autrement
> qu'en caricature – les différentes parties de ce tout. Et l'idée que des personnes dif-
> férentes peuvent cultiver leurs points communs et appartenir à une même société, en
> somme être des citoyennes et des citoyens, a avancé pendant ces années. La liberté
> de chacun, autant que la cohésion sociale, y ont gagné. (Pouliquen and Quinqueton
> 1999)

Before considering what this alternative Republic might look like in the aftermath of the PaCS law, we need to analyse more closely the reactions to this law of the political right.

In the run-up to the PaCs law the right (characterised by the UDF, the RPR, the DF and the FN) has been constant in its opposition to the PaCS law, and generally united on the crucial issue of the sanctity of the family, with only degrees of difference distinguishing parties. The National Front views the family as the organic foundation of the nation, a belief that is couched in the language of a utopian yesteryear; as a threat to 'l'âge d'or de la famille', the PaCS is described by Bruno Mégret as 'un mariage bis destiné à détruire la famille, mais aussi une porte ouverte à l'immigration par le biais de PaCS de complaisance' (Chombeau 1999). Other viewpoints from the moderate and central right are opposed to the law on the grounds of it being 'inadapté aux besoins de la famille', but in comparison with the FN, these views are less inflammatory in tone. The official position of the right has been to question, on the one hand, the constitutionality of the new law given that its parliamentary passage was plagued with delays, and was perceived not to have followed correct procedures (Fabre 1999). On the other hand, its essential critique focuses on the content of the law. Central concerns relate to the open-ended nature of the contract between two 'pacsés', the lack of definition around the notion of 'vie commune', and the rupture in the principle of equality, where married couples and single people are seen to be disadvantaged in fiscal and inheritance matters in comparison with their 'pacsé' counterparts. Other points of concern for the right (from a legal perspective) are the lack of compensatory arrangements in the case of the termination of a PaCS (a decision that can be taken simply by sending a letter to one's partner and then by informing a judge) and thus the affront to human dignity, as well as the absence in the law of provision for the child. In short, the right believes that the socialist government has come up against one of the intractable issues of contemporary life, that of providing a balanced *legal* framework that will take into consideration the complex social developments. In the absence of this balance, there is, according to the right, only the illusion of protection.

These are valid and significant concerns which will be addressed in due course. However, within the context of the debate on the family, it is possible once again to detect a point of covergence between the positions of the right and the Church on the important issue of social tolerance towards homosexuals but a denial of legal status. We recall, for example, the contradictory stance of the Church in its compassion for the homosexual, but its refusal to recommend any legal equivalence or indeed real social recognition. A similar stance is taken by prominent politicians of the right, notably Nicolas Sarkozy, secrétaire général of the RPR. In a speech to young members of the RPR, he states:

> *Notre idée et notre vision de la famille devront s'ouvrir, se moderniser, s'actualiser. J'aime la famille. Je crois en la famille [...] car réussir sa famille c'est réussir sa vie. Mais il nous faudra être plus à l'écoute et plus tolérants à l'endroit de ceux qui ont fait un autre choix, par exemple celui qui consiste à s'aimer en dehors du mariage et qui sont porteurs du même amour, de la même sincérité, de la même confiance en l'avenir. J'étais contre le PaCS et je le demeure. Mais je regrette que nous n'ayons pas pu nous faire davantage entendre ou comprendre d'une communauté homosexuelle qui a parfois pu être blessée par ce qu'elle a cru entendre. Nous devons être à l'écoute de toutes les différences parce qu'elles sont parfois synonymes de souffrances. (Le Monde, 30 août 1999, p. 5)*

Behind his conciliatory tone, Sarkozy's modern vision is still undermined by stereotype (to be different is synonomous with suffering) and by legal prejudice in his fundamental opposition to the PaCS law. While appearing to want to find solutions to the problems created by social evolution (including the financial difficulties of 'concubins' and the need for 'une attestation de vie commune' for homosexuals), throughout the PaCS debate the right has remained officially opposed to the social recognition of homosexuals (in the same way that the Church has), whom it perceives as a threat to marriage and the family. The intransigeance of the right on the issue of legal status is further reinforced in its refusal to address seriously sexual difference, preferring to hide behind the term 'vie commune'. In this respect, the political right is seen to echo the sentiments not only of the Church but also lays its own claim to the values of the Republic: 'C'est la logique de la *sensibilité républicaine*, qui dans la culture française préfère toujours ce qui est universel à ce qui est spécifique' (Théry 1997b, p. 164).

It has only been post PaCS that attitudes on the right have shown signs of change. Douste-Blazy, président of the UDF, has expressed regret for 'la tonalité du débat, mais pas sur le vote'. The level of argument during the course of the debate on the PaCS in the National Assembly descended into invective and homophobia on the right, which the latter only later conceded had damaged its image.[1] And yet this public confession – whether it be interpreted as political or media-influenced posturing – only belied deeper and more serious divisions within the right to which the PaCS gave rise. For instance, the homophobic pronouncements by, and the very appointment of, Christine Boutin as spokesperson for the UDF during the PaCS debate were questioned by young militant members of the party who considered her to be too removed from issues relating to contemporary life. Indeed, in the fallout after the PaCS law, the right has perhaps perceived itself to be out of touch with contemporary life and the PaCS debate has exposed divisions within the right, bringing to light evidence of an internal ideological split between a defence of its 'emblèmes' and a search for a modern face. These divisions, in turn, have provided an opportunity for the right to reassess its own identity, particularly in relation to issues about lifestyle and 'les sujets de société'. As Dominique Paillé, député (UDF) des Deux Sèvres, has stated: 'Il y a, à droite, sur les sujets de société, des conservateurs et des progressistes' (Courtois, Fabre and Montvalon 1999). How permanent this conservative/progressive split is and how far it will develop is open to conjecture. However, it is clear that the PaCS has revealed a crisis of identity within the right 'en matière de moeurs', from which two scenarios might emerge. The first points in the direction of a socio-cultural shift within the republican guard, which may prove significant in terms of a rethink on issues relating to universal equality. The second points to the question of the willingness and capacity of the French political and legal machinery to adapt to social and cultural change.

The left

While the right viewed the aftermath of the PaCS as an opportunity to re-examine its traditional values and shake off the label of a 'droite ringarde', the left promoted the implementation of the PaCS law on several levels. Firstly, based on the statistics on the decline of marriage and the increase of 'unions libres', highlighted earlier, the left was seen to be responding to dramatic social and demographic transformations. According to L'INED, of a sample of ten married couples, nine had already lived together before marriage. Also, of couples formed in the 1990s, 30% were still living together ten years later and L'INED also predicts between 150,000 to 200,000 requests for PaCS every year.[2] In short, two major social phenomena have changed notions of the family and marriage. Marriage has ceased to be 'l'acte fondateur du couple', and replacing it is 'l'union

---

1. The following comments were made by a range of députés from the the political right: 'Il n'y a qu'à les stériliser!'; 'En guise d'innovation, le PaCS annonce le retour à la barbarie'; 'Les homos, je leur pisse à la raie' (quoted in *Le Monde*, 26 juin 1999, p. 10).

2. *Le Rapport annuel de l'institut national d'études démographiques*, décembre 1999 (not covered in this report are the results of the recent 1999 census).

libre' which has become 'un mode de vie durable'. Hand-in-hand with these phenomena is the fallout from broken marriages and the increase of divorce, one-parent families and recomposed families. According to L'INED, some 120,000 divorces take place each year in France and 39% of marriages end in divorce. As a consequence of these separations, there has been a steady increase in one-parent families 'qui ont cessé d'être stigmatisées'. Other statistics point to 10% of children living with only one parent, and according to the 1990 census, it was estimated that 950,000 young people below the age of twenty-five (out of a total of 15 million) lived with a step-father and that, of the 7.8 million couples with children, 660,000 were 'familles recomposées'.

Such figures show a new face to the French family. They reflect a different picture to that of the one on the right with its slogan 'un père, une mère et des enfants'. The French family today is a mutating form, a distant relative of its nineteenth-century creation. The French family has evolved in the light of 'nouvelles formes de vie'. It is in direct response to these and other social evolutions that the Socialist government has shown the foresight to implement radical legislation. Not, however, without its detractors, the government was heavily criticised by the right for the lack of importance it placed on the child in the PaCS legislation and the implications for family life. The right claimed that a child needs the stability of a 'family', particularly in times of social change. However, whereas opponents of the PaCS appeared to equate stability with a traditional and exclusive definition of how a 'family' is constituted, the government placed the emphasis on the 'cadre de stabilité' in the context of several types of family unit. In other words, the PaCS law, first and foremost, offered a 'cadre juridique' for unmarried couples – individuals who were themselves possibly brought up in recomposed families or by same-sex parents – and thereby reinforced the stability of a union (previously precarious) and the sense of a 'family' for couples with children.

It is clear that the sophistication of the ideas of those on the left have reflected more accurately the complexity of our socio-cultural climate. While, for instance, the right criticised the social and legal recognition of 'concubins' as an attack on marriage and the family, the response on behalf of those in favour of the PaCS was to affirm that the law referred only to couples, and not to children, and thus was not a threat to the family because it did not concern children directly. Indeed, in the opinion of some commentators, the law goes even further on this point:

> Le PaCS introduit une distinction entre la relation amoureuse, stable et durable, et la famille; il introduit l'idée que la relation amoureuse n'a pas obligatoirement pour finalité la procréation, mais doit tout de même être considérée comme un lien commun parce qu'elle permet aux êtres, quel que soit le choix sexuel, de se construire et de s'épanouir. (Derycke and Bel 1999)

Far from undermining marriage, the PaCS constitutes a supplementary status between 'union libre' and marriage, a loving and legally recognised alternative for those for whom marriage is either inappropriate or against the law.

The Intellectual left

Where the ideology of the left has, in fact, stolen ground on the right in its implementation of the PaCS law is through the harmonisation of legislation with social evolution, and in its capacity to re-invent the links between 'la politique' and 'les droits de l'homme'. Claude Lefort, for example, has suggested new ways of approaching the relationship between social interaction and the State. According to Dominique Rousseau, Lefort strips the notion 'les droits de l'homme' of its Marxist and liberal presuppositions, and proposes an alternative social model based on the 'les droits de rapport' which are defined in terms of their public space:

> En mettant les hommes en relation, ils produisent, en effet, un espace de rencontres, d'échanges, de débats où se définissent les règles de la vie commune et où se construit la légitimité. Pour autant, L'Etat n'est pas nié; il est seulement remis à sa place comme instance de pouvoir ne détenant pas le principe de sa légitimité et comme simple partie d'un tout qui ne peut prétendre à devenir la totalité. (Rousseau 1999)

With the State 'reduced' in its republican function as 'Supreme Being', and conditional on the public space as the site where it must earn its right to act, 'l'espace public' becomes the locus of legitimacy, structured on the principle of discussion around issues relating to 'l'organisation des formes de vie': 'c'est par le débat et la mobilisation de l'espace public que l'égalité des sexes a pu être prise en charge, que la femme comme composante de l'universel humain et non comme catégorie a pu être pensée' (Rousseau 1999). By shifting the focus away from what he would see as an out-dated notion of the republican State as the bearer of wisdom to all its citizens, Lefort appears to redress the balance of power by relocating the agency of change within the community, a process which the left has effectively mirrored in its legislative policy on the PaCS.

If we pursue Lefort's philosophy further, we can use it as a means of interpreting the right's political, social and cultural responses to the implementation of the PaCS law. With the right's tendency to privatise sexuality (particularly homosexuality which it views as a 'problème d'ordre privé'), the dominant role of the State as moral enforcer is even more important in that it is seen to maintain a control over what happens in the public space. What underpins this power dynamic is the monopolisation of the moral discourse and the continuation of a socio-political status quo; it is a dynamic that is conservative rather than progressive, narrowly *republican* rather than *democratic*. Indeed, in the context of the PaCS law, the republican credentials of the right have appeared to have been undermined in that, as a consequence of the strides taken by the Socialist government in implementing the PaCS, and in the light of the post-mortem that took place within the right afterwards, the perception remains that the right was seen to have shifted ground (politically, socially and ethically) towards accepting a form of 'statut' for 'concubins' and homosexuals. By contrast, where the left has appeared to lead the way from the right on the issue of the PaCS is in its embrace of socio-cultural change and the acceptance within the law of 'un droit de cité pour les concubins et les homosexuels'. With homosexuality, for instance, gaining in public tolerance (indeed being seen as of 1997 as 'une manière acceptable de vivre sa sexualité'[1]), the left is seen to have responded to the evolution of public opinion. Furthermore, it has taken the notions of freedom of choice and mutual engagement out of the domain of the private, and given them public license not in any self-serving way but in the interests of a democratic Republic: 'Le PaCS intéresse *aussi la République et la société*, puisqu'il reconnaît le couple et installe une plus grande stabilité des relations' (Tasca 1998) (my italics).

One vital area where the 'democratic' dimension to the PaCS debate has challenged republican 'stonewalling', is in the contrasting perspectives on the *future* of the family. A key phrase in the PaCS legislation is 'organiser une vie commune' which points to two central ideas. The first, is the notion of order. From a traditional republican perspective, new 'figures relationnelles' coupled with the decline of the symbolic family, have been seen to have contributed to social fragmentation via the absence of any semblance of a familial order. Such a premise, of course, is founded on the notion of the ideal family which, as recent figures have shown, is losing its prominence as the primary social unit. By contrast, the philosopher Sabine Prokhoris deflates this mythical order of the ideal family, referring to the 'totalitarisme familial' in its projection of a 'nostalgie d'éden' on to the child, in its indoctrination of the father, mother, child institutions, and in the prolongation of lifelong 'étiquettes' which prevent the individual from 'pouvoir inventer des liens et de s'inventer soi-même à travers ces liens' (Prokhoris 1998). It is increasingly clear that the concept of the traditional order of the family must be seen in the context of other orders that organise new solidarities which themselves reinforce new social links.

In this respect, the second central idea underlining the PaCS debate is the unprecedented opportunity offered to some on the intellectual left to name an alternative symbolic order to that of the family. In sociological circles, this process has been ongoing in France since the 1960s. One of the powerful messages of the 1960s was the way in which individuals defined themselves first and foremost through themselves, and not in terms of their familial labels. Individuals were perceived to have rights other than the rights ascribed to them by the institution of the family. The aftermath of the 1960s revolution has witnessed a tension between these conflicting roles. While the traditional family has provided a system where the individual has been able to realise his/her identity via the support and love of those within the family, this system has also been seen to fall short in terms of its ability to satisfy the principles of autonomy and freedom. As the sociologist Singly has suggested, there is an undeniable 'mouvement d'individualisation' in the human condition, the force of which has not only contributed to a destabilisation of the family institution, but which has characterised the conjugal relationship post 1975 (with divorce by mutual consent) as a new space of multiple lives and multiple partners:

---

1. *Le Nouvel Observateur* (3 juillet 1997) compared the results of two surveys carried out in 1981 and 1997. Among other revelations, it was noted that the percentage of those polled who believed that homosexuality had become a more acceptable way of living had increased from 29% in 1981 to 55% in 1997.

Le modèle de la famille recomposée ne sera plus l'exception, mais la norme. Les valeurs qui sont en oeuvre aujourd'hui vont continuer à agir de plus belle, c'est-à-dire la logique affective et la logique de l'individualisation [...]. La fin du XXe et le début du XXIe siècle sont marqués par la mondialisation et en contrepartie par un très grand attachement à la réalisation de soi dans la vie privée. (Singly 1999)

Singly recognises that the traditional family has evolved and will continue to evolve into a reconstituted form in order to accommodate the new affective and individualist 'logics' of the day. In identifying these two logics as the primary values operating in our contemporay society – thus bridging a gap between the emotional needs provided by the proximity of a family and the self-fulfilling concerns of the modern 'individu mobile' – Singly highlights the dilemmas of many thousands of individuals (childless or not, homosexual or heterosexual) who want to organise and legalise a common life with one another, based not on binding obligations and institutional demands but on a mutual respect for the freedom of the individual.

Equality: 'l'oeuf fécondé' in the Republic

Where the debate on the left has been particularly controversial is on the notion of equality. The sociologist Irène Théry and Professor of Law Evelyne Pisier have both been critical in their assessments of the shortcomings of the PaCS law, perceiving it as a 'minimum symbolique' and 'un projet en demi-mesures' (Théry 1999a, p. 140). Théry views the PaCS as a missed opportunity to discuss the central issue of 'la spécificité du lien de couple', and, according to her, the fundamental lack of recognition of the homosexual who is granted a 'status' almost by dispensation. Pisier, on the other hand, while agreeing in principle with Théry, addresses the issue from historical and philosophical perspectives. Her views reflect a debate within a debate; in other words, within the context of the political to and fro of right and left on the PaCS law, there has been an equally important and ongoing debate that goes to the heart of French society and culture, and which questions the role of the principle of universalism (and sexual equality in the name of the universality of the Republic) in a modern pluralist society. The universal applicability of such a notion as equality in France, a founding principle of the Revolution, has been shown to be problematic. Despite the legal promise of its intent and the abstraction of its rationality, universalism has been seen to be blind to discrimination and confined to a reductive notion of equality, based frequently on 'natural' gender differences. In the context of the PaCS debate, the right has been keen to invoke this difference (or alterity) as the foundation of the couple, the family and society. Another, and more problematic word which has often replaced the word 'difference' is 'nature', the latter being perceived as the true barometer in the debate over the universalism of rights.

In this context, nature is seen as that which dictates law and therefore includes and excludes. 'La différence des sexes' becomes a means to legitimate 'l'exclusion de l'homosexualité hors de l'enceinte sacrée du mariage et de la famille' (Borillo, Fassin and Iacub 1998). As a further tactic of exclusion, this notion of the 'différence des sexes' is perceived to be grounded anthropologically, giving it the force of the law of nature and culture. Pisier questions the arbitrariness of constructing a law on this natural difference, asking: 'Si l'altérité sexuelle est une loi de nature, que faire du "même" dans la paire?[...] La revendication égalitaire défie la limite que la nature est censée imposer à l'universalisme des droits' (Pisier 1998). Indeed, Théry adds weight to this counterattack in her response that the notion of 'la différence des sexes' is constructed by culture and institutions, hence transitory and open to negotiation. Furthermore, she claims that what may undermine anthropological comparisons is the very historical rootedness of their presuppositions. She argues that, over the course of time, societies progress to remodel the institutions that define them, responding to new circumstances and interactions.

For Théry and Pisier, then, the PaCS represents something of a half-way house. On the one hand, it can be interpreted favorably as a step towards recognition, but it can also be seen as an inadequate and demeaning legal settlement. As far as equality is concerned, the PaCS can be perceived as a regression in the face of a new modernity characterised by a 'radical' universalism, since in their view the republican tradition puts universal equality of all individuals before any difference between them. The sociologist Schmuel Trigano concurs to a degree with Pisier and Théry in his judgment that the PaCS is 'un reste d'archaïsme s'opposant à la modernité dont l'universel abstrait serait l'unique modèle' (Trigano 1998). Pisier founds her notion of a new *universel abstrait* on a revaluation of the concept of nature: 'pour l'ordre moral, il vaut mieux qu'une différence de nature justifie la similitude des droits du moment que la norme suprême ne fait pas l'économie de cette différence qui continue de la fonder' (Pisier 1998). She goes on to suggest that it is the role of modernity to rethink the role of nature and invent a new policy based on 'les droits d'une multitude d'êtres différents partageant ensemble une commune humanité, quels que soient leurs races, leurs sexes et...leurs sexualités' (1998). On one level, Trigano agrees with Pisier in the vital claim to reinvent the idea of the 'universel' which he defines as '(l'égalité des droits, l'unité du genre humain) avec la différence (les identités singulières)' (Trigano 1998). However, their respective viewpoints diverge significantly on the emphasis each places on the relationship between 'commune humanité'/'genre humain' and difference. Pisier appears to privilege difference at the centre of humanity and Trigano privileges the centrality of the human being from which difference derives.

What might seem on the surface a minor distinction highlights, in fact, two crucially important issues that faced those who scripted the legislation for the PaCS law and the homosexual 'community' at large. Firstly, arguing from the standpoint of what could be seen as radical and individualist Jacobinism (in which the State liberates the individual and remains morally neutral but normalises in the absence of a norm), the PaCS legislators 'ont fait valoir que la tradition républicaine (c'est-à-dire révolutionnaire) française s'opposait à toute organisation communautaire, par nature discriminatoire' (Yonnet 2000, p. 108). By valorising this 'tradition républicaine' (a radical move in itself, given the pride in the notion of a homosexual 'community'), they sought to identify with the Republic first as individuals and, in so doing, were able to appropriate for their own 'communal' benefit, what Yonnet calls, 'le mécanisme spécifique dont la Révolution française a offert une variante radicale et volontariste' (p. 106). In other words, the PaCS strategists embraced the republican model on its own terms (i.e. on the basis that a Republic recognises, emancipates and assimilates within the French nation individuals ('des personnes individuellement citoyennes' (p. 108)) and not groups, communities, or nationalities. This strategy to position homosexuals in particular within an assimilationist French Republic 'de nature individualiste' has been seen, as Paul Yonnet would suggest, to have been influential in the justification and approval of the PaCS legislation. In describing the PaCS law as 'une révolution', Yonnet situates it within a republican tradition that is essentially 'anticommunautaire', and suggests that this legislation represents 'une *matrice révolutionnaire* dont l'oeuf fécondé réside dans l'équivalence posée entre hétérosexualité et homosexualité' (p. 108).

The assimilationist pathway is contested on the grounds that the republican argument does not redress the problematic issue of the difference of sex, which, as we have seen, Pisier and Théry wish to renogotiate in their argument for a legal and specific recognition of homosexual union. They go this far because they both view the republican tradition as inherently unjust in its promotion of a symbolic (heterosexual) order of human relations, hence Pisier's attempt to decentre the 'natural' centre. However, while the legal recognition of homosexual union may be perceived as one of the more obvious 'benefits' of the PaCS legislation, the legislation eschews the crucial issue of equality between heterosexual and homosexual unions. From the persepctive of republican universalism, everyone is equal regardless of their differences, hence the notion of assimilation. However, within this all-encompassing idea, difference can be seen to matter, both practically and legally (contrast Roudinesco 1999). Two homosexual 'pacsés' can enjoy legal status (akin to marriage) but the status of their union is not equal to marriage in terms of respective rights, particulary in the area of parenting where homosexual parenting is a taboo subject (this is not to say that marriage, and particularly the French model, is an ideal to which homosexual unions should aspire. Eric Fassin has highlighted its normalising and patriarchal roots (Fassin 1999)). In other words, under traditional universalism, when sex and sexuality are removed from their private categorisations and lay claim in various forms to public and legal recognition, it seems that everyone is more unequal, not regardless of their differences but because of them. The PaCS is in effect an illustration of the riddle of traditional French Republicanism, a riddle with serious injustice/ inequality at its centre and which is summarised concisely by Paul Yonnet: 'Cet échec à être entendu nous montre en effet que la France reste structurellement attachée à un trait de mentalité historique qui lui interdit de rendre égal autrement qu'en rendant identique' (2000, p. 108).

In France, this historical mentality has been slow to shift. When it does, it is usually in the context of constitutional declarations. The 1948 Universal Declaration on *Les Droits de L'Homme* has been seen to have modernised the relationship between the individual and State by inscribing 'le principe de non-discrimination fortement marqué par une pratique anglo-saxonne qui préfère l'empirisme des garanties concrètes au lyrisme des idéaux révolutionnaires' (Decaux 1998). Revised declarations and constitutional revisions have been viewed as welcome clarifications (indeed, in the context of equality between men and women, the 1946 Constitution is particularly important). On the other hand, as Emmanuel Decaux has argued, to enumerate categories of discrimination is itself to classify groups, thus to create discrete parts of the 'equal' whole, in the end to omit others from the whole. In short, the practice of appropriating the issue of equality to fit socio-political and sexual agendas can often be self-serving, reductive and counter-productive.

By contrast, in the current parity debate, Roudinesco seeks to distance herself from 'agenda' politics by confirming anatomical sexual difference between men and women as 'fact' and therefore impossible to efface. She goes on to highlight the dangers of conflating sexual difference with identity, and 'repositions' the emancipation of women within 'une conception de l'inconscient qui refusait toute forme d'ancrage dans la psychologie des peuples, des ethnies ou des identités' (Roudinesco 1999). This philosophical, feminist and deeply universalist position, however, seems to fly in the face of the practicalities of everyday life, like unequal pay and the myriad forms of discrimination that surface from the PaCS legislation. This is why today the focus of the debate on equality must revisit the republican notion of universalism as a catchword not for sameness but for specificity (based on diversity and difference). In the words of a recent manifesto entitled '*Pour l'égalité sexuelle*':

> *L'égalité affectera notre ordre sexuel dans son entier, c'est-à-dire notre manière d'organiser à la fois les sexes et les sexualités. Ainsi, quand on ne définira plus le mariage et la famille, comme naturellement, par la différence des sexes, l'inégalité des sexes apparaîtra moins naturelle. L'égalité des sexualités aura donc un effet en retour sur l'égalité des sexes. Nous revendiquons l'égalité. Non pas pour les femmes, non pas pour les homosexuels, mais pour tous, et donc pour toutes; il n'est d'égalité qu'universelle. Il en va de l'intérêt général. Nous sommes les universalistes. (www. egaliteifrance.com: accessed June 1999)*

Conclusion

The PaCS debate has thrown into sharp focus the republican/democratic opposition at the heart of French socio-cultural discourse. The political right has been seen to have upheld and desired to preserve the traditional values of the Republic, particularly in areas relating to the family, moral order and the uniqueness of civil marriage, all three predicated on what we have seen to be an increasingly controversial definition of the word 'nature'. While not overtly hostile to homosexuality, the Republic's 'right' arm has expressed tolerance of it within the confines of love as a matter of 'private' concern, but not an issue for public debate, let alone legislation. The democratic opposition (current Socialist government and leading left-wing intellectuals) has succeeded through the PaCS in renegotiating the republican 'veto' on sexuality, and shifting the discourse on sex and sexuality into the public domain. However, the changes and freedoms that have ensued as a result of the implementation of the PaCS law, have also given rise to concerns (the limitations of the PaCS[1]) and ideological splits about how the new legislation addresses (or fails to address) the issue of equality. Homosexual groups claim that the legislation does not go far enough on equality, and that it represents nothing more than a republican ruse to appease sexual difference. Intellectuals, notably Pisier, Théry and Trigano, support these sentiments from an anti-anthropological perspective, claiming that the PaCS law presents homosexuals with a stark choice between the struggle to negotiate equality on the basis of sexual difference and sexuality (the new/abstract universalist position), and marginalisation. That is to say, keeping faith with what the PaCS has delivered in terms of a valid and legally recognised lifestyle, but not delivered in terms of equality with heterosexuality. Paul Yonnet sides with the former option, and, in characterising the PaCS legislation as 'révolutionnaire', he goes a step further by responding to the challenge of 'taking on' Republicanism from within by re-appropriating its very universalist credo.

Bibliography

Borillo, D., Fassin, E. and Iacub, M. (1999) 'Au-delà du PaCS: pour l'égalité des sexualités', *Le Monde*, 16 février, p. 17.

Borne, D. (1992) *Histoire de la société française depuis 1945*, Paris: Armand Collin.

Chombeau, C. (1999) 'M. Mégret se pose en défenseur de la famille traditionnelle', *Le Monde*, 13 avril, p. 11.

Courtois, G., Fabre, C. and Montvalon, J.-B. (1999) 'La Droite partagée entre défense de ses "emblèmes" et quête de modernité', *Le Monde*, 12 octobre, p. 8.

Decaux, E. (1998) 'Non-discrimination', *Le Monde*, 5 décembre, p. 10.

Derycke, D. and Bel, J.-P. (1999). *Sénateurs votez pour le Pacs* [online]. Accessed 3 May, 2000: www. multimania.com/psdoc/recherche/discours/bel/pacs.html

Fabre, C. (1999) 'Le Report du PaCS révèle les embarras parlementaires du gouvernement', *Le Monde*, 2 juillet 1999, p. 8.

Fassin, E. (1999) 'Le Mariage des homosexuels', *French Politics, Culture and Society*, vol. 17, nos. 3-4, Summer/Fall, pp. 165-79.

Hume, B. (1995) La Documentation catholique no. 2115. *L'Homosexualité; qu'en dit l'Eglise?* [online]. Accessed 6 April, 2000: www://pricip[al.14"http://www.portsnicolas.org/soc/soc30.html.

Laudet, C. and Cox, R. (1995) *Le Peuple de France aujourd'hui*, Manchester University Press.

Laurence, F. (1998) 'L'Union libre, ces millions encore négligés par le droit', *Le Monde*, 30 mai, p. 10.

Pisier, E. (1998) 'PaCS et parité: du même et de l'autre', *Le Monde*, 20 octobre, p. 18.

Pouliquen, J.-P. and Quinqueton, D. (1999) 'Le PaCS est-il républicain?', *Le Monde*, 15 octobre, p. 19.

---

1. It is worth mentioning that the PaCS can only cope with one-to-one relationships while many people who have responded to post-60s social changes live in looser clusters – or even 'families' – than a couple-based law allows.

Prokhoris, S. (1998) 'Inventer de nouvelles formes de vie, cela ne veut pas dire qu'il n'y a pas d'ordre', *Le Monde*, 3 novembre, p. 15.

Roudinesco, E. (1999) 'Une Parité régressive', *Le Monde*, 11 février, p. 12.

Rousseau, D. (1999) 'Fonder la politique sur les droits de l'homme', *Le Monde*, 16 juillet, p. 16.

Singly, F. de (1999) 'Le Renforcement du mariage est dû à l'existence d'autres formes de la vie commune', *Le Monde*, 2 mars, p. 12.

Tasca, C. (1998) 'Un Nouveau cadre, un nouveau regard; *Le Monde* pour ou contre le PaCS', *Le Monde*, 10 octobre, p. 7.

Tincq, H. (1998) 'L'Eglise de France accentue sa pression contre le pacte civil de solidarité', *Le Monde*, 3 novembre, p. 17.

Théry, I. (1999a) 'PaCS, sexualité et différence des sexes', *Esprit*, no. 257, octobre, pp. 131-81.

Théry, I. (1997b) 'Le Contrat d'union sociale en question', *Esprit*, no. 236, octobre, pp. 159-87.

Trigano, S. (1998) 'Les Droits de l'(autre) homme', *Le Monde*, 18 novembre, p. 16.

Weill, N. (1999) 'Une "société de pensée" proche des traditionalistes au service d'une mission politique', *Le Monde*, 13 octobre, p. 7.

Yonnet, P. (2000) 'PaCS: un mariage républicain', *Le Débat*, no. 112, novembre-décembre, pp. 105-08.

L'Exception française as Culture

Georges Salemohamed

The debate about 'exceptionalism in France' is most often pitched at the level of the organisation and functions of the state. The French state is thought to be the principle agent of opposition to change and modernisation. In what follows it is argued that the issue is far more complex and requires that one takes account of culture as a determinant of political practices, interpersonal relations and collective beliefs.

The expression 'exception française' evokes a history fraught with difficulties which accompanied the creation of the modern French state. Whereas in most European countries the formation of more or less homogeneous societies preceded the creation of the state, in France it was the reverse. The revolution of 1789 started the process which continued with accelerated momentum throughout the Third Republic (1870-1940) after the final demise of the monarchy. It led to the secularisation of public education, hitherto a church monopoly, followed by the secularisation of the state in 1905. Both types of secularisation are fundamental principles underlying a 'republican model of integration' which generally considers multi-culturalism, particularly when bolstered by religion, as disruptive and divisive. They both seek to unify origin, belief and circumstance into equality before the law and the state, and they are both linked to a culture of unmediated relationship between the individual and the state whose legal foundation goes back to the Le Chapelier Law of 1791. In addition, they explain the citizen's dependency with respect to the state, which is one important feature of 'exceptionalism'.

Another feature of 'exceptionalism' touching on the nature of the state is its aspiration, from the beginning, to a 'universalist' function in relation to society (Debré 1989, p. 33). The classic expression of this is *La Déclaration des Droits de l'Homme et du Citoyen*. The spirit of this continues in the principle of equality characterising in particular state education. In the French system, a vigorous selection and grading process operating through a uniform examination system preserves candidates' anonymity. It eliminates the possibility of preferential treatment, guaranteeing that anyone can in theory rise to the top.

A third feature, by far the most important nowadays in the controversy over French exceptionalism, is state intervention in the economy. Although intervention has been in decline with privatisation, an awareness remains of how the state successfully embarked on reconstruction after the war, rationalising moribund industries, planning the economy and creating a comprehensive social security system (Saint-Etienne 1992, p. 23). This modernising and wealth-creating state was reinforced by an army of functionaries and administrators. With the help of an informal coalition of workers and teachers which gave it political support, it succeeded in creating a strong industrial base, and the conditions for improved living standards and welfare provision. It was thereby able, in conjunction with public and social services, to assume a redistributive function. Redistribution plays an important part in the ideology of exceptionalism, bringing all its various features together and welding them into a particular notion of democracy, based not on the confrontation of opposing interests, but on an objective image of the general interest.

This Colbertist interventionist and protectionist tradition of the French state has been challenged by a new rationality which views intervention as a hindrance to progress and innovation. To the opponents of French exceptionalism, modernisation and progress, however defined, are products not of the human will, but of market forces, not of wealth distribution, but of resource allocation. Competition thus replaces protection, and the laws of economics, blind to issues of rights and duties, seem to spell the demise of the republican model (Touraine et al 1996, p. 16).

Criticism of 'exceptionalism' focuses principally on the economic function of the state, taking it to task for subordinating economic and financial stability to political and social ends. The state is seen as dissipating resources in helping unprofitable industries, and its distributive practices are considered harmful to wealth creation, as well as encouraging indolence and wasting resources. A punitive tax régime of 70 francs to every 100 francs paid out in wages is similarly thought harmful to competitiveness and initiative. In this way, it is claimed, capital and human talent are forced to flee overseas. Not least, it is argued that the 'exceptionalist' state creates havoc amongst traders, shopkeepers, small and medium-sized industries, and encourages rebellion and strikes when powerful interests, often nurtured by the state itself, such as civil servants, find their demands frustrated.

These are familiar objections. Just as familiar is the exceptionalist defence against these charges (Touraine 1999, pp. 42-5). The attack on the republican state, based as it is on a notion of general interest, by the forces of globalisation and free market economy, is condemned as a surrender to the interests of powerful countries like the U.S.A. and Japan. To subscribe to this neo-liberal agenda, it is argued, is to accept damage to the ethos of solidarity which would be injurious to the integrity of civil society. Economically, globalisation and neo-liberalism are seen as shifting resources away from the needy to the wealthy. Together, they damage employment, increase profits and depress wages; they entrap the unwary into a belief in an ideology of economic freedom from which only the powerful can benefit. They create insecurity, foster selfishness and threaten social order with a hegemonic culture of greed.

In 1995, public service workers went on strike and paralysed France for three to four weeks. The strike gained great public support. It has been described as a 'republican' strike to denote its symbolic as well as real importance in the continuing defence of a fast-eroding public sector, the lynchpin of economic exceptionalism. In a famous address to a gathering of railway workers during the strikes, Bourdieu reminded a whole nation that what was at stake was rather more important than the strikes themselves; in other words, the destruction of a civilisation linked to the existence of a public service sector. In short, it was the erosion of the republican equality of rights: rights to education, to health, to culture, to research, and above all, to work (Touraine et al, 1996, p. 173). Bourdieu, along with other intellectuals such as Luc Boltanski, summed up the fears of many exceptionalists in the face of free competition and the global market economy. They saw these as inducing 'la quête d'une rentabilité à court terme' which, in turn, posed for them the question of knowing 'dans quelle société nous voulons vivre' (*Le Monde*, 6 décembre 1995, p. 30).

Despite the hyperbolic tone of his address, Bourdieu's intervention is in the tradition of intellectual reflection in France on questions relating to political culture – equality, rights etc. – and also to culture, both as this term is usually understood and with respect to intellectual culture. Intellectuals, after all, were the principle agents of the republican model. The strength of feeling in defence of the culture and civilisation that this model embodies is nowhere more evident than, for example, in the denunciation of the so-called 'Macdo-civilisation' or 'culture Disney' (Guerlain 1996, p. 54). However, to appreciate what is fundamental to the conceptual framework and mentality that distinguish the 'exceptionalists' from their adversaries, a different notion of culture is required, and organisation theory supplies this. The conception of culture here is just as inclusive as it is with culture within the conspectus of art and civilisation (Trompenaars & Hampden-Turner 1998, p. 21). Organisation culture embodies, inter alia, ideas about social interaction, mutual expectations, shared meanings, norms and values, how people behave individually or in groups, and how these groups relate to each other, co-operate and consider each other. Politics is an important element in all these, although it tends to be de-emphasised in organisation studies. French theorists, by contrast, give more emphasis to the power dimension of inter-relations between groups and individuals. This political approach is useful because it makes it possible to compare two opposing models of French organisation culture and two different responses to French exceptionalism as the repository of social and political norms. One response, by Michel Crozier, stressing the role of bureaucracy, is well known. It has contributed to a widespread notion of French society, influenced by the state, as riddled with bureaucratic anomalies. The result, according to the proponents of this view, is incompetence, inefficiency and tension. The other response, championed by Philippe d'Iribarne, which emphasises the role of informal procedures as the hidden mechanism of collective action in French life, articulates an entirely different case.

The bureaucratisation of French life thesis

Few in France would question the thesis that bureaucracy runs through all types and all aspects of French organised life. An often quoted instance of the effect of bureaucracy that compares France unfavourably with the United Kingdom, Germany or Japan, is the payslip. Consisting of an average of three lines in the United Kingdom, it reaches a staggering sixteen in France. Bureaucracy seems to be universally called into question and yet, as Domenach puts it: 'Il est probable que si un référendum proposait aux Français l'intégration de tous les travailleurs dans la foncion publique, la réponse serait "oui", à une très forte majorité' (Domenach 1997, p. 161). Domenach calls France a 'forteresse bureaucratique' and compares it, from this standpoint, with the Soviet Union. He would agree with Allègre's characterisation of France as a 'luthériste' not – as Allègre insists – a 'luthérien' country. Contrasting France with the United Kingdom, Allègre argues that the former is as resistant to reforms as much the latter thrives on them. The British, he says, have no constitution but practise reforms constantly. They are continually changing laws and building up new traditions without writing a line of a constitution: 'Ils inventent le présent.' The French, by contrast, live in the past, a past that harks back to a feudal order, pointing up the anachronism of the French situation: the combination of an aristocratic with an egalitarian principle (Allègre 1996, pp. 265-7).

Much of the discussion of bureaucracy in France as the main obstacle to reform is inspired by Michel Crozier. French bureaucracy, he says, has an enduring capacity because everyone conspires to its continuance, even its victims (Crozier 1970, p. 99). A consensus exists, conscious or not, about the virtues of a bureaucratic regime. To show why this is so, Crozier highlights a number of permanent traits of French behaviour (Crozier 1963, p. 279). He emphasises two of them: the fact that, on the one hand, the French crave absolute authority, holding it as a requisite for all formal collective activities, but that, on the other hand, they hanker after personal autonomy. Crozier builds on this contradiction to show how it results in a bureaucratic style which permeates organised life in general. French organisation is highly centralised and this satisfies the drive towards absolute authority because power is concentrated at the top. At the same time, organisation is highly stratified and there is no face-to-face contact between superiors and subordinates. Power, therefore, does not bear directly on the individual and autonomy is in this way preserved. The cost, however, is bureaucracy because, in the absence of contacts between superiors and subordinates, everything must to the greatest extent possible be catered for in advance; every contingency must be accounted for. Rules, regulations and paperwork are the result, leading to routine and immobilism.

Crozier's analysis points out one great advantage of the system: equality. According to Crozier, lack of face-to-face contact guarantees equality in the sense that it eliminates all possibility of favouritism. No one is able to seek privileges or favours from a superior; the very hint of a contact between a superior and a subordinate would raise suspicion. However, this can be seen as equality in a negative sense. It encourages mistrust, which is one feature of the bureaucratic climate and which hovers over everything that departs from established practice. This mistrust, Alain Peyrefitte argues, has historically hampered French economic development (Peyrefitte 1995, pp. 22-3). Crozier subscribes to this view and also lambasts the lack of French readiness to undertake change. A second consequence of bureaucracy, according to Crozier, is the growth of parallel power systems in the shape of groups. These groups put pressure on the individual, but limit themselves to the defence of existing interests. When these are not threatened, the group functions as a collection of isolated individuals; when they are, the individual is pressured to conform. A third consequence is the practice of the so-called 'système D', the tendency of individuals to detect and exploit flaws in the organisation for their own personal advantage. A fourth consequence, amongst many others, is the problem of communication and information; the likelihood that information required of a subordinate will be distorted for fear that it might hurt his interests, which means that little is asked of subordinates by way of important information. Crozier characterises French organisational practice from this point of view, as 'la non-communication institutionnalisée' (Crozier 1970, p. 96).

In the light of these dysfunctions, Crozier concludes that French society and institutions tend towards conservatism rather than change and modernisation. These are resisted because groups fear that any alteration to the status quo might be damaging to them in particular. Change is, therefore, usually the result of conflict. A well-known illustration of this, familiar even to those who have never read Crozier, is the prevalence of strikes in France. These are most often an index of an employer's refusal to negotiate rather than, as in countries like the United Kingdom, the outcome of failed negotiations. Strikes are thus, in a curious way, a means of communicating, of conveying information about grievances (Coutrot 1998, p. 82). The cumulative effect of difficulties of this nature, inherent in bureaucratic culture, is to stultify initiative and dynamism. It is what Crozier means when he refers to France and its institutions as 'une société bloquée'. Movement is difficult within the 'stalled society' because, in addition, group co-operation is lacking. Consequently, innovation, modernisation, flexibility and readiness to take risks are also lacking, although these are conditions thought vital for survival and progress in a constantly changing environment.

Culture, elites, change and resistance

If the anti-exceptionalist critique of the relationship between the state and groups or individuals can be summed up in one word, it is dependency. Appeal to the state for subsidies and grants, regulations and protective legislation on a scale unseen in countries like the United Kingdom is its most visible expression. Even those who are in principle opposed to the state are not averse to seeking state intervention when the occasion suits them. Trade unions provide a classic example. For a long time, a minority union movement, first of anarcho-syndicalist, then of Marxist persuasion, sought or welcomed state subsidies and legislation. These gave it the only means of protecting the interests of its members in the face of recalcitrant employers. Critics have always seen this situation as counter-productive, arguing that it prevented a less politicised and less ideological movement from emerging. For the most part, however, state intervention is simply condemned as inefficient, a waste of resources (Crozier and Tilliette 2000, p. 57).

The reference to dependency with respect to the state appears at first sight to clash with Crozier's observation that lack of face-to-face contact originates in individuals' desire to flee dependency. However, attitudes towards, and respect for, the state are not the same as attitudes towards organisations or institutions, public or private. The latter fall under the category of government (the French even talk of government in relation to business firms). Whereas the state as 'abstract ethics', to borrow Hegel's term, commands unconditional loyalty, governments do not (Pitts 1981, pp. 292-3). Uncivic behaviour stems in part from this dichotomy (Safran 1995, p. 52). It includes rebellion and strikes against governments, the most recent example being the 1995 public service strikes. The question for those who oppose the republican/exceptionalist model then, is how to remove dependency on the state and encourage inter-dependency at the organisational level. One factor they perceive as common to both is the existence of an elite which is homogeneous in background, training and temperament: an elite whose vested interest lies in preserving the status quo (Sérieyx 1994, p. 157).

Elite criticism is not new in France. It first arose after the war when the conduct of state affairs, but, more particularly, the way management behaved, came under close scrutiny by American experts sent to France to administer Marshall Aid. There was no mention of elites, but the reference was clear. Thus French managers were taken to task for their arrogance and for the distance they kept between themselves and their workforce. Boltanski states a similar point of view when he refers to 'le paternalisme sans père' of the bosses at the largest companies (Boltanski 1982, p. 39). To the Americans this was one of the great obstacles to the rise in French productivity and economic welfare. These in turn were thought vital if France, threatened by the existence of a strong Communist Party, was to resist the lure of an alliance with the Soviet Union. The Americans thought French managers were ignorant of the importance of human factors in the drive for increased productivity. They did not consult, they did not delegate, and they remained aloof from their workforce, directing everything from the top. In other words, the French did not manage but 'directed', hence the term 'direction' or 'gestion'. Both these terms, but especially the latter, denote hierarchical, quasi-military rule rather than the more convivial relations, transgressing status and rank, which the word 'management' evokes.

Elite rule is now considered by its critics as the lynchpin of the republican model, the bulwark of conservatism and resistance to modernisation (Crozier 2000, p. 42). To this extent, the attack on the elite is an extension to other fields – e.g. public administration, governments – of the critique launched under Marshall Aid against private enterprises. This elite is called into question because its access to power at the top of organisations and institutions arises not from demonstrable competence but from educational success. It is an elite chosen on the basis of a rigorous selection process with an emphasis on academic achievement assessed by competitive examinations. Equality of access to elite positions is thus ensured but it is only formal equality. The education system from the early stages through to the *Grandes Ecoles*, from which the brightest students will graduate, having been successful at a number of competitive examinations, is a creaming-off process. The best from the best *Grandes Ecoles* will automatically gain access to the most sought-after public administration posts with some of them subsequently moving into the private sector. This education process which favours a particular type of knowledge – largely theoretical – is thought to favour a type of disposition and a type of knowledge which bias success towards membership of certain social classes.

Bourdieu remarks with some acerbity that these are people for whom success is a 'consécration' and the education content merely a way of 'enseigner aux poissons à nager' (Bourdieu 1981, p. 20). It is easy to see why this elite is deemed incompetent (Fauconnier 1996, p. 17). Its 'sélection-élection' as Bourdieu puts it (1981 p. 49) is in effect the culmination of a process that seeks only to create 'distinction'. Bourdieu never tires of pointing out the strong influence of the ownership of cultural capital on the educative action as the principal means of conferring or confirming distinction (Bourdieu 1979, p. 89). But different educational systems define success leading to disinction differently. In the United Kingdom, for example, public schools used to provide the means of doing so via sports. In so far as the personality of this elite is concerned, the individualism bred into its members by the need to come out best in competitive examinations is thought to make them somewhat isolated with respect to human relations. This, in turn, translates into a hierarchical sense of self-worth that hinders fluid interpersonal encounters. Group work, informal co-operation, particularly when this involves crossing boundaries of status and rank, are said to be anathema to the elite. Nor is the knowledge gained from their formal education of much use to them in the positions they are chosen to occupy, since it is an education mostly of an abstract, theoretical nature. It makes them spurn the concrete or the practical (Fauconnier 1996, p. 80). Whilst it is conceded sometimes that this is not of necessity an obstacle to efficiency in public administration, the fact that administration is the privileged route to senior posts in the private sector raises an important objection. It is that the process – termed 'pantouflage' – assumes an equivalency between those qualities required of work in the public and those required in the private sector. This is one of the reasons given for the slow march of management procedures in France.

The argument about the elite has some merit but reduces organisation to the habits of mind and behaviour of those at the top. It is surprising to see that even Crozier, who has an organisational view of behaviour, indulges in this type of reductionism (Crozier 1995, p. 8). Elite reductionism ignores the complexity of cultural norms which permeate the tissue of organisations: that is to say, the expectations of those lower down in the hierarchy and whether they find improved cross-hierarchical relations attractive. Elite critics argue that it is enough for elites to modify their posture and initiate change affecting themselves for others to follow suit. They overlook the fact that advantages which are proposed as a justification for change may be viewed differently by subordinates. In short, they fail to recognise that the cultural orientation on specific issues relating to organised life usually provokes different responses from different positions of the organisational structure. These responses may even be contradictory and so make situations more difficult. Thus, as Hofstede observes on the question of hierarchy, French employees tend to express disrespect for bosses who ask for their advice before taking a decision (Bollinger and Hofstede 1992, p. 82), although, contradictorily, the same employees wish for more participation. Hofstede has also shown, on the basis of a comparative study of forty countries, that France has a very high degree of 'distance hiérarchique' (power distance). The term refers to the fact that in some countries like France the distribution of power in organisations and institutions is extremely unequal. It favours those at the top who determine in great measure the behaviour of others. France has also, according to the same study, a high degree of 'contrôle d'incertitude' ('uncertainty avoidance'), a point Crozier touches on as well when when he observes that lack of face-to-face contact is actually a way of avoiding contact. A high degree of 'uncertainty avoidance' in France means that as little as possible is left to chance in organised life, as witnessed by the predominance of laws and regulations, not to mention the existence of identity cards or of bureaucratic arrangements in which it is imperative that everyone knows their place.

Both 'distance hiérarchique' and 'contrôle d'incertitude' have come into play in a series of programmes for change initiated either by the state or by employers since the war. In so far as these touched on the interests of those situated in the middle rungs of the hierarchical ladder, they raised objections to do with status. Not surprisingly, the attempt to import the principle of Japanese quality circles into the structure of companies met with middle-manager resistance. Quality circles are supposed to encourage in organisation members the habit of what are called 'transversal relations'. These seek to cut through hierarchical lines of division and get people to co-operate on specific projects. Middle-managers, although involved indirectly, saw them as a threat to status when those of a lower rank approached them for information required for quality circle projects. 'Management by objectives', imported from the U.S., was similarly resisted because it involved assessment of middle-manager work by senior managers. It brought fear of control over a group that had traditionally prized its independence. Nor have workers shown much enthusiasm for management novelties brought in from outside. They have not so much resisted as shown indifference to them and this is why experiments with Swedish industrial democracy on participatory schemes of various kinds have failed in their ultimate aim of integrating the workforce (Chevalier 1989, p. 202). Work, as one goes down the hierarchical ladder of French organisations, becomes more instrumental, aggravating yet another tendency highlighted by both Crozier and Hofstede: individualism.

Is French exceptionalism crisis-generating?

There is no lack of examples quoted of dysfunctions related to state activities and the culture associated with these. Hierarchy is portrayed as the main culprit. One recent example focuses on lobbying activities within the European Community. French state representatives, it seems, instinctively address themselves to senior civil servants when those in charge of a particular dossier which interests them may be at a lower level. Time is thus wasted and other countries' representatives gain an advantage over their French colleagues (Revol 2000, p. 87). A similar phenomenon occurs when French firms buy out foreign firms and seek to re-shape the hierarchy in order to conform to their own vision of organisational structure. The penchant for risk avoidance also brings disadvantages. French firms choose on the whole to invest much more in Europe, where markets are more secure and stable, than in the Third World markets. State bureaucracy, for its part, with the proliferation of rules and regulations that it generates, hinders foreign investment in France.

It is once again Crozier who seeks to expose the more deep-seated cause of the 'exceptionalism' at the root of these and other counter-productive results. Beyond bureaucracy and the culture that legitimises it, he finds an obsessive attachment to a particular identity in the way, for example, that the French seek derogation from European legislation that threatens them, rather than simply ignoring it (Crozier 2000, p. 36). The French, and most notably the elite, are exponents of *la pensée unique*: they think there is only one way of thinking which is unique to the French. In so far as organisations are concerned, the elite runs them according to principles that can be traced back to a primitive Cartesian fundamentalism (Crozier 1995, p. 41). This elite behaves as if problems can be broken into their constituent elements and unique solutions deduced from them. Crozier elaborates on this to say that, in fact, it is solutions that define problems for the elite rather than the other way round. In short, he accuses them of dogmatism. The mechanism at work in this, he says, is a deductive rationality that pre-supposes detachment from problems to be solved on the part of those seeking the solutions. Needless to say, this putative detachment nurtured in the elite by an education system which prizes objective thinking, justifies in its turn all manner of hierarchical practices in French organisations and institutions. It buttresses, in the eyes of its critics, the distinction between those who think and those who act. Since, as Crozier argues, it also involves an intellectual way of thinking which is linear and causal, it is unsuited to a world defined by complexity. Complexity requires by all accounts that one understand the systemic determinants of every action, event or decision. Crozier therefore concludes that the prescriptive models to which *la pensée unique* is wedded are wholly inappropriate in a world in which, in addition, everthing is immaterial and relational (Crozier 1995, p. 41).

In defence of the French model: exceptionalism redeemed

When invoking complexity, adversaries of French 'exceptionalism' think, as a contrast, of lean, fluid organisations where actors are said to have autonomy and where decision-making is devolved and team-work becomes the norm. The vertical, traditional pyramid organisation, Sérieyx claims, has been shown to be out-dated and inflexible (Sérieyx 1994, p. 101). The modern organisation, on the other hand, is horizontal, and in its ideal form seamless. It is a network organisation, transitory in so far as the combination of its constituent parts are concerned, and therefore more responsive to changes in the environment. It is driven by time, forever remoulding itself to meet the challenge of technical innovation and new market conditions. Aoki, the Japanese theorist, calls it the 'J' model (Aoki 1991, p. 1). This model is said to be superior to the hierarchical, bureaucratic model (the H model) built on Taylorist principles of division of labour and job specialisation. H, thriving in times of long-term stability of production technology, manpower skills and market conditions, has, in Aoki's

view, served its purpose. The army model conceived by Taylor, one of whose aims was to stop workers 'soldiering', that is to say malingering, must give way to the family-community model of the firm which is convivial and co-operative.

Not all French thinkers or management practitioners are convinced by this argument. Nor are those who adopt these models conscious of the problems they raise in their own countries of origin. Fashion more than necessity seems to dictate the need to import them. Fashion itself is the creation of a legion of management consultants and of specialised management journals. Midler refers to their output as steeped in a rhetoric that associates the universal and the everyday (Midler 1986, p. 75). However, the rhetoric has been influential. Even a weekly news magazine like *Le Point* regularly publishes articles of two to three pages under the rubric of 'management'. It is useful to mention this because the interest in France in management and company reforms has been greater than in any other European country. For example, Tom Peters' *In Search of Excellence* sold 140,000 copies when it first appeared in French.

The objection raised by those who question the usefulness of importing foreign management models is that these, not to be confused with scientific paradigms, are culture-specific. Their success depends on the specific resources, human and material, available to particular cultures. When there is no fit between models and cultures, models are no more than techniques which, when applied to human relations, become instruments of social engineering (Villette 1996, p. 83). This is central to the contention of those who insist on the French model's capacity to change and adapt to new conditions. They insist that it must not be through transplantation from without but by way of evolution within. They argue that the fact France is the fourth most powerful industrial country in the world, would indicate a degree of dynamism and efficiency that opponents of the French model all too easily ignore. The champion of this standpoint, Philippe d'Iribarne, offers both a coherent defence and, in a tangential way, a critique of the bureaucratic thesis.

Iribarne, like Crozier, stresses the importance of tradition in French organisation culture. He even agrees that this brings the French model close in appearance to a feudal or a caste system. But he does not agree that the result is a backward or a dysfunctional system. It may seem that tradition belongs to a distant era but this is merely because it represents a historic compromise between groups arrived at centuries ago, the manifestation of a French way of living together in society (Iribarne 1989, p. 56). The French model is, in other words, a social compact that defines relationships between different social groups, drawing boundaries between them of what is acceptable or not acceptable, and thus setting the conditions on which co-operation takes place. These conditions have nothing to do with avoiding face-to-face relations. Nor do they entail centralisation or impersonal rule (Iribarne 1990, p. 263). They indicate that there is something other than bureaucracy as the operational logic of organisation. This logic, Iribarne says, is the 'logic of honour'.

To illustrate what he means by 'logic of honour', Iribarne contrasts it with the 'logic of contract' typical of American organisations. Both have to do with authority relationships. In the U.S.A., Iribarne says, authority relationships are based on contracts between superiors and subordinates. A contract stipulates in detail what work is expected of a subordinate, and inefficiency or non-fulfilment of what the contract prescribes invites sanctions and ultimately dismissal. The 'logic of honour' is different in that it is not a superior who defines what a person's work consists of but the 'work tradition' itself, and it is not fear of dismissal or desire for reward that motivates the employee, but rather a sense of honour which membership of the various work traditions engenders.

The notion of work tradition is central to Iribarne's explanation of how work works – or organisation organises – according to the French model. Apart from setting out what a person's functions are, his work tradition assigns him, as in a feudal system, to an order which marks his status and position. This in turn has a bearing on the type of authority relationships he has with his superior. Qualifications and training are decisive in this respect. The higher the qualifications and the level of training attained, the more 'noble' an occupation, the more relaxed relations between superiors and subordinates. For instance, maintenance workers have easier relationships with their superiors than production workers. Their work and their occupational status mark them off as more 'noble' in a skills-based hierarchy which includes everyone in the organisation; the most 'noble' at the top and the least 'noble' – e.g. unskilled workers, the serfs, as it were – at the bottom. This is one aspect of the 'logic of honour'.

A second aspect is a sense of duty which accompanies the fulfilment of the tasks set for everyone by their work tradition. A person does his work because this is what is expected of him. He may interpret how he does it, but as long as the result is of a high quality, that is what matters. Consequently, the American contract with its attendant sanction or reward is out of place in the French context (Iribarne 1989, p. 20). It is not fear or ambition that motivates the employee but a sort of ethical impulse to fulfil what his work tradition prescribes. Compulsion is of course not entirely absent but applies mostly to those at the bottom of the hierarchy.

The diversity of authority relationships which the 'logic of honour' expresses and the different work traditions that underlie them means that the organisation is effectively decentralised. Iribarne refers to the various groups with their respective work traditions as 'territories'. However, this type of diversity with the existence of quasi-autonomous groups creates its own problems, and inter-group co-operation is not one of them. As long as the symbolic code of honour and status are respected, co-operation routinely takes place. Problems, however, arise when two contiguous groups or 'territories' disagree; for example, when a demarcation dispute crops up or else a new technological development blurs responsibilities between two groups. In such instances conflicts, heavily laden with symbols, take place, but they are conducted with a sense of moderation which governs the outcome. Conflicts, most of them no more than verbal, are a frequent occurrence in the organisation which Iribarne describes. But they achieve an important aim:

they are the principle motor of change, the way the whole system adjusts to pressure both from inside and outside. Iribarne calls this process self-adjustment.

Conclusion: ideology and power

What the process of self-adjustment and negotiations within the parameters of the logic of honour shows is that motivation, co-operation and even flexibility are not the preserve of imported management models. They have flourished in French organisations as well but in different forms. The issue raised by Iribarne in relation to modernisation in France, beyond his insistence on the fact that the French system is self-adjusting, is how one introduces changes that have potentially dislocating effects but are nevertheless vital. This rules out as intolerably dislocating most of the organisation/management models imported from outside of France. They have different cultural codes from that of the French with which they clash. They therefore tend to offend sensitivities, create suspicion and cause resistance. By contrast, Iribarne shows how new technologies which are potentially dislocating in that they threaten conflicts generated by clashes with the code of honour of a noble occupation – e.g. that of electricians in relation to mechanics – can be, and have been successfully negotiated in French industries (Iribarne 1987, p. 14).

According to Iribarne, even when the dictates of the logic of honour are followed, change is accompanied by pressure. Success depends on how this is countered. However, other countries experience pressure too. Sweden, for example, has a reputedly consensual culture in contrast to its hierarchical French counterpart, which is noted for being conflictual. But consensus in arriving at decisions is not without pressure; there is pressure to conform and in addition the possible exclusion of those who do not (Iribarne 1998, p. 93). To ask that France becomes like Sweden and Japan is to assume the superiority of some models of co-operation or decision-making over others. It is also to forget that some of the very aspects of French culture, so often condemned, have significant advantages. Thus France is said to have a culture of ascription – the attribution of status – and is therefore less efficient than countries like the United Kingdom which have an achievement culture. However, at least one effect of ascription is that it may in some instances lead to higher performances, as when a person tries to live up to his status. This may explain the high calibre and dedication of French engineers and technicians or the French focus on long-term projects, as against the short-termism and bottom-line obsession of the Anglo-American countries.

Ascription is usually associated with a bureaucratic, hierarchical command structure. In the often-made distinction between countries where managers are said to view the organisation as political system and those where they are said to view it as a network, France is placed in the former category. The distinction is useful, since at the very least it demonstrates an increasing tendency of those who postulate the superiority of network organisations to elide the question of power. To many of its critics, the network principle is for this reason pure ideology. In any case, some of the qualities attributed to the network organisation – autonomy, integration, dynamism, adaptability – are mutually contradictory. How, for instance, is autonomy to be reconciled with altruistic co-operation and teamwork in the pursuit of collective benefit? The solution has been to postulate the unity of diversity around a new function of managers as leaders. Leadership is thus substituted for power as the new binding element of organisational unity.

In reality however, leadership does not banish power but is a subtle version of it. Kindleberger shows how in international relations, theoretically a system of mutual dependencies, the function of leadership assumed by the United States allows it to establish its hegemony through its capacity to impose its strategies on other nations (Kindleberger 1988, p. 150). In internal relations as in the global economy, the attempt to re-engineer the French model is looked on by its opponents as one further step towards French alignment with the American distribution. The danger is all the more present to the French exceptionalists since, as Enriquez points out, management models increasingly supply the norms and values applicable to institutions and organisations (Enriquez 1990, p. 205). Were they to succeed and the state to retreat, the argument goes, justice and solidarity would disappear. And so the door would be left open to economic exploitation justified by a belief in a philosophy of the market as the determinant of resource allocation. It would result, as in the U.S.A., in indifference by those who succeed to depressed wages and living conditions for those who do not (Coutrot 1998, pp. 214-5).

The new ideology of the network firm and the market philosophy that supports it – neo-liberalism – is also condemned for extracting co-operation out of coercion. Fear of unemployment disciplines a workforce, makes it more docile and, therefore, co-operative in a perverted sense of the word. The most radical champions of exceptionalism fasten on to on this idea, taking their cue from Foucault who elaborates the notion of discipline to show that the new management models are the end-game of a process which preceded Taylorism. This process started as discipline, leading to a process of normalisation which tied every worker to a machine: the age of 'man-machine'. It went on with Taylor and the division of labour to become the age of 'man-system' when each worker assigned to a job took his place in a totality of operations, i.e. a system of interdependence that ensured continuity of the work process. We are now in the age of 'man-organ': the organisation is no longer, as in a system, limited to internal co-ordination but has now become one in which each member is like an organ in a body acting automatically with other organs in response to stimuli from inside and outside. Discipline in the age of man-machine and man-system was action on the body. Discipline now, in the age of managerialist ideology, is action on behaviour and on attitudes in order to change mentality. This involves normalisation of the mind and of representations (Jorda 2000, pp. 162-3). From 'savoir faire' (knowing how to) the emphasis has changed to 'savoir être' (knowing how to be) which has cultural implications, referring as it does to general protocols of behaviour amongst other things. It is this that the protagonists of 'exceptionalism' fear the most: the danger of cultural homogeneity and the loss of singularity through indoctrination into a different way of life. Alternatively, they fear the break-up of a social contract which Iribarne seeks to express through the 'logic of honour'.

Bibliography

Allègre, C., and Jeambar, D. (1996) *Questions de France*, Paris: Fayard.

Aoki, M. (1991) 'Le Management japonais: le modèle J de Aoki', *Problèmes Economiques*, no. 2225, 15 mai, pp. 1-14.

Bollinger, D. and Hofstede, G. (1992) *Les Différences culturelles dans le management*, Paris: Les Editions d'organisation.

Boltanski, L. (1982) *Les Cadres: la formation d'un groupe social*, Paris: Minuit.

Bourdieu, P. (1981) 'Epreuve scolaire et consécration sociale: les classes préparatoires aux Grandes Ecoles', *Actes de la recherche en sciences sociales*, no. 39, septembre, pp. 3-70.

Bourdieu, P. (1979) *La Distinction: critique sociale du jugement*, Paris: Minuit.

Coutrot, T. (1998) *L'Enterprise néo-libérale, nouvelle utopie capitaliste?* Paris: La Découverte.

Crozier, M. (1963) *Le Phénomène bureaucratique*, Paris: Seuil.

Crozier, M. (1970) *La Société bloquée*, Paris: Seuil.

Crozier, M. & Tilliette, B. (1995) *La Crise de l'intelligence: essai sur l'impuissance des élites à se réformer*, Paris: Inter Edtions.

Crozier, M. & Tilliette, B. (2000) *Quand la France s'ouvrira*, Paris: Fayard.

Debré, R. (1989) *Que vive la république*, Paris: Odile Jacob.

Domenach, J.-M. (1997) *Regarder la France: essai sur le malaise français*, Paris: Perrin.

Enriquez, E, (1990) 'L'Entreprise comme lien social: "un colosse aux pieds d'argile"' in R. Sainsaulieu (ed.) *L'Entreprise une affaire de société*, Paris: Presses de la fondation nationale des sciences politiques, pp. 203-28.

Fauconnier, P. (1996) *Le Talent qui dort*, Paris: Seuil.

Guerlain, P. (1996) *Miroirs transatlantiques: la France et les Etats-Unis entre passions et indifférences*, Paris: L'Harmattan.

Iribarne, P. d'. (1989) *La Logique de l'honneur: gestion des entreprises et traditions nationales*, Paris: Seuil.

Iribarne, P. d', et al (1998) *Cultures et mondialisation: gérer par-delà les frontières*, Paris: Seuil.

Jorda, H. (2000) *Travail et discipline: de la manufacture à l'entreprise intelligente*, Paris: L'Harmattan.

Kindleberger, C. (1988) *The International Economic Order*, Brighton: Harvester.

Martin, D. (ed.) (1989) *Participation et changement social dans l'entreprise*, Paris: L'Harmattan.

Midler, C. (1986) 'Logique de la mode managériale' *Gérer et comprendre*, juin, pp. 74-5.

Peyrefitte, A. (1995) *La Société de confiance*, Paris: Odile Jacob.

Pitts, J.R. (1981) 'Les Français et l'autorité', in J.D. Reynaud and Y. Grafmeyer (eds.) *Français qui êtes-vous?* Documentaion française, pp. 285-300.

Revol, M. (2000) 'Lobbying: la regrettable exception française', *Le Point*, no. 1433, 3 mars, pp. 86-8.

Safran, W. (1995) *The French Polity*, London: Longman.

Saint-Etienne, C. (1992) *L'Exception française: pour un nouveau modèle démocratique de croissance*, Paris: Armand Colin.

Sérieyx, H. (1994) *L'Effet Gulliver: quand les institutions se figent dans un monde tourbillonnaire*, Paris: Calmann-Lévy.

Touraine, A., et al (1996) *Le Grand refus: réflexions sur la grève de décembre 1995*, Paris: Fayard.

Touraine, A. (1999) *Comment sortir du libéralisme?* Paris: Fayard.

Trompenaars, F. and Hampden-Turner, C. (1998) *Riding the Waves of Culture: Understanding Cultural Diversity in Business*, London: Nicholas Brealey.

Villette, M. (1996) 'Le Management jetable: récits du 'management réel'', Paris: La Découverte.

Food in France: From la nouvelle cuisine to la malbouffe

Ben Taylor

The term *la malbouffe* was included in *Le Petit Larousse* for the first time in the 2001 edition, endorsing the word's currency as an expression of anxiety about the quality of certain types of contemporary food. The journalist Gilles Luneau has commented on the aptness of the term in conveying a sense of the inedible:

> Un article féminin devance un préfixe masculin accouplé à un mot féminin fleurant l'argot: l'ensemble a une allure étrange. On fait tourner le mot en bouche sans trop oser le laisser sortir. Une impression bizarre, de faute de langage. A l'entendre, et plus encore à le prononcer, on a déjà un début de nausée. De celles qui peuvent vous assaillir à la vue du plateau-repas d'un fast-food. Et on se dit que le mot sonne juste. (Luneau 2000, p. 7)

The expression was popularised by José Bové, a sheep farmer on the Larzac plateau in Aveyron and, in 1987, one of the founder members of la Confédération paysanne. Bové came to prominence in August 1999 when he was arrested and imprisoned, along with four others, following a demonstration at a McDonald's restaurant under construction in Millau in south-west France. Bové's rejection of *la malbouffe* of McDonald's (he described it as 'la nourriture industrielle, dégradée, sans saveur, qui détruit complètement le goût des consommateurs' (Rollat 1999)) struck a chord. Not only did it seem to represent a rebuke to American fast food, it also seemed to be a legitimate expression of many of the contemporary anxieties surrounding food. In the wake of such crises as BSE in beef, dioxins in chicken and the introduction of genetically modified (GM) produce, anxieties about the quality and safety of food are prevalent (Henley 2000b). In the light of such concerns, Bové received widespread public support and generous media coverage where, with his large, droopy moustache, he was feted as a modern day Astérix (Bové 2000, p. 6; Rollat 1999; Sabatier 2000). Two books of interviews with him were published and went on to become best-sellers (Bové 2000; Bové and Dufour 2000). 'Durant l'été 1999,' Bové has proclaimed, 'l'alimentation est devenue un débat politique' (Bové and Dufour 2000, p. 78). This chapter will focus on the debate about *la malbouffe* instigated by Bové's protest. I will argue that this debate is principally organised around two concerns: first, the issue of French national identity, and second, the issue of modernity and its impact on food practices.

Asked to explain the popularity of Bové, Jean Viard has suggested that it arises from the fact that he is 'vu come porteur des valeurs de cette République. Bové et Marianne, avec ses gerbes de blé, feraient un couple superbe!' (Viard 2000, p. 5).

That the scourge of *la malbouffe* should be linked with the figurehead of the Republic is interesting, and not only because when Bové was voted the most popular man of 1999 in France, the most popular woman was the supermodel, Letitia Casta, on whom the updated image of Marianne for the new millennium was modelled. It is also interesting because food has so regularly been regarded as 'perhaps the distinctive ingredient of French identity' (Sonnenfeld 1999, p. xvii; quoting Jean-Louis Flandrin). The growth of the fast food market in France, and with it the increasing availability of *la malbouffe*, is viewed by many as a form of 'McDo-mination' (Belleret 2000; quoting José Bové), as an affront to France's own gastronomic traditions and as a challenge to her national identity. At the same time, however, fast food is a key example of 'la modernité alimentaire', as Jean-Pierre Poulain has described it (Normand 1999). While pre-modern societies were largely consigned to consuming seasonal foods produced within the immediate locale, modern societies have gradually been able to consume foods from ever more distant places, which have often been preserved over long periods of time (see James 1996; Lee 1993). Anthony Giddens has identified one of the principal processes of modernity as the 'development of disembedding mechanisms' (Giddens 1990, p. 53), in other words, the mechanisms whereby places are disembedded from their locale, and brought into contact with other distant and disparate places. The development of transport systems, and of techniques for processing and preserving foodstuffs, belongs to this modern process of disembedding. Bové's response to McDonald's is articulated in relation to questions about the impact of such processes upon the food system. Indeed, he has used his high profile to develop and publicise a wide-ranging critique of globalisation, modern farming and contemporary food production. His account of *la malbouffe* is elaborated in relation to a critique of the World Trade Organisation (WTO), of intensive farming practices, and of associated recent food crises.

In the course of this chapter, I will examine accounts of the development of 'Mc-Domination' within French culture. I will then turn to Bové's critique of *la malbouffe* and the debate which it has generated. I will begin, however, by reflecting on one of the principal controversies about food in France in the 1970s and 1980s: the debate about *la nouvelle cuisine*.

La nouvelle cuisine

The relatively recent emergence of *la malbouffe* as the most pressing food-related issue within French culture can be illustrated by turning to two recent analyses of post-war France, both of which focus instead on *la nouvelle cuisine* as the principal culinary issue. In *French Culture Since 1945*, for example, Stephen Mennell considers the degree of continuity between *la nouvelle cuisine* and the culinary codes established by Escoffier and Montagné (Mennell 1993, pp. 176-91). Meanwhile, in *France Today*, John Ardagh discusses the extent to which *la nouvelle cuisine* poses a threat to traditional forms of French *haute cuisine* (Ardagh 1990, pp. 388-402). Just as *la malbouffe* provokes questions about French tradition and national identity, then, so too did *la nouvelle cuisine*.

As the *Larousse Gastronomique* explains, *la nouvelle cuisine* dedicated itself to 'authenticity and simplicity in cooking'[1] (*Larousse Gastronomique* 1988, p. 732). In 1969, Henri Gault and Christian Millau founded the Gault-Millau food guide, which championed this new culinary style, propelling chefs such as Paul Bocuse, Michel Guérard and the Troisgros brothers into the limelight. Rejecting the heavy sauces and rich flavours of *haute cuisine*, *la nouvelle cuisine* favoured a lighter style predicated on freshness, rapid cooking techniques and natural flavours. It was, importantly, a *cuisine du marché*, constructing dishes from the best ingredients available in the market each day. Philippe Faure, the current director of Gault-Millau, has suggested that this principle would have garnered the support of José Bové himself: 'face aux conséquences désastreuses de l'agriculture intensive, Gault et Millau ordonnaient en effet de ne travailler que des produits dont l'origine et la qualité soient absolument irréprochables'(Faure 1999). In this respect, *la nouvelle cuisine* can be seen as an attempt to resist certain aspects of a modernised food system. At the same time, however, *la nouvelle cuisine* represented an attempt to modernise French culinary tradition itself. In this respect, as Mennell explains, *la nouvelle cuisine* should be seen as the latest in a series of culinary revolutions which have taken place since the seventeenth century (Mennell 1993). Mennell argues that such innovations have tended to combine resistance and renewal, rejecting certain aspects of the dominant culinary style while at the same time reaffirming certain inherited principles (Mennell 1993, p. 182). As the example of *la nouvelle cuisine* suggests, the process whereby culinary traditions are established is itself extremely complex. As Julia Csergo has argued, the various styles of French regional cooking were themselves only properly defined as recently as the nineteenth and twentieth centuries. Initially this belonged to a wider process of celebrating the diversity of the Republic after the revolution. With the development of the tourist industry in the late nineteenth century, however, it received added momentum. In an attempt to marry tourism and gastronomy, tourist guidebooks were keen to codify the culinary specialities a traveller could expect to encounter within each region (Csergo, 1999).

It is in its inclination to challenge received culinary tradition that the controversial potential of *la nouvelle cuisine* resided, shocking the French public with its appetite for novelty. The *Larousse Gastronomique* approves of certain examples of such novelty,

> for instance, Jacques Manière's eggs Céline, with caviar and a little vodka; Pierre Vedel's lobster soup with sweet garlic; Michel Guérard's aubergine (eggplant) purée cooked in saffron-flavoured steam; or Alain Senderen's calf's sweetbread in sea-urchin cream. (*Larousse Gastronomique*, 1988, p. 732)

However, it also argues that there is a point at which the novelising imperative 'oversteps the mark':

> the "pink at the backbone" rule can mean a fish oozing with blood; small vegetables become fragmented; and mousses and purées are added to every sauce. Although

---

1. All citations are taken from the English language edition of *Larousse Gastronomique*.

novel, such combinations can become pretentious, like the "mad" salads, where lobster may find itself sharing a plate with foie gras, or herring is paired with pineapple. Where then is the much-vaunted simplicity? (Larousse Gastronomique, 1988, p. 732)

Since the 1980s, the controversy surrounding *la nouvelle cuisine* has largely subsided. Nevertheless, the spate of recent food scares and concerns about the globalisation of food continue to generate debate within the field of professional cookery in France. In November 1999, *Le Monde* hosted a roundtable discussion between some of France's top chefs to debate the issue of *la malbouffe* (Belleret 1999). While most of the chefs involved remained generally confident that French consumers were well informed about the problems and risks that it posed, not all chefs are so optimistic. For example, Alain Passard, a chef with three Michelin stars to his name, has all but removed meat from the menu of his Arpège restaurant in Paris as a result of anxieties about its declining quality (Henley 2000a). It is not simply questions about food safety and quality which the debate about *la malbouffe* has provoked, however. Faure has raised questions about the very future of the French restaurant in a global economy:

Un conservatoire des arts et traditions populaires? Un diorama "France éternelle" pour riches clientèles étrangères, avec toute la difficulté qu'il y a à évaluer ce type d'établissements remplis de Japonais, d'Allemands et d'Américains, venus se ressourcer dans des lieux pour ainsi dire désertés par les Français? Ou alors un espace de résistance active à la mondialisation, à la malbouffe, aux aberrations transgéniques, aux volailles à la dioxine, aux attaques de prions? (Faure 1999)

What Faure's inquest demonstrates is that, although the debate about *la nouvelle cuisine* might have now largely dissipated, the concerns about national identity and culinary tradition which that debate broached are still resonant. In order to examine such concerns further, however, I want to turn to consider the issue of 'Mc-Domination' within French culture.

'Mc-Domination'

The first McDonald's opened in Paris in 1972, and it is now the largest restaurant chain in France with some 800 outlets (Normand 1999). George Ritzer has argued that the form of rationalisation that we find in the structures of the McDonald's enterprise – its global ability to provide standardised products – has now replaced the bureaucratic imperative identified by Samuel Weber as the paradigm of rationality in modern society. According to Ritzer, the success of McDonald's is based upon the principles of efficiency, calculability, predictability and control (Ritzer 1993, pp. 9-12). He contends that, in applying these principles, McDonald's has 'not only revolutionized the restaurant business, but also American society, and ultimately, the world' (Ritzer 1993, p.xi).

Ritzer's thesis has its critics. While some have complained that it ends up as 'a lament on modernity and industrialism' (Finkelstein 1999, p. 80), others have contested the status of McDonaldization as a new form of rationalisation, rather than simply an extension of the processes distinguished by Weber (Smart 1999). Nevertheless, Ritzer's account of McDonald's global success provides an ideal starting point for a consideration of the impact of McDonald's within French culture. Ritzer quotes an anonymous French socialist politician expressing concern about the opening of Euro Disney by suggesting that it will 'bombard France with uprooted creations that are to culture what fast food is to gastronomy' (Ritzer 1993, p. 12). As Richard Kuisel has shown, such reactions to American culture, which treat it as a shoddy, foreign threat to French traditions, have arisen frequently within the course of post-war French history. In the period after the end of the Second World War, for example, there was a campaign, orchestrated chiefly by the French Communist Party, against the import of Coca-Cola (Kuisel 1991, 1993).

Rick Fantasia provides the most detailed analysis of the fast food industry in France. Drawing on a series of interviews with McDonald's employees and customers, he argues that it is precisely the Americanness of fast food which sustains its allure (Fantasia 1995, pp. 228-30). As a result, he suggests, the French hamburger chains which have attempted to capitalise on McDonald's success, tend to market themselves under 'American-sounding names' ('France-Quick, FreeTime, Magic Burger, B'Burger, Manhattan Burger, Katy's Burger, Love Burger, and Kiss Burger') (Fantasia 1995, p. 206). Alongside such chains, there are other companies (La Brioche Dorée, La Croissanterie, La Viennoiserie) who offer fast food à la française, providing traditional French snacks on a McDonaldized basis (Fantasia 1995, p. 207; Ritzer 1993, p. 3). As Fantasia argues, however, while such chains have managed to establish themselves with some success in the USA, 'the exchange of croissants for hamburgers has not represented anything approximating an equal cultural exchange':

> they have been produced and marketed not by professional French "boulangers" or "patissiers" drawing upon local raw materials and family recipes, but in mechanized kitchens, supplied by centralized warehouses, using standardized recipes and processes, and sold in restaurants designed for their efficiency and visual hyperbole. (Fantasia 1995, p. 234)

Such developments add weight to Ritzer's thesis about McDonaldization as a global process whose effects are felt beyond the McDonald's Corporation itself.

While the Americanness of McDonald's might contribute to its popularity, it is also often a principal target for its detractors. As Barry Smart notes, when resistance to McDonald's has arisen, it is usually motivated primarily by anxieties about 'American economic and cultural imperialism' rather than about the processes of rationalisation identified by Ritzer (Smart 1999, p. 17). For its critics, as Jean-Michel Normand suggests,

> le pavillon rouge et jaune de McDonald's est la nouvelle version de la bannière étoilée de l'Amérique, dont l'hégémonie commerciale menace l'agriculture et dont l'hégémonie culturelle mine insidieusement les comportements alimentaires, effets sacrés de l'identité française. (Normand 1999)

Normand provides a succinct summary of the concerns typically expressed about 'Mc-Domination' within French culture. I will now examine the manner in which such concerns are played out in the debate about *la malbouffe*.

Bové and *la malbouffe*

On 12 August 1999, Bové led a demonstration to dismantle ('démonter' is the verb Bové uses (Bové 2000, p. 76)) a McDonald's restaurant that was being built in the town of Millau. The action had been organised by la Confédération paysanne in response to measures taken by the USA following the European Union's decision to prohibit the sale of American beef which had been treated with hormone supplements. The US responded by imposing a 100 per cent import tax on a range of European products, including Roquefort cheese, a policy which was endorsed by the WTO. Roquefort is made on the Larzac plateau, close to Millau, and Bové's own herd of sheep produce milk for its manufacture. The protesters targeted McDonald's, as Bové explains, as an expression of opposition to the logic of globalisation which the American levy represented (Bové 2000, p. 74). Following the demonstration, Bové was arrested, along with four other demonstrators, and imprisoned, eventually spending nineteen nights in jail. A photograph of him wearing handcuffs, smiling and raising his arms aloft has since become one of the most familiar media images of Bové (Luneau 2000, p. 8).

Bové already had a long history of political activism of this sort, and in interviews he has sought to characterise his political philosophy as a form of anarcho-syndicalism, situating himself within a tradition incorporating la Fédération jurasienne in 1870s France, figures such as Fernand Pelloutier and Emile Pouget, who were involved in founding la Confédération Générale du Travail (CGT), and the strategy of la Confederación Nacional del Trabajo (CNT) during the Spanish Civil War (Bové 2000, pp. 33-4; Bové and Dufour 2000, pp. 187-8). Ideologically, he declares himself 'plus proche de Bakounine que de Marx' (Bové 2000, p. 33), and the anarcho-syndicalist emphasis upon direct action can be seen in the development of Bové's own political commitments. He had originally settled on the Larzac plateau in the early 1970s, part of a collective attempt to wrestle the territory from the French Army, which in 1971 had declared its intention to extend its activities in the area, a proposal eventually cancelled by President Mitterrand in 1981 (Bové 2000, pp. 11-22; Bové and Dufour 2000, pp. 53-6; Ardagh 1990, pp. 326-7). He had also participated in the anti-nuclear movement in the 1980s, and in 1995 joined the Greenpeace demonstrations against France's nuclear tests in the Pacific. In January 1998 he had helped to destroy a silo of GM maize in the town of Nérac in the course of a protest which was organised by la Confédération paysanne (Bové 2000, pp. 45-54). Bové received a suspended sentence along with eight others. It was the demonstration at McDonald's, however, which not only propelled Bové into the limelight, but also ensured the debate about *la malbouffe* a prominent position within the French public arena.

By the time Bové was released from prison, on 6 September 1999, he had become a potent political symbol, championed by groups from across the political spectrum. From the moment that he was imprisoned, an assortment of unions and political organisations on the left offered their support, identifying Bové's actions as a necessary step in the struggle against globalisation, and demanding his release (Bové and Dufour 2000, pp. 29-30; Monnot 1999). The regional press in south-west France, *Midi Libre*, *La Dépêche du Midi* and *Sud-Ouest*, also endorsed Bové. As Jean-Paul Besset explains, they found in Bové 'le héros national d'une France inquiète de ce qu'elle mange et de la manière dont elle pourrait être dévorée' (Besset 1999b). On the extreme right, Bruno Mégret and Jean-Marie Le Pen of Le Front National sympathised with Bové's attempt to defend French traditions against Americanisation (Besset 1999a; Bové 2000, pp. 68-9). Within government, Bové's actions were denounced for their illegality, but his widespread popularity nevertheless necessitated a conciliatory approach. While condemning the tactics used by la Confédération paysanne, for example, Jean Glavany, the agriculture minister, claimed to share the farmers' anger at 'la prise d'otages inacceptable' which the decision of the USA represented (*Le Monde*, 25 août 1999, p. 28). Shortly after Bové's release, President Jacques Chirac similarly denounced the American policy, proclaiming, 'Nous sommes tous des paysans!' (*Le Monde*, 18 septembre 1999, p. 1). He has also been filmed reading one of Bové's books (Burke 2000, p. 24).

Bové's campaign did not end at Millau. Following his arrest, a series of similar protests against McDonald's were launched by farmers around France (Webster 1999; *Le Monde*, 25 août 1999, p. 28). In November, Bové went to Seattle to join demonstrations against the WTO, where he led a protest against GM food which culminated in a McDonald's restaurant being targeted by protesters (Vidal 1999). At the end of June 2000, Millau itself was turned into 'Seattle-sur-Tarn' as thousands of demonstrators turned up to support Bové and nine other defendants as they stood trial for the original attack on McDonald's. The judge eventually announced his verdict on 13 September 2000, sentencing Bové to three months in prison, a decision whose severity was lambasted by trade unions, legal groups and a range of political parties (*Le Monde*, 15 septembre 2000, p. 12). Bové launched an immediate appeal against the verdict.[1]

That Bové's campaign should have acquired such notoriety and provoked such a sympathetic response – one commentator characterises it as 'la "bovémania"' (Viard 2000) – is important, for it demonstrates the extent to which there is widespread concern about the prevalence of *la malbouffe* within French culture. It is also apparent that such concerns are imbricated with anxieties about national identity and tradition. Bové is thus constructed as an Astérix character protecting French culinary conventions from the joint threats of Americanised and GM foods, as the 'Robin des bois du Larzac' (Benguigui 1999) defending artisanal traditions against the homogeneity of globalised produce. However, in the light of the apparent ease with which Bové has garnered support from across the political spectrum, in spite of his own uncompromising political analysis, it is worth examining in more detail the manner in which he has pursued his critique of *la*

---

1. At the time of writing, Bové's appeal had yet to be heard.

malbouffe. My particular focus here will be the interviews which appear in Bové's two books, *La Révolte d'un paysan* (Bové 2000) and *Le Monde n'est pas une marchandise*[1] (Bové and Dufour 2000).

The first issue to consider is the targeting of McDonald's itself. In his survey of French responses to American culture, Kuisel argues that, 'while there will be those [...] who continue to urge resistance to modernity by attacking America' (Kuisel 1993, p. 234), such suspicions of Americanisation have now been replaced by a mistrust of globalisation. Bové's attitude to McDonald's bears out Kuisel's analysis. In spite of the fact that the action at Millau was designed as a response to the USA's surcharge on European food imports, Bové argues that McDonald's is a legitimate target not because it is American *per se*, but because it is a key symbol of globalisation. As he explains, the campaign launched by la Confédération paysanne is not 'contre les Américains mais contre les règles du commerce mondial qu'ils veulent imposer' (Chiquelin 1999, p. 41). For Bové, McDonald's represents the industrialisation of both agriculture and food retailing (Bové and Dufour 2000, p. 15), offering a centralised system of food production and distribution and a completely standardised range of products (Bové and Dufour 2000, pp. 78-8). In an analysis which concurs with that of Ritzer, Bové presents a critique of the standardised anonymity of McDonald's:

> *C'est une nourriture complètement standardisée, avec les mêmes formes et les mêmes compositions de hamburgers partout dans le monde; en fait, c'est une bouffe de nulle part, pas même issue de la culture américaine [...]. Voilà pourquoi à nos yeux McDo symbolise la mondialisation anonyme, vidée du sens de l'alimentation. (Bové 2000, p. 79)*

If the disembedding mechanisms of modernity threaten the specificity of local cultures, then McDonald's represents the power of globalisation to generate deterritorialised, anonymous forms of culture.

Central to the threat of 'la mondialisation anonyme' is its impact upon French national identity, a problem which Bové recognises: 'l'alimentation est en train de devenir un sujet social et politique extraordinaire du fait que dans une période de mondialisation comme la nôtre, nos identités sont menacées' (Bové 2000, p. 39). Insofar as some of Bové's supporters champion him as a defender of French tradition, it is worth examining in greater detail Bové's own response to such issues. The reactions of the far right to the anti-McDonald's campaign, and Bové's reply to them, are instructive here. Asked about apparent support from le Front National in the form of a 'jambon-beurre anti-McDo' pact, as one interviewer puts it (Bové 2000, p. 69), Bové has responded with a critique of the nation state upon which the far right's concept of national identity rests. For Bové, the problems of globalisation cannot be resolved simply by a defiant appeal to French patriotism: 'l'agriculture et l'alimentation ne seront pas sauvées dans le cadre de l'Etat-nation contre le reste du monde' (Besset 1999a). Bové's argument can be thrown into

---

1. Here Bové is interviewed jointly with François Dufour, the national secretary of la Confédération paysanne.

sharper relief here by turning to the relationship between the largest farmers' union, la Fédération nationale des syndicats des exploitants agricoles (FNSEA), and la Confédération paysanne. In 1983, la Fédération nationale des syndicats paysans was established as a breakaway group from the FNSEA, and la Confédération paysanne emerged from that group in 1987, with Bové one of its co-founders (Bové and Dufour 2000, pp. 69-73). For Bové, one of the problems with the FNSEA is its commitment to a protectionist notion of sovereignty. As a result, it seeks to resolve difficulties by invoking French sovereignty. Here, Bové cites the French government's embargo introduced in 1996 against imports of British beef in the wake of the BSE crisis, a policy supported by the FNSEA. Bové argues instead for a European solution to such problems:

> *Dire qu'on protège le consommateur français sans protéger le consommateur anglais, cela n'a pas de sens. Nous sommes dans la même Europe [...]. L'attitude de la FNSEA, avec ses menaces de boycottage des viandes anglaises, ne fait qu'ajouter à la confusion et exacerber le corporatisme et le chauvinisme. (Bové 2000, p. 140)*

The extent to which the dispute between Bové and the FNSEA revolves around the issue of sovereignty can also be seen in the reaction of the FNSEA to Bové in the aftermath of the McDonald's protest in Millau. While certain departmental FNSEA groups had expressed support for Bové (Bové and Dufour 2000, p. 22), nationally they distanced themselves from the action. One FNSEA official reproached Bové for presenting France as 'le pays de la malbouffe' (Belleret 2000). In a similar vein, the FNSEA's Luc Guyau has dismissed Bové as 'un "agent double américain", puisqu'il ne défend pas la "vocation exportatrice" de l'agriculture française' (Chemin 1999). Bové's response to such criticisms is to contest the very basis of the FNSEA's standpoint: 'Il ne s'agit donc pas de défendre les Français, ou les agriculteurs français – lesquels? – mais un mode de développement' (Bové 2000, p. 209). In distancing himself from traditional notions of sovereignty, the dispute between Bové and the FNSEA reveals Bové attempting to develop an internationalist perspective on the problems of globalisation, a perspective which he has sought to amplify by expressing solidarity with a range of groups across the world who share in similar struggles against the forces of globalisation (Bové 2000, pp. 43-4; pp. 55-62).

Bové also distances himself from the FNSEA's commitment to 'la logique du productivisme', the industrialised model of agriculture endorsed by the European Union which is, for him, the same logic which underpins the dynamic of globalisation (Bové and Dufour 2000, p. 209). La Confédération paysanne challenges the rationale behind this form of intensive farming, proposing an alternative agricultural model, 'l'agriculture paysanne', which seeks instead to organise agriculture around the principles of social need and environmental responsibility (Bové 2000, p. 44; Bové and Dufour 2000, pp. 231-5). Bové traces the industrialisation of French agriculture back to the 1950s and 1960s (Bové and Dufour 2000, pp. 88-90), a period which was, as Jean-Jacques Chiquelin argues, a crucial moment in the modernising of French food practices (Chiquelin 1999, p. 44). From this point on there has been an escalating drive towards the provision of processed foods, and a marked decline in the amount of time given over to preparing meals in the home.[1] The first hypermarket opened in 1963, where one would go 'en famille embrasser une modernité qui avait le sourire inoxydable de la Vache qui rit et des Trente Glorieuses' (Chiquelin 1999, p. 44).

In spite of such promise, culinary modernity has also brought with it a range of food crises and, arguably, an increasingly homogenised provision of foodstuffs, provoking widespread anxieties about the safety and quality of the foods we eat. Bové argues that it is precisely the globalising thrust of modernity which has precipitated such problems today, and that the strategy now must be to contest the economic, environmental and ethical legitimacy of globalisation (Bové 2000, pp. 36-8). As the scale of the protests at the WTO talks in Seattle suggest, Bové is not alone here. The success of the anti-McDonald's protest in raising such questions within the public arena, along with Bové's subsequent campaigning, suggests that this strategy has been effective, if only in provoking a debate within the French media about the economic, ethical and environmental consequences of globalisation.

Bové is keen to distance himself from the charge that his position necessarily leads him 'à l'envers de la modernité' (Bové 2000, p. 36), but his analysis nevertheless expresses a profound sense of disenchantment with modernity: 'Je vivais aussi bien ici quand je n'avais ni l'eau ni l'électricité ni le téléphone', he claims (Bové 2000, p. 40), and he frequently attempts to find solace in pre-modern practices, often invoking examples from the culinary realm. He argues that modernity threatens the rich diversity of food cultures, and that modern food practices have lost the collective, festive symbolism which they once enjoyed:

> l'alimentation a trop souvent perdu son aspect collectif, sa dimension festive quotidi-
> enne. Plaisir et nourriture sont indissociables, ou devraient l'être, mais dans les
> familles, on ne se retrouve pas forcément le soir pour manger tous ensemble. (Bové
> and Dufour 2000, p. 81)

Along with the processes of birth and death, Bové concludes, food has increasingly been stripped of its spiritual significance (Bové and Dufour 2000, p. 82). For all that he resists the suggestion that his analysis is anti-modern, it is clear that Bové often finds himself evoking a pre-modern potential within food practices to which globalisation poses a considerable threat. His analysis of contemporary food is not wholly pessimistic, though, for in a final flourish, Bové attributes to food a key role in sustaining a sense of optimism in the course of political struggle:

> Il n'y a pas une manifestation du Larzac où les gens n'ont pas leur pique-nique dans
> le coffre de leur bagnole! À midi, on fait une pause et on bouffe! Si on milite et qu'on
> s'ennuie, il vaut mieux arrêter. On ne peut pas durer si on n'y trouve pas un certain
> bonheur de vivre. (Bové 2000, p. 91)

---

1. According to Chiquelin, between the 1950s and the 1990s, the average time spent cooking a meal fell from two and a half hours to twenty minutes (Chiquelin 1999, p. 44).

There can be no doubt that the anti-McDonald's protest at Millau helped to arouse public concerns about *la malbouffe*. While the courts responded in a punitive manner, elsewhere, as we have seen, the campaign received a more favourable reception, and Bové has used this popularity to publicise a sustained critique of food production, agricultural policy and globalisation.

Conclusion

In the course of this chapter, I have focused on the terms of the debate about *la malbouffe* undertaken by Bové. I have argued that previous culinary debates within French culture, such as the controversy surrounding *la nouvelle cuisine*, have tended to broach questions about national identity and about the impact of modernity upon gastronomic tradition. In this, the debate about *la malbouffe* is no different. A standardised, globalised and, frequently genetically modified food regime is seen to imperil the very sanctity of French cuisine. Claude Fischler has suggested that in contemporary society the rules which traditionally governed our food choices are increasingly being undermined. This 'crisis of gastronomy', he argues, 'leads to a state of *gastro-anomy*' (Fischler 1980, p. 948). Bové has exploited this state of affairs in his attack on *la malbouffe*. The campaign launched by la Confédération paysanne against McDonald's, and Bové's success at promoting that campaign to a broad constituency, has ensured, for the time being, the prominence of *la malbouffe* as a source of public anxiety.

John Tomlinson has argued that, while some theorists have conceived the way in which we encounter modernity in terms of a dramatic shock to the senses, the experience is actually rather more mundane. For all that globalisation seems to pose a threat of cultural estrangement, such transformations 'are, on the contrary, rapidly assimilated to normality and grasped – however precariously – as "the way life is" rather than as a series of derivations from the way life has been or ought to be' (Tomlinson 1999, p. 128). The achievement of Bové lies in the success with which he has called into question the apparent normality of *la malbouffe*, raising in turn questions about the economic logic from which it springs.

Bibliography

Ardagh, J. (1990) *France Today* (revised edition), Harmondsworth: Penguin.

Belleret, R. (1999) 'La Bataille du goût contre la "malbouffe"', *Le Monde*, 15 novembre, p. 10.

Belleret, R. (2000) 'José Bové ou le goût du contre-pouvoir', *Le Monde*, 1 janvier, p. 12.

Benguigui, R. (1999) 'Le Parquet demande le maintien en détention de José Bové', *Le Monde*, 1 septembre, p. 7.

Besset, J.-P. (1999a) 'José Bové plaide pour une "alliance" des paysans et des consommateurs', *Le Monde*, 9 septembre, p. 6.

Besset, J-P. (1999b) 'José Bové, héros de la presse du Sud-Ouest', *Le Monde*, 14 septembre, p. 38.

Bové, J. (2000) *La Révolte d'un paysan*, Villeurbanne: Golias.

Bové, J. and Dufour, F. (2000) *Le Monde n'est pas une marchandise: des paysans contre la malbouffe (entretiens avec Gilles Luneau)*, Paris: La Découverte.

Burke, J. (2000) 'Burger rebel faces token jail sentence', *TheObserver*, 2 July, p. 24.

Chemin, A. (1999) 'Le Premier ministre ne veut pas de photo avec José Bové', *Le Monde*, 23 octobre, p. 9.

Chiquelin, J.-J. (1999) 'Comment sauver la bonne bouffe', *Le Nouvel Observateur*, no. 1819, 16-22 septembre, pp. 40-6.

Cook, M. (ed.) (1993) *French Culture Since 1945*, London: Longman.

Csergo, J. (1999) 'The Emergence of Regional Cuisines', in A. Sonnenfeld (ed.) *Food: A Culinary History from Antiquity to the Present*, New York: Columbia University Press, pp. 500-15.

Fantasia, R. (1995) 'Fast Food in France', *Theory and Society*, vol. 24, pp. 201-43.

Faure, P. (1999) 'McGault: un chef peut-il s'affranchir du temps, de la géographie et des saisons?', *Le Monde*, 23 november, p. 15.

Finkelstein, J. (1999) 'Rich Food: McDonald's and Modern Life', in B. Smart (ed.) *Resisting McDonaldization*, London: Sage, pp. 70-82.

Fischler, C. (1980) 'Food habits, social change and the nature/culture dilemma', *Social Science Information*, vol. 19, pp. 937-53.

Giddens, A. (1990) *The Consequences of Modernity*, Cambridge: Polity Press.

Henley, J. (2000a) 'French bons vivants take a battering as superchef takes meat off the menu...', *The Guardian*, 30 December, p. 3.

Henley, J. (2000b) 'The year of eating dangerously', *The Guardian*, 30 December, p. 3.

Kuisel, R. (1991) 'Coca-Cola and the Cold War: The French Face Americanization, 1948-1953', *French Historical Studies*, vol. 17, no. 1, pp. 96-116.

Kuisel, R. (1993) *Seducing the French: The Dilemma of Americanization*, Berkeley: University of California Press.

James, A. (1996) 'Cooking the books: global or local identities in contemporary British food cultures?', in D. Howes (ed.) *Cross-Cultural Consumption: Global Markets, Local Realities*, London: Routledge.

Larousse Gastronomique (1988) London: Paul Hamlyn.

Lee, M. (1993) *Consumer Culture Reborn*, London: Routledge.

Luneau, G. (2000) 'Avant-propos', in J. Bové and F. Dufour, *Le Monde n'est pas une marchandise: des paysans contre la malbouffe (entretiens avec Gilles Luneau)*, Paris: La Découverte.

Mennell, S. (1993) 'Food and wine', in M. Cook (ed.) *French Culture Since 1945*, London: Longman, pp. 176-191.

Monnot, C. (1999) 'La Gauche "mouvementiste" soutient la Confédération paysanne', *Le Monde*, 23 août, p. 5.

Normand, J.-M. (1999) 'McDonald's, critiqué mais toujours fréquenté', *Le Monde*, 24 septembre, p. 29.

Ritzer, G. (1993) *The McDonaldization of Society: An Investigation into the Changing Character of Contemporary Social Life*, Thousand Oaks: Pine Forge Press.

Rollat, A. (1999) 'Vive le roquefort libre!', *Le Monde*, 9 septembre, p. 32.

Sabatier, P. (2000) 'Editorial', *Libération*, 30 juin, p. 3.

Smart, B. (1999) 'Resisting McDonaldization: Theory, Process and Critique', in B. Smart (ed.) *Resisting McDonaldization*, London: Sage, pp. 1-21.

Sonnenfeld, A. (1999) 'Preface', in A. Sonnenfeld (ed.) *Food: A Culinary History from Antiquity to the Present*, New York: Columbia University Press, pp. xv-xviii.

Tomlinson, J. (1999) *Globalization and Culture*, Cambridge: Polity.

Viard, J. (2000) 'José Bové, pont entre le rural et l'urbain', *Libération*, 30 juin, p. 5.

Vidal, J. (1999) 'How the young battalions hatched the Battle of Seattle', *The Guardian*, 30 November, p. 1.

Webster, P. (1999) 'Arrest hardens French action against burger chain', *The Guardian*, 24 August, p. 10.

Republic of Cinema or Fragmented Public Sphere: the Debate between Film-makers and Critics

Martin O'Shaughnessy

The angry debate that opposed (some) French film-makers and cinema critics towards the end of 1999 seemed, at first sight, a hackneyed remake of a multitude of previous disputes between artists and critics, and, moreover, a narrowly Parisian affair, and thus one of little potential interest to a broader constituency. It also had a touch of the absurd about it, both in the inflated importance it seemed to take on for its participants and for its confused beginnings and decidedly anti-climactic dénouement. Yet much of interest emerged from it concerning competing visions of cinema and cultural debate and, beyond that, of the nature of exchange in the public sphere. It also threw light on current French cultural responses to the rise of a seemingly all-pervasive and all-conquering capitalist global order. However, before these broader questions are broached, some ground needs to be cleared concerning the context of the debate and the way it played itself out.

The context

This brief contextualisation will show how, if French film directors have reached new heights of public prominence, their traditional base (their presence on cinema screens) is entering a period of considerable uncertainty.

Michel Trebitsch (1999) has recently written of the contemporary mobilisation of *cinéastes*, noting their involvement both in broad humanitarian issues (support for the *sans-papiers*, *prises de position* on Bosnia or Algeria under the broad banner of human rights and democratic freedoms) and in a more specific defence of culture against perceived threats.[1] Constructed as a struggle for cultural diversity and freedom of expression, the latter can clearly be aligned with other democratic and humanitarian commitments rather than being seen as simply a form of corporatist intervention. Trebitsch seems happy to accept such an alignment, describing the directors' mobilisation as primarily ethical and suggesting that the cosmopolitan sub-culture of the world of cinematic production may partially explain it. He suggests that their engagement can be seen as a continuation of the classical French tradition of intellectual commitment whereby a group moves out of its specific area of expertise and uses its public

---

1. These range from the Front National through economic internationalisation to changes to the insurance regime of the many *intermittents* upon which the cultural industries depend.

visibility to support a broad political or humanitarian stance.[1] However, he also recognises that the same commitment could be seen as a clear example of what Finkielkraut (1987) describes as *la défaite de la pensée*, the engulfing of the intellectual domain and its capacity for critical thought by the world of spectacle, by *le tout culturel*. This is broadly the line taken by cultural commentator Judith Lazar (2000) in *Le Débat*. Lazar sees the whole *sans-papiers* affair as a media produced event, a *feuilleton*, that failed to generate informed public debate. Presenting film-makers' defence of the *exception culturelle* and the quotas it implies as proof of their protectionism, corporatism and disregard for the public's rights to watch what it wants, she refuses to accept that their support for the *sans-papiers* is a humanitarian gesture. She suggests instead that they wanted to imitate their Hollywood counterparts' use of public participation to enhance their own visibility. Whichever stance one chooses to adopt, the generous or the deeply cynical, it does seem clear that the film-makers have to some extent taken on the mantle previously worn by prominent writers, artists and university-based intellectuals.

Trebitsch suggests that this is because cinema is a popular art (i.e. it is seen as an art but can also claim a broad appeal), thus combining intellectual respectability and a publicness no longer possessed by other artists and intellectuals. It is not an accident that the committed *cinéaste* has emerged in France, a country whose highly developed *cinéphilic* culture is a clear precondition for the visibility and respectability of the film-makers. François de la Bretèque (1999) suggests that the current prominence of film-makers can be explained in part by the long struggle by cinephiles and a broader intellectual community to install cinema as *the* art of the twentieth century. Prominence won for it means that it now plays a key role in socio-political debates, even to the extent that comment on films may replace discussion of the social issue to which they relate. Film-makers are, at least temporarily in the van, a position perhaps most clearly symbolised by the fact that it was they who marched directly behind the *sans-papiers* in the 22nd February 1997 demonstrations in Paris.

Reaching new heights of political prominence has not prevented French cinema from feeling a sense of crisis. The clearest symptom being that while cinema audiences have been rising against long-term historical trends, the French share of their domestic market has been in decline, dipping in 1999 below thirty

1. Bourdieu rehearses various types of intellectual commitment in a recent piece (2001, pp. 8-12). He identifies two traditional types of commitment. Firstly, one which sees intellectuals being used to window-dress a political cause. Secondly, one whereby they put their specific expertise at the service of a struggle. To these inherited models, Bourdieu opposes a new dialogical and collective variant which would see intellectuals and militants come together to produce 'applied' critical knowledges which would feed into new forms of mobilisation. The directors' mobilisation is clearly nearer to the first of the two traditional models. What was new about it, and what Bourdieu's different categories do not cater for, is, firstly, their pro-active role in mobilisation around the *sans-papiers*, a feature that is symptomatic perhaps of the shift of the locus of political mobilisation away from parties to less structured movements, and, secondly, their bridging role, as *cinéastes-citoyens*, between the world of intellectuals and that of a broader public. Feeding off cinema's own cultural in-betweenness, this role could clearly be cast as either a democratisation or a dissolution of intellectual involvement.

per cent, with a good share of that low figure being claimed by *films événements* such as *Astérix* or *Jeanne d'Arc*. Despite drawing audiences back to the cinema, the growing number of mutliplexes allow a narrower range of films to circulate. With production flourishing (due to the state-sponsored system of levies and grants and compulsory funding by the television companies) more films are competing for reduced distribution and exhibition slots with a resulting acceleration of turnover times. Whereas films used to have more time for word-of-mouth to function, they may now be pulled from circulation at the end of the first week, with admission figures on the opening day being a decisive factor. Under such circumstances, a bad pre-release review may seem to condemn a film to quick oblivion, while critical support can play a crucial role in allowing films to move from Paris onto the narrower national *arts et essais* circuit. Not only are 'minority' films under threat, well-budgeted ones that seek to reach a broad audience also seem in danger, with the relative failure of several in the Autumn of 1999, notably Kurys's *Les Enfants du siècle*, being one of the key triggers for the debate between (some) critics and film-makers, with the former being accused of killing quality popular cinema. If blockbusters – like *Jeanne d'Arc* – and many Hollywood films were pitched at *Génération Canal +* (a young audience reputedly uninfluenced by critical opinion), this French 'quality' cinema was felt to need critical support to reach its intended adult audience. Crucially also, the entire French system of state-led support is underpinned by cinema's dual character, its massness and its cultural status. If the middle ground (the cinema which aimed to attract a popular audience yet also produce works of cultural value) could not attract public and critical support, French cinema seemed in danger of splitting irremediably between a purely commercial sector and an art sector with little popular appeal. Cinema's claim to constitute an *exception culturelle*, to make an essential contribution to the cultural life of the nation, would be profoundly undermined.

The key critics that came under attack were those that form what is known as the *Triangle des Bermudes*, the graveyard of those films that do not find favour. The triangle, of dubious geometry, is made up of *Le Monde*, *Libération*, *Les Inrockuptibles* and, depending on sources, *Télérama* and *Cahiers du Cinéma*. These journals are reputedly both the most demanding and the most respected, two qualities that are perhaps not unrelated. What gives them a special prominence is the decline of critical culture elsewhere, notably on television. French television, which had once given air-time to cinema criticism, is now seen to be dominated by the culture of promotion whereby magazine programmes and national news allow film-makers and stars to sell their films unchallenged. This is all the more suspect because of television's heavy involvement in the production of films that it will itself recycle with a clear vested interest in earlier screen success.

Beyond television, producers also draw on a range of uncritical printed media where advertising per se blends into indirect promotion in the form of complicit interviews with actors and directors and location or progress reports. Starting long before the finished article ever hits the cinema screens, but culminating in the eight o'clock Monday night pre-opening news report on national television, film promotion does all it can to secure a successful launch. The traditional critics' preview is the potential spanner in the works, for it opens the possibility of poor pre-launch reviews that may partially undo the months of promotional activity. Directors such as Besson and Leconte have banned some papers from the preview, thus appealing over the heads of the 'elitist' critics to the public. Triggered by shifts in the cinema industry that generated a feeling of crisis, the debate that was to emerge between film-makers and critics also clearly fed off long-standing tensions which had most recently boiled over in the controversy surrounding the 1999 Cannes festival where the austerely serious *Rosetta* (the Dardenne brothers) and *L'humanité* (Bruno Dumont) had been awarded the chief prizes leading to press claims that the festival had betrayed public tastes.[1] As both international bazaar and prestigious competition, Cannes clearly concentrates the opposition between the promotional and the critical.

The debate itself

The debate proper began when a letter from the director Patrice Leconte to his fellow members of the ARP (Société des Auteurs, Réalisateurs, Producteurs), was sent accidentally to 'le tout Paris politique et culturel'. Leconte accused unnamed critics, of conniving to kill 'le cinéma commercial, populaire grand public'.[2] Invited by *Libération* to comment further, Leconte explained that he considered the violence of some reviews unbearable, especially at a time when French cinema's market share was falling. He accused critics of displaying *a priori* judgments and *mauvaise foi* and of not loving the cinema viscerally. He suggested that continued assaults on French cinema would eventually lead to an American cinematic monopoly and more specifically accused the Bermuda triangle of systematic disregard for 'les films populaires de qualité'. Reiterating Besson's comment, 'un film ne veut de mal à personne; c'est un objet gentil', he rejected critics who demonstrate hatred for films, asking for them to be 'des partenaires attentifs' without becoming 'une armée de lèche-bottes' (25/10/99, BIFI: 3-4).[3]

Leconte's statements were more than a little inept. They revealed a line of argument that was protectionist, corporatist and naïve. They also opened him to accusations of wishing to restrict freedom of expression and critical thought. All that the accused journals had to do was to claim the principled high ground (defence of free speech, of critical thought and of internationalism), demonstrating their sincerity by opening their pages to a range of supportive and critical comment and their web sites (*Libération, Télérama*) to uncensored comment.

---

1.   Two contrasting takes on the Festival can be found in Camy (1999) and Lavoignat (1999). Writing in *Jeune Cinéma*, Camy applauds the jury's selection, suggesting that the Festival has fulfilled its role as 'découvreur,' by bringing to public attention two films that break radically with the dominant 'dream-factory' mould. Jean-Pierre Lavoignat suggests that the Festival's austere, radical and politically correct prize list effectively splits cinema between minority cinema and popular Hollywood fodder with nothing left in between.

2.   The full text of the letter is published in *Libération*, 25/10/99 and in BIFI (2000: 2).

3.   Where a text from a periodical is included in the BIFI dossier on the debate, I give both its initial date and source and its page reference in the dossier.

Leconte also left himself wide open to accusations of scapegoating, of blaming the critics for the effects of profound mutations in the cinematic terrain, or, worse still, of using them to avoid acknowledging that French cinema was out of touch with the public. This was essentially the position taken by Michèle Stouvenet (*Journal du Dimanche*, 15/11/99, BIFI: 15), who was very happy to side with Leconte and his allies against the 'intellectual terrorism' of the elite critics, but continued by accusing French cinema of offering too much grim realism and too little moving, amusing or escapist fare. *L'Evénement du jeudi* (2/12/99, BIFI: 45-9) took a similar populist line. Accusing the critics of promoting their own visibility at the expense of the films, it advised them to learn to love what the public loves, to defend popular as well as elite tastes. It saved its harshest attacks for a French cinema split between a mediocre commercial sector and a hermetic avant-garde. It thus relaunched a wave of assaults that had begun the previous February when *Figaro Magazine* had accused the state-led support system, the FEMIS (the national film school) and 'fundamentalist' critics of having taken French cinema 'jusqu'au bout de l'ennui'. *L'Evénement* had itself followed up this attack by accusing over-intellectual critics of encouraging a deeply self-indulgent auteurist cinema.[1]

L'Humanité (15/11/99, BIFI: 12-14) was the journal that opposed this populist line most overtly, unsurprisingly perhaps, as it still lays claim to a popular readership despite its diminished influence. Equating appeals to the popular with populist scorn for the people and refusing to accept the tyranny of viewing figures, it proclaims the health of French cinema, citing its high output of films and diversity of themes and styles. Declining to accept Besson's *Jeanne d'Arc* as the measure of the popular, it proposes a counter canon embracing Poirier's *Western*, Guédiguian's *Marius et Jeannette* and the two Cannes prize winners mentioned earlier, and widely cited as proof of the out-of-touchness of elitist critics. *L'Humanité*'s clear strategy was to propose a definition of the popular that allows for the inclusion of socially committed and aesthetically challenging films. The paper also hit at the heart of the nationalist corporatism implicit in Leconte's statements by pointing out the contradiction between political support for the *sans-papiers* and a failure to consider the need to defend foreign films, not merely French ones.

Le Nouvel Observateur, the prestigious left-of-centre political weekly, took up some similar positions, while showing much less inclination to struggle for the soul of the popular. It castigated the nationalism of Leconte's position and the scapegoating of the critics, before an editorialist, Jérôme Garcin, launched into a somewhat improbable idealisation of the critics in a fable about the struggle between a householder and property speculators keen to build 'une cité du cinéma idéale' where all films are extraordinary and all actors handsome and kind. The last householder refusing to sell up and the hero of the piece is the critic who won't be a 'partner' in a world where money makes the rules and the public sphere is

---

1. For a summary of the positions taken by *Le Figaro Magazine* and *L'Evénement*, see *Libération*, 25/10/99 (BIFI: 4).

given over to 'l'empire de la bande-annonce généralisée'. Through the pen of Garcin, the debate opens onto a manichean struggle between the mercantile values of a triumphant capitalism and those who defend alternative principles (*Le Nouvel Observateur*, 18/11/99, BIFI: 20-2). Garcin's argument is picked up approvingly by Josyane Savigneau in *Le Monde* (30/11/99, BIFI: 37) who suggests that, as art itself is necessarily a form of critical expression, film-makers cannot eliminate negative criticism without abolishing their own right to exist. She writes:

> la société, en passe de devenir totalement marchande et médiatique, souhaite nier l'existence et la possibilité même de l'art comme [...] expression irréductible d'un individu [...] pouvant être jugée par un autre individu au nom de son goût, de son désir ou de son talent.

Although it feeds off a clichéd mythology of creative and critical individualism in opposition to a one-dimensional massified society, this piece also relocates the debate in the light of the contemporary rise of capitalism and its increasing penetration of the cultural sphere, suggesting that, given the decline of traditional oppositional ideologies, recalcitrant individualism may take on new life.[1]

A similar intervention is made by Christophe Gallaz (*Le Monde*, 10/12/99, BIFI: 61) who refuses the idea of a block of film-makers opposing a block of critics, preferring to see the struggle (in equally manichean terms!) as between those in thrall to the codes of commerce and media visibility and those who defend authentic values. In rather apocalyptic terms, and along broadly Baudrillardian lines, Gallaz suggests that the world is becoming a huge, image-dominated 'Festival de Cannes' where only the production and consumption of images allows people and things to 'exist'. We will soon not be able to differentiate between a (good) cinema that modifies how we see the real and a (bad) cinema that encourages us to fit the world to a look that it has formed.

Contributions from Gallaz and Garcin illustrate how, although still ostensibly about the relation between critics and film-makers, the polemic was overspilling in all directions to embrace a series of interlocked cultural, political and ethical issues while simultaneously revealing a complex set of oppositions and alliances around them. Neat it was not.

Tavernier takes over

The second phase of the debate began when the film-maker Bertrand Tavernier took over the leading role from the less combative Leconte. Once a critic himself, the veteran left-leaning director had been prominent in the campaign over the *sans-papiers* as well as a range of other causes that had mobilised elements of the

---

1. In a retrospective piece on the debate, Vincent Dieutre (2000) suggests that individual subjectivity has become '(une) idéologie d'urgence salvatrice, après l'échec patent des partis pris esthético-politiques d'antan'. While Dieutre would rightly seem to suggest a key cause for the rejuvenation and rehabilitation of individualism, he seems insufficiently attentive to its obvious downside. Cast as hero to promotional culture's villainy, individualism is dispensed from an examination of its own assumptions and prejudices.

film-making world. If Leconte represented the apolitical wing of the *cinéma populaire de qualité*, Tavernier was on its political edge, a figure who makes hard-hitting, socially engaged films that self-consciously reach out for both an older audience and the younger public that French cinema is in danger of losing.[1]

Tavernier's initial intervention was in *L'Humanité* (15/11/99, BIFI: 13). He protested that he was not attacking the critics but their excesses, be they insults such as *collabo* or *vichyste*, and acts such as the pre-release demolition of a film or the condemnation of ten films in order to defend one. Tavernier was the initial drafter of the text which emerged from the 4th November meeting of the ARP which was itself a response to Leconte's initial missive. Having circulated among ARP members for their approval and signature, and intended apparently for a direct appeal to the public via cinemas and cine-clubs, the text was leaked by *Le Monde* on 25th November, still in draft form and unsigned. Tavernier himself said that an operation for a detached retina had prevented him rereading it.

The text itself (BIFI: 24-32) is a direct appeal to the cinema spectator. It is a bundle of contradictions, although it shows clear signs of trying to reclaim some of the high ground that Leconte had lost through his overtly corporatist appeal. It ends by calling for the objectivity, humility and lucidity necessary for a debate but begins by speaking of the irrational blend of disgust, rage and scorn that the directors feel when faced with certain critical articles. It protests its attachment to *esprit critique* and freedom of expression but reiterates the wish that negative criticism of a film should be held back until the weekend after release. It accuses the critics of self-promotion but also boasts about the admirable achievements of the *cinéastes* in a range of areas. It finds convincing examples of personal attacks against directors and actors but then makes personal assaults on named critics while suggesting that they are collectively part of an inward-looking clique that takes a sadistic pleasure in destroying films. Accusing them of an inability to promote the films they love, it then notes that many film-makers owe the continuation of their career to critical support. It notes that the support system the ARP fights to defend also works in favour of foreign film-makers such as Loach, Almodóvar, De Oliveira or Kiarostami. But in the light of the transparently corporatist wish to postpone negative criticism, this can easily seem an attempt to hide baser motives and collective grievances behind internationalist principles and support for cultural diversity.

In follow-up interviews, Tavernier indicated that he would have amended certain areas of the letter without substantially distancing himself from it. In an interview in *Libération* (2/12/99, BIFI: 50-1), he reaffirmed his attachment to a diverse and challenging French cinema that welcomed foreign directors, while distancing himself from any measure of its value in terms of market share. He repeatedly tried to put the ball back into the critics' court, by telling them that they needed to unite and fight both for more critical space in the media and to ensure that the films they defend have a chance for general exhibition. He also accused them of failing to support the struggles over *l'exception culturelle*,

---

1. see Bretèque (1999).

suggesting that they had played into Jack Valenti's hands by accusations of protectionism. He nonetheless reaffirmed the corporatist position that negative reviews should be held back, apparently seeing no contradiction between this call for self-censorship and his welcoming of the vigorous debate that the film-makers had unleashed. Another interview published the same day in *L'Evénement* made some similar points. Revealingly, Tavernier suggested that the critic's main role was to be a *passeur*, to communicate enthusiasm.

The debate did not go much further. A counter-text was issued by the other directors' union, the SRF (Société des réalisateurs de films). It read:

> *Le texte anonyme publié le 25 novembre, abusivement intitulé dans* Le Monde
> *'La critique des cinéastes' et dans* Libération *'Nous cinéastes [...]', nous paraît
> inepte. Nous tenons à faire savoir que nous n'en sommes pas solidaires. Nous ne
> l'avons pas signé. Nous pensons que cette polémique (cinéastes / critique) est vaine.*
> *(Le Monde, 6/12/99, BIFI: 53)*

Its initial 63 signatories embraced different generations and tendencies within French cinema. They would later be joined by others. Two of them, Pascal Thomas and Jacques Rozier, explained themselves in *l'Humanité* (8/12/99, BIFI: 55). They commented that criticism was either free or muzzled, and that no in-between position was possible. Rozier added, 'la critique n'est constructive que quand elle est destructive. Assez avec cette pléthore de respect qu'on voudrait lui imposer'. This vision of vigorous dialogue between creator and critic, between self and other, contrasts sharply with Tavernier's tamed model of cultural interaction.

Matters were drawing to a close. The main business ended with the resignation of Claude Miller from the presidency of the ARP. Distancing himself from 'un combat douteux' he abandoned the battlefield 'aux haineux, aux malins, aux coupe-jarret et aux gens de guerre' (*l'Humanité*, 10/12/99, BIFI: 59). The ARP itself called for the end of the debate, regretting that the leaking of the draft letter had prevented a serene and democratic discussion and reaffirming its status as a forum for film-makers' opinions, be they polemical or contradictory. The orderly debate that had been called for at various times was as elusive as ever, while the acknowledgement that film-makers, far from forming a compact body, were profoundly divided was an admission that orderliness was unattainable.

Competing definitions of the public sphere

The debate over the role and behaviour of cinema critics repeatedly opened, as I have suggested, onto broader issues about the nature of public interaction. Three broad positions can be identified. The first being that, as part of the public sphere, cinema is a site of major disagreements and tensions which need to collide with vigour and with few if any holds barred. The second, accepting the need for robust disagreement, opted for a more rule-governed model, while the third sought, in one way or another, to remove cinema from the cut and thrust of public debate.

Jean-Louis Comolli, film-maker, prominent film analyst and erstwhile editor of *Cahiers du cinéma*, was the most eloquent proponent of the first position, his own commitment to vigorous public debate being clear from the description of the

ARP text in his title, 'A propos d'un torchon-manifeste' (*Le Monde*, 1/12/99, BIFI: 43). Describing the notion of cohesive critical or film-making communities as an ideological deceit, he asserts that films are inevitably engaged in struggle with each other, a struggle that is not simply for market share but which expresses profound differences at the level of economics, film-making practices, and film style. Critics are willy-nilly participants in these same struggles which have their root in profound divisions in French society. Choices of means, form and style are never merely aesthetic questions, but inevitably have a moral dimension which it is the critic's task to identify. Because of this impurity of aesthetics (its connection to other questions), criticism can never simply decide that a film is aesthetically good or bad. The 'Bessonian' notion of 'innocent' films requiring an 'innocent judgement' would be laughable were it not for the broader context of attacks on critical thought in the cultural sphere. Rather than seeking a confirmation of what he or she has already said in his or her films, the film-maker should welcome the encounter with 'le regard des autres' and especially with that of the critic, who can locate a film in the context of other films (and thus, by extension, in the struggles that they express). The critical encounter ('le choc critique') can thus reveal the 'shadows' that a film bears, even the shadow of the film-maker when she or he becomes the promoter of a film.

Comolli's intervention helps reframe the debate by tying it into a broader, implicit, ethico-political interchange that is constantly underway in cinema and which in turn feeds off social divisions and ideological conflicts. In this analysis, criticism takes on a key role by making explicit what was implicit, thus facilitating the vigorous public clash of ideas that is vital for democratic interchange and which is threatened both by what Comolli calls 'un lepénisme rampant' and by the consumerisation of cinema.

Comolli's vision prolongs that of many other participants in the debate both in its refusal to separate cinema from broader socio-political struggles and in the value it attaches to the public collision of 'looks' that it allows for. This second point was echoed by quite a number of the *internautes* who added their voices to the debate. Writing on the *Telerama* site, Franzou (1999), for example, commented, 'je lis les critiques après être allé voir le film. Comme ça, je suis à égalité avec celui qui a écrit, je sais de quoi il parle et ça permet, même en cas de désaccord profond, de réfléchir sur ce que je viens de voir'. [1] The critical encounter, conceived in egalitarian terms, helps generate a reflexive self-awareness that allows this viewer to reconsider his own response and to engage with that of the critic. Other *internautes* expressed similar thoughts, often stating, like Franzou, that they used the critics retrospectively in order to engage on equal terms with another look.

---

1. The *Télérama* site uses a web-board format which means that correspondants respond to individual letters thus constituting identifiable subsidiary themes within each major debate. Access to the debate is gained by opening the *Télérama* web site (*www.Télérama.fr*) and then selecting 'Forums' and entering the details requested (e-mail address etc.). Liberation's site, which is open access, simply gives all letters upon a particular topic in reverse chronological order.

The internet became the site for robust confrontations of outlook. Partisans of a no-holds-barred approach to public debate expressed their views through free use of insult directed towards both the directors (Besson being a frequent target) and towards the critics, who came in for considerable abuse. The word 'cul' was a key part of some of the most used expressions ('lèche-cul', 'torche-cul', and 'trou du cul'!). This disrespect, echoing that already shown by some critics to directors and actors, was countered by a large number of interventions that called in one way or another for rule-governed but still freely expressed cinematic exchanges. Many *internautes* said that critics should provide reasoned analyses giving arguments in support of their positions. Criticism of the critics provided, by implication, a list of vices that prevented fair judgement of films (chief amongst these being *parti pris*, *nombrilisme*, elitism, sadism, self-promotion or wit at the expense of film, membership of narrow Parisian coteries, and attachment to fashion and fad rather than to artistic value). More than one commentator likened criticism to a legal judgement, remarking on the lack of a defence for the films or the critics' capacity to pass 'sentence' with no right of appeal. Several contributors drew a sharp line between attacks on films (considered legitimate) and *ad personam* assaults which were felt to be an infringement of human rights. Contributing to the *Télérama* debate, hzb (1999) aligns the critics' insults with 'une tradition d'extrême droite qui consiste à avilir l'adversaire en cherchant dans son physique les disgrâces qui reflètent son âme'. These various positions (only sketched here) all suggest that *internautes* are drawing on a vision of how power should be exercised and how judgements should be justified that feeds off a broader sense of the norms of democratic public interaction.

If the first two lines of argument considered agreed about the need for vigorous exchange, a third suggested that discussion of cinema should be removed from full and open debate. We have already examined some variants of this position in our consideration of the *cinéastes*' initial text which, apart from its call for a postponement of adverse reaction, suggested a role for criticism somewhere between cinephilic love and pedagogic explanation, so that a good critic is one who transmits enthusiasm to the public while educating its taste. This position was echoed by more than one of the directors who came out in support of Tavernier and Leconte. It received some support on the internet. Martine, a Toulousaine cyber-critic, writes:

> *Exprimer au plus juste la joie, le plaisir que l'on a éprouvé à voir un film est notre devoir. Cet avis n'engage que nous mais il permet de donner l'envie et la curiosité de voir et peut-être un peu d'encouragement aux créateurs qui nous font tant de plaisir'* (on the *Libération* site, 29/11/99).

Censoring dislike, this reverential enthusiasm effectively removes film from public debate.[1] It contrasts strongly with the very different construction of the pedagogic role that is found in contributions from Comolli and many others who see criticism in terms of the generation of reflexivity and the support of diversity.

---

1. 'Economisons nos pages pour les films auxquels on tient', said Tavernier (*Libération*: 2/12/99, BIFI: 51).

Its tame *cinéphilie* can also be contrasted with the more robust vision of *Inrockuptibles* associate editor Serge Kaganski who commented: 'on confond passion et amour. Dans passion, il y a amour, désamour, et détestation'. Kaganski defended a radical subjectivist position in the debate, claiming 'les lecteurs savent aussi faire la part des choses. La prétention à l'objectivité revient au discours promotionnel ou publicitaire. Donc la mauvaise foi, la subjectivité, ça fait partie de l'agitation des idées' (*Libération*, 17/11/99). Adding passion and prejudice to the domain of legitimate discussion, Kaganski's stance implied that those models of the public sphere centred on rational argument required their own form of self-censorship. It also supported the suggestion that a radical and perhaps dangerously unreflexive individualism had gained a new lease of life as a form of resistance to market generated uniformity.

The impure publicness of cinema

One of the positive outcomes of the debate was the way in which it obliged critics and journals to ground their understanding of their own role in a broader sense of what cinema might mean. What emerged surprisingly often was an egalitarian, 'republican' model which placed all films, whatever their origins or wealth on the same footing in the face of criticism which then assumed a role of republican defence faced with the inequalities and violences of the market. *L'Humanité*'s Jean Roy provided one striking example:

> A *L'Humanité*, nous continuerons à porter sur les films, quelle que soit leur durée, leur budget ou leur pays d'origine un regard curieux, éveillé, humble et averti à la fois [...] nous continuerons à ouvrir nos colonnes aux créateurs dans le cadre d'entretiens, hors toute pression du box office, des productions et de la publicité. (26/11/99, BIFI: 33)

Télérama's Jean-Claude Loiseau expressed a not very dissimilar position:

> *Télérama* [...] a été créé [...] pour parler des films, de tous les films, chaque semaine. Pour mettre en lumière la création là où elle était [...] nous refusons le dogme, l'exclusion. Le cinéma, c'est, pour nous, tous les cinémas. (1/12/99, BIFI: 39)

Le Monde's Frodon was the most vocal defender of this filmic republicanism. He explicitly grounded it in the principles of 1789, justifying their extension to cinema by saying:

> tous les films relèvent en droit du même ensemble qu'on appelle le cinéma [...] en droit tous pouvaient être vus dans le même lieu, la salle de cinéma, pour le même prix, au même moment [...] tous recèlent potentiellement une qualité artistique qui les rend éligibles au regard critique. (*Le Monde*: 8/11/99, BIFI: 7).

It is this egalitarian unity of the cinematic republic that has meant, for example, that genre films by Hitchcock or Ford could be judged of greater value than prestige literary adaptations by the *Cahiers'* critics in the 1950s. Moreover, the most ambitious auteurist films profit from belonging to the same technical, sociological and cultural universe as films aimed at a wide public. It keeps them from disappearing into a self-imposed ghetto and losing touch with the public. The unity of cinema has meant too that the aura of authentic artistic achievements has spread to embrace areas on the edges of cinema and allowed for defence of the *exception culturelle* which in turn has allowed France to provide (the only) support for many directors around the globe and to stand as a beacon for a non-mercantile approach to human relations. It is this generous edifice that has been placed in jeopardy by the corporatist nationalism of a privileged minority of directors.[1]

Frodon draws on Bazin's notion of the ontological impurity of cinema to ground his argument. In his essay 'Pour un cinéma impur', Bazin (1990) had suggested that cinema's propensity to draw from other arts rather than to pursue its own internal logic was a decided advantage, allowing it to develop by digesting advances from other forms even at the cost of lagging well behind them or watering them down. Cinema was thus a bridge to other arts (providing them with new readers and spectators) while at the same time bringing elements of them to the mass public with which they had increasingly lost touch since the Renaissance. Bazin's piece does not share Frodon's republican bagage. If anything, one can find in it traces of the Personalist roots which push him to view cinema as a replacement for a lost common culture through its fusion of the elite and the popular. In any case, he was writing at a time when cinema could still claim to be shared by all. Its position as dominant public spectacle was still unchallenged while its audience and directors had yet to split between art house and industrial consumption. Any claim for a common cinematic culture is now much harder to ground in evidence. Frodon admits this himself, noting that the split begun around 1960 is now at crisis point. In these circumstances, the critic becomes a stubborn defender of cinema's impurity, refusing to acknowledge the separation between commerce and art and defiantly applying aesthetic criteria to all films. By Frodon's own admission, the result is that the middle-brow creator risks the same genre of comment as 'un fabricant de posters s'il était jugé à la même aune que Matisse' (*Le Monde*: 8/11/99, BIFI: 7).

Frodon's position ultimately leads to a paradox familiar to those accustomed to looking for the hidden exclusions and hierarchies lurking behind republican universalism. Defense of the equality of all films ends up looking suspiciously like the imposition of the tastes of an elite group on the cultural practices of other groups. This is not to say that one should jettison his generous defence of a diverse, inclusive and internationally open cultural sphere. But it does suggest that we need to examine the sociological shadows that critics may bear and fail to see. This is what many of the *internautes* would seem to be saying when they remind

---

1. Further insight into Frodon's republican conception of cinema can be gleaned by a reading of the interview devoted to him in Houben (1999). Interviews with other critics in the same volume, notably Michel Ciment, help cast light on some of the major faultlines that divide French film critics and confirm that they are no more of a united body than the directors to whom some sought to oppose them en bloc. But, on the other hand, no corporate position was ever taken by the critics.

them that despite their role as intermediaries of the international and defenders of critical thought, they sometimes look suspiciously like an elitist Parisian clique.

In the end, we have to prefer Comolli's vision of plural cinemas in collision, to Frodon's republic of cinema which is at best a generous fiction and at worst an alibi for elitism. Yet even by Comolli's reckoning, different cinemas do still engage with each other and thus still constitute a connected public sphere, one in which different taste regimes, politico-ethical positions and economic and industrial practices collide, generating not a shared culture, but a common space, where despite its many asymmetries of power and access, reflexive exchanges can occur following a set of rules that is at best under constant negotiation. Perhaps the notion of a public debate about the role of critics was, like the Republic of cinema, at best a generous fiction, an active idea that inflected actions and reactions, but one which had to jostle for space among the chaos of colliding passions, interests, prejudices, grievances and principles.

Conclusion

It is doubtful whether cultural debates ever arrive at neat conclusions. Mobilising shifting alliances around clusters of issues rather than tightly defined questions, they help bring out some of the faultlines and underlying tensions of a specific field at a given moment (as well as revealing the many shadows that individuals and groups may bear when exposed to the spotlights of their opponents). Avoiding any totalising conclusion, I would like to sum up by focusing on tensions over three key issues, *l'exception culturelle*, the impurity of cinema, and competing conceptions of public debate, suggesting finally how they may be linked by the sense of an overarching clash between core democratic values and the culture of a globalising capitalism.

Discussion of cultural exceptionalism revealed that those supporting it were torn between corporatist, protectionist positions and defence of internal and international diversity of expression. Michel Trebitsch (1999) would do well to temper his generous assessment of the cosmopolitan tendencies of filmmakers' subculture. A more rounded analysis of this issue would consider how directors and critics negotiated their interaction with international film markets, national and international publics and national institutions and media.[1] Debate over the nature of cinema and its socio-cultural role revealed a surprisingly widespread republican model of a cinematic republic within which all films, rich and poor, French and foreign, were presumed equal (if not innocent!). Welcoming this model's support for a diverse and open cinema, I nonetheless suggested that it

---

1. Such an analysis might begin by considering the geographical and politico-cultural location of the critics (on this, see Hedetoft (2000)). Predominantly based in the capital, they are exposed to an unrivalled selection of world cinema which strong French cinephilic traditions push them to view positively. Yet, at the same time, their address is primarily to a national audience, as evidenced among other things by repeated references to Vichy, Poujade or Le Pen during the debate considered in this piece. Narrow Parisian coterie, cosmopolitan elite, national sages, their complex position faces them with clear tensions and potential contradictions, to which Frodon's very French republican universalism is one possible response.

failed to recognise its own potential elitism as well as clinging to an increasingly tenuous sense of cinema as a unitary sphere. I expressed my preference for a vision of cinema as a multiply divided but nonetheless connected sphere within which radically incompatible styles, production practices and values compete and collide, not least when brought together by critics in their columns. Debate over the nature of the debate itself revealed strong tensions between no-holds-barred, rule governed and sharply curtailed models. What was of particular note was how often people drew on a broader sense of the norms of democratic interaction to describe not only the debate itself but also the encounter between film, critic and viewer, an encounter in which the critic played a key role by allowing both film-maker and viewer to achieve enhanced reflexivity through explicit (verbal) engagement with another look.

The three issues considered converge in that discussion of each seemed inevitably to return to capitalism whose increasing reach and penetration in the cultural arena was felt to threaten international diversity, the 'republican' equality of films, and the type of free and open exchange that the critical encounter exemplifies. To move from this convergence to a manichean opposition of a 'promotional' and a critical culture is to flatten out the wide diversity of oppositional voices and of cinematic practices. However, it would seem that because of its 'Bazinian' impurity, because of its status as art and industry, as commercial product and cultural intervention, cinema may be a site where tensions between commercial and alternative values will be particularly sharply felt. This would in part explain the passionate nature of the debate.

Bibliography

Bazin, A. (1990) *Qu'est-ce que le cinéma*, Paris: Editions du Cerf.

BIFI (la) (2000) *Polémique autour de la critique* (Les dossiers d'actualité de la BIFI, no. 1), Paris, la BIFI (a collection of press cuttings covering the debate). Available from Centre d'Information et de Documentation, Bibliothèque du film, 100, rue du Faubourg Sainte-Antoine, 75012, Paris.

Bourdieu, P. (2001) *Contre-feux 2*, Paris: Raisons d'Agir.

Bretèque, F. de la (1999) 'Le Cinéma, les intellectuels, l'engagement sur la scène publique: le syndrome de la sorcière', *Cahiers de la Cinémathèque*, no. 70, octobre, pp. 3-7.

Camy, G. (1999) 'Cannes: la compétition', *Jeune Cinéma*, no. 256, été, pp. 11-3.

Dieutre, V. (2000) 'Nous cinéastes…Critique de la critique de la critique', *La Lettre du Cinéma*, no. 13, mars, pp. 88-95.

Finkelkraut, A. (1987) *La Défaite de la pensée*, Paris: Gallimard.

Franzou (1999) 'A propos d'un objet gentil', 28/10, *www.telerama.fr/culturama/forums*

Hedetoft, U. (2000) 'Contemporary cinema: between cultural globalisation and national interpretation', in M. Hjort, and S. Mackenzie, (eds.) *Cinema and Nation*, London: Routledge.

Houben, J.-F. (1999) *Feux croisés sur la critique*, Paris: Cerf.

Hzb (1999) 'Délit de sale gueule', 25/11, *www.telerama.fr/culturama/forums*

Lavoignat, J.-P. (1999) 'Retour sur Cannes', *Studio*, no. 147, juillet-août, p. 79.

Lazar, J. (2000) 'Cinéastes: de nouveaux "intellectuels"?', *Le Débat*, no. 112, novembre-décembre, pp. 48-53.

Martine (1999) 29/11/99, *http://www.liberation.com/cinema/archives/critique/ reactleconte.html*

Trebitsch, M. (1999) 'Les Cinéastes contemporains se mobilisent sur des thèmes sociaux', *Cahiers de la Cinémathèque*, no. 70, octobre, pp. 85-93.

L'Affaire Sokal

John Marks

This chapter will attempt to outline the parameters of the debate around the so-called *affaire Sokal* in France. Particular attention will be paid to the fact that much of the debate, although taking the initial arguments advanced by Alan Sokal and Jean Bricmont as a starting point, tends to use *l'affaire* as a pretext for talking about wider issues. In this way, *l'affaire Sokal* becomes a genuinely French cultural debate. Ultimately, it seems that many of the contributions to the debate are framed – consciously or not – within ongoing issues with regard to the Republic. For example, in the wake of the 1995 public sector strikes, the question of the duties of intellectuals within the Republic has become particularly pertinent, and these issues have appeared in the debate around *l'affaire Sokal*. It is difficult not to be aware of an urgent call for accessibility, commitment, rationality and clarity within certain sectors of the French intellectual class. It also seems clear that this call to arms constitutes a rejection of, and a settling of accounts with, the structuralist and post-structuralist trends of previous decades.

The chapter starts by looking at reactions in France to what was perceived as an attack on French thought as a whole. It then moves on to consider the question of scientific metaphors and analogies within philosophical or cultural work. This particular aspect of the debate might appear at first sight to be limited to the initial questions raised by Sokal, but it actually provides important indicators of the way in which the debate transformed itself into a way of talking about other issues. This capacity of *l'affaire Sokal* to attract and absorb broader discussions is discussed in the light of Yves Jeanneret's notion of 'la dimension triviale de la culture' (Jeanneret 1998). In simple terms, Jeanneret suggests that it is inevitable that the transmission and diffusion of cultural knowledge will entail transformations. The very fact that ideas are communicated means that they will be 'détournées, réinventées' (p. 11).

What became known in France as *l'affaire Sokal* had its origins in a series of events which initially took place within American academic circles. Alan Sokal, a professor of physics at New York University, submitted a spoof article to the American cultural-studies journal *Social Text* in 1994, entitled 'Transgressing the Boundaries: Toward a Transformative Hermeneutics of Quantum Gravity' (Sokal, 1996a). The article presents a 'relativist' reading of contemporary physics, drawing on quotations by French and American intellectuals relating to mathematics and physics. The quotations were authentic but, as far as Sokal was concerned, nonsensical. The editors were apparently unaware that this was a hoax, and subsequently published the article in 1996. Sokal revealed the hoax in *Lingua Franca*, claiming that the article was accepted because it 'sounded good' and 'it flattered the editors' ideological preconceptions' (Sokal, 1996b). He claims to have been motivated in part by a sense of political anger when confronted with 'silliness' being propounded by academics who are supposedly part of the left. More precisely he is concerned by what he sees as the proliferation of a certain kind of 'sloppy thinking'. According to this 'epistemic relativism', 'postmodern science' has effectively abolished the concept of objective reality, of a 'real' world which exists independently of human cognition. He invites anybody who really believes that physical reality 'is at bottom a social and linguistic construct' – as he claims in 'Transgressing the Boundaries' – to try transgressing those conventions by jumping out of his twenty-first floor apartment window. For Sokal, the acceptance of his hoax article by the editors of *Social Text* illustrates the arrogance of 'Theory' and the claims it makes for epistemic relativism, according to which all is 'discourse' and 'text'.

Sokal had only used a small fraction of the material he had originally collected to compile his spoof article, and decided to publish the remainder. So, in 1997, after the *Social Text* and *Lingua Franca* articles had generated much controversy in the English-speaking world Sokal published *Impostures intellectuelles*, co-authored with Belgian physicist Jean Bricmont. Here, passages were cited from a variety of French thinkers (Baudrillard, Deleuze & Guattari, Julia Kristeva, Paul Virilio, etc.) in which scientific concepts are used erroneously. This book was subsequently published in English in 1998 (Sokal & Bricmont 1998). What had initially appeared to be an academic quarrel that had its roots in a series of circumstances specific to the United States – namely the epistemic relativism implied by the 'multicultural' approach which has been a powerful movement in American higher education in the past fifteen years or so, along with a sociological or 'constructivist' view of science – was now seen in some quarters as an all-out attack on French intellectuals. So, for example, the title page of *Le Nouvel Observateur* for September 25 1997 asked 'Les intellectuels français sont-ils des imposteurs?', and inside Julia Kristeva interpreted *Impostures intellectuelles* as a glaring example of American 'francophobie':

> *Après une période d'intense francophilie, pendant laquelle les intellectuels aux États-Unis se sont appuyés sur certains courants de la pensée françise moderne au risque d'outrances politically correct, nous assistons actuellement à une véritable francophobie. De peur d'être "colonisés", quelques-uns se laissent aller à une attitude de rejet. La compétition économique et diplomatique entre l'Europe et l'Amérique entraîne un nouveau partage du monde opposant des intérêts farouches et des replis identitaires. La virulence anachronique de ce débat pseudo-théorique s'inscrit dans un contexte politique chargé. (Kristeva 1997)*

Jacques Derrida, writing in *Le Monde*, adopts a generally more moderate tone, but also implies that the attack on French intellectuals is somewhat arbitrary:

> *Il aurait été intéressant d'étudier scrupuleusement lesdites métaphores scientifiques, leur rôle, leur statut, les effets dans les discours incriminés. Non seulement chez "les Français"! Et non seulement chez ces Français! Cela aurait exigé qu'on lût sérieuse-*

*ment, dans leur agencement et dans leur stratégie théoriques tant de discours diffi-
ciles. Cela n'a pas été fait. (Derrida 1997, p. 17)*[1]

Défense nationale

Of course, not all French commentators saw *Impostures intellectuelles* as an
unjustified attack on French thinkers. For some, *l'affaire* seemed to provide a focal
point for wider frustrations with a certain strand of French intellectual life and its
public role. One of the most interesting interventions in defence of Sokal and
Bricmont is that of Jacques Bouveresse, in his book published by Raisons d'Agir[2],
Prodiges et vertiges de l'analogie (Bouveresse 1999). Bouveresse is scathing about
what he regards as a nationalistic defence of 'philosophy' in the face of an anti-
intellectual onslaught from America. The spectacle of French intellectuals, like
Kristeva, 'playing the martyr' and claiming that the attack carried out by Sokal
and Bricmont is vindictively directed at them rather than at the content of their
work is, Bouveresse finds, somewhat ridiculous (pp. 18-20). He considers the
sudden appearance of an intellectual consensus, 'la grande idée de la paix et de la
concorde universelles qui sont censées régner désormais au sein du monde
intellectuel', to be nothing more than an 'idealist fiction' which wilfully ignores
the conflicts, inequalities and injustices that pertain to intellectual activity in
France (p. 114). The 'République des Lettres' is, Bouveresse claims, the least
republican of institutions, organised as it is along tribal lines, and demonstrating
many of the faults that it pretends to condemn in the political field. What is more,
the defenders of the tribe tend to accuse any critic who points out these faults as
a small-minded puritan:

> *Tout ce que l'on pourrait suggérer d'entreprendre pour essayer de les limiter relève
> précisément du genre de moralisme répressif que cultivent les aigris et les puritains*

1. Christopher Norris indicates that he has some sympathy with those who feel that Sokal and
Bricmont have unfairly directed their scorn at French intellectuals (Norris 1999). He feels that
the 'distinctively French tradition' of a philosophy of science – a line which comes down
through Bachelard, Canguilhem and Derrrida's essay 'White Mythology' – is ignored because it
does not fit with the typecast image of a 'French' intellectual. Sokal and Bricmont tend to ignore
this approach, which shows how certain scientific concepts develop out of a 'matrix of intuitive
or metaphoric thought', preferring to attack a more generalised 'postmodern' tendency to treat
all knowledge as a form of cultural construct (p. 92). Similarly, Norris argues that the groupings
that Sokal and Bricmont use are loaded, with French, or French-influenced, intellectuals
portrayed as adopting relativist positions, ranged against scientists and anglophone defenders of
common sense. Hilary Putnam, for example, has moved from a realist position to a doctrine of
'internal realism' which is, Norris claims, 'little more than a relativism that dare not speak its
name' (p. 101). It is, Norris claims, an oversimplification to claim that French intellectuals are
chiefly responsible for undermining the value of objectivity or for creating conditions where
science is misused in support of relativist or anti-realist arguments. (p. 102)
2. Editions Raisons d'Agir is an independent publishing venture, set up by Pierre Bourdieu
and associates in the mid 1990s. To date, Raisons d'Agir has published twelve inexpensive and
relatively short pocket-sized books which deal with a range of issues including unemployment,
education, neo-liberalism, the media and the 1995 public-sector strikes. The aim of these
publications has been to challenge the vulgate of what Pierre Bourdieu and Loïc Wacquant
have recently called 'NewLiberalSpeak'.

qui, pour des raisons qui leur sont personnelles, ne sont pas convaincus des vertus objectives éclatantes du système. (p. 123)

In short, Bouveresse feels that Sokal and Bricmont are justified in pointing out errors in the work of Deleuze, Lacan, Kristeva etc., and he is shocked by what he regards as the duplicity of some of these criticisms, which refuse to engage with the precise textual problems highlighted by Sokal and Bricmont. However, as has already been suggested, Bouveresse has a wider target, a point which will be expanded on in the second half of the chapter.

La métaphore et l'analogie

Before dealing with some of the wider political and cultural implications of *l'affaire*, implications for which *Impostures intellectuelles* often seems merely to be merely a springboard, it is worth dealing with at least one substantive issue which is closely linked to Sokal and Bricmont's argument. Much of the discussion concerning *l'affaire Sokal* in France has focused on the question of the legitimacy of using scientific metaphors in the fields of philosophy and social sciences. Speaking to the 'Société romande de philosophie' in 1998, Jacques Bouveresse considers that the crucial question is whether it is admissible that, in philosophy, there is nothing more than a resemblance in the language used to the original scientific material. He suggests that, on the contrary, it is reasonable to expect from the philosopher a somewhat more serious treatment of scientific material which is being transposed or generalised. In *Prodiges et vertiges de l'analogie*, Bouveresse explores this particular question in some detail. Essentially, he claims that those who have rejected Sokal and Bricmont as intellectual 'cops' [flics] have claimed a *general* right to metaphor, rather than defending *specific* uses of metaphor. Just because a thinker is 'creative', it should not follow that he or she should be above criticism (p. 147). He considers that the authors criticised by Sokal and Bricmont use two principles which are particularly effective in the philosophical and literary domains, but potentially extremely misleading in terms of the appropriation of scientific material. Firstly, these authors highlight superficial resemblances between a scientific theory and literary or philosophical work. Secondly, they systematically ignore profound differences between the two fields, dismissing them as unimportant (p. 22). Moreover, it is implied that such differences are only points of detail which could only be of interest to 'les esprits pointilleux, mesquins et pusillanimes' (p. 22).

As an example of this, Bouveresse examines at some length Régis Debray's application of Gödel's theorem to the theory of social or political systems. According to Bouveresse, the method used by Debray is similar to that applied by most of the authors cited in *Impostures intellectuelles*. Debray claims that in the same way that Gödel's theorem demonstrates that formal systems include statements which cannot be determined by the system, so social and political systems include statements which cannot be justified by the internal resources of the system (pp. 22-3). Therefore, as far as Debray is concerned, from the point that Gödel showed that Peano's arithmetics could not be formalised within the framework of its own theory (1931), so political scientists could understand why the Soviet authorities found it necessary to preserve and display the body of Lenin. Bouveresse is unequivocally dismissive of Debray's reasoning, recommending that this assertion should figure in the next edition of the *Dictionnaire de la stupidité*. If nothing else, Bouveresse argues, Debray simply does not need Gödel's theorem to illustrate what is nothing more than the philosophical commonplace that there is no possibilty of absolute reflexivity, truth or foundation (p. 25). Put simply, Bouveresse considers that in recent decades any number of French intellectuals have employed this method, whereby A is shown to be the same as B, when A and B have very little in common (p. 29).

In contrast to this, Jean-Marc Lévy-Leblond, a Professor of Physics at the University of Nice, defends the use of scientific metaphor, and makes precisely the accusation – that Sokal and Bricmont are seeking to police knowledge – that Bouveresse finds so ridiculous (Lévy-Leblond 1997). Lévy-Leblond mobilises the argument that Sokal and Bricmont have confused ontology with epistemiology, and he accuses them of creating a strawman on which to focus their attacks on 'relativism', since no serious critic of contemporary science would consider a scientific theory to be a 'pure production of ideology'. Why should, he asks, the physical sciences claim the unique privilege of producing purely *formal* knowledge, when *signification*, as opposed to *validity*, is always socially produced? For Lévy-Leblond, Sokal and Bricmont are zealous purists, who seek to police the boundaries and defend the illusory epistemological purity of the physical sciences. He suggests that it is only by running the permanent risk of mutual misunderstanding that human communication can take place, and the creation of a *cordon sanitaire* around science can only lead to a harmful sterility.

Similarly, Max Dorra, writing in *Le Monde*, is convinced of the legitimacy and even the necessity of the use of metaphor which draws upon scientific concepts (1997). He considers metaphor to be a sort of 'carrefour germinatif', necessarily a representation based upon analogy which is created by an individual. Scientific models are themselves more often than not metaphors that are then taken up within a field governed by absolute objectivity. In this way, the metaphor is a sort of crossroads, which leads in one direction to the poetic, and in another direction to a philosophical or scientific theory. A 'third way' is also possible, whereby metaphor is allowed to run its own course within an associative chain. This would be the case with certain forms of psychoanalysis, for example, which would lead towards some sort of interpretative hypothesis.

In his *Défense des sciences humaines*, Marc Richelle presents the argument for the use of scientific metaphor by social scientists in rather more conciliatory terms, but also suggests that the appropriation of metaphor is necessary for thinking and communicating (1998). Richelle suggests that the 'jeux gratuits de métaphores' which are so severely criticised by Sokal and Bricmont should be viewed as an extreme form of a necessary intellectual activity, which is essential both to everyday thinking and to scientific thought:

L'analogie, la métaphore, Aristote déjà l'avait observé, sont des outils essentiels dans nos efforts de compréhension du réel aussi bien que dans notre exploration des potentialités du langage. Chacun à sa manière, le scientifique en use autant que le poète. (p. 44)

Metaphors should have, as far as 'science' is concerned, (Richelle's term refers to both the human and the exact sciences) a heuristic or didactic value. They should help us to make ourselves understood or to do research. This sounds straightforward, Richelle admits, but it is in fact extremely difficult to draw the line between uses of metaphor which fulfil this role and those that do not. However, he feels sure that prescriptions should not be made, and that researchers in the social sciences should not be afraid of using scientific metaphors in the light of Sokal and Bricmont's interventions. Richelle proposes as an example his own area of expertise, psychology, which has frequently made use of current technologies, such as magnetism, fluid dynamics and computers. Each 'model' has helped to construct a representation of the particular object of study that was useful at a given point in time.

La dimension *triviale* de la culture

It can clearly be seen that the way in which this particular part of the debate is framed points towards wider issues, such as the position of intellectuals in public life. In this way, it is clear that *l'affaire Sokal* can often act as a pretext for talking about a much wider series of issues. Of course the fact that the debate is, in part at least, sensationalised by the media, opens it up to issues not directly connected with the initial matters at stake. Baudouin Jurdant, for example, in the introduction to the collection *Impostures scientifiques: les malentendus de l'affaire Sokal*, claims that the mediatised nature – 'tout ce battage médiatique' – of *l'affaire* frequently makes measured and useful reflection difficult, if not impossible (Jurdant 1998, p. 11). Yves Jeanneret, similarly, in *L'Affaire Sokal ou la querelle des impostures* traces the development of *l'affaire* between 1996 and 1998, and is particularly struck by the protean nature of the debate (1998). As far as Jeanneret is concerned, the proliferation of interventions in this period – his book is based on somewhere in the region of three hundred texts[1] – do not constitute a structured 'debate' as such. The majority of the texts may well refer to 'l'événement fondateur', Sokal's original hoax, but it is as if each intervention starts the debate afresh: 'Chaque intervention semble être un commencement absolu, juxtaposant l'article d'avant-hier avec l'événement fondateur; elle se dispense de faire référence à la confrontation des idées, toujours plus copieuse, qui la précède' (p. 9). However, Jeanneret is ultimately more sanguine about the way in which *l'affaire* develops in mediatised terms. In terms of both form *and* content, Jeanneret regards 'l'affaire Sokal' as a genuinely *cultural* debate to the extent that it is framed within a public space and necessarily reflects upon what he calls the 'trivial' – a term which he claims is in no way pejorative – dimension of culture:

---

1.   Jeanneret only draws on one Internet site, that of *Libération*.

Toute culture, savante ou populaire, scientifique ou littéraire, légitime ou contestée, peut être dite en quelque mesure triviale, en ce sens que la qualité des savoirs y est indissociable de la façon dont ils circulent, s'échangent, se publient, se réinterprètent. Les œuvres, les représentations et les savoirs ne se constituent en effet qu'en connaissant, par diverses méditations, diverses formes d'appropriation et de détournement. Les idées deviennent savoirs, sciences, idéologies, croyances en étant diffusées, reconnues, détournées, réinventées. (pp. 10-11)

In this way, Jeanneret feels that what has been generated by Sokal and Bricmont is 'une *querelle des impostures*' rather than 'affair' or a 'controversy'. It is naïve to expect that this *querelle* can provide any real sociological or philosophical lessons. The interest lies rather in the fact that it offers an overview of a series of texts which provide an exceptionally rich commentary on a range of 'trivial' – in Jeanneret's non-pejorative sense – issues: the ideologies of science, the representation of the relations between science, authority and knowledge, and the reinscription of scientific categories within culture. That is to say, a range of issues which constitute the background to scientific and cultural matters, but which are frequently not discussed (pp. 11-12). For Jeanneret, this highlights a paradox which lies at the heart of 'le sokalisme'. That is to say, Sokal and Bricmont have – by taking texts from their normal context and exposing them to 'un *forum* protéiforme' – brought to light 'la question de la trivialité'. However, they have done this precisely in the interests of preserving the 'utopia' of a form of thought which is completely isolated from its social exposition (pp. 251-2).

Science in post-war France

As far as the relations between science and authority are concerned, the question of politics is crucial, and the network of political issues within which the debate functions is obviously different in France and the United States. The fact that Sokal and Bricmont are in part aiming their attack at what they see as the relativism of 'cultural studies' in American universities – a phenomenon which does not occur to the same extent in France – is well-established. Patrick Petitjean, however, takes things a stage further by claiming that Sokal and Bricmont are also involved in defending science against the American religious right, and creationism in particular (1998, p. 118). It is worth looking at Petitjean's argument at some length, since he offers an account of the position of science in French public life in the twentieth century. He sees Sokal in an American context as defending science against the religious right, whilst at the same time responding to cultural relativism. However, since there is no significant conservative or religious rejection of science coming from the political right in France, and the relativism/realism dichotomy does not have the same cultural or political relevance in France as it does in the United States, he is initially puzzled by the impact of l'*affaire* in France.

In part, his answer is that the political debate around science in the French public sphere remains essentially within the framework established in the 1930s, and that Sokal can easily be located within the lineage of 'une certaine gauche' in

France, which saw socialism as essentially scientific, and which rejected any criticism of science as potentially 'obscurantist and prefascist' (p. 120). Petitjean argues that the political situation in the 1930s brings together a particular set of circumstances that encourage the resurgence of neo-positivism. Essentially, science suffers a 'moral crisis' in the wake of its association with the mass slaughter of the First World War. Against this, the irrationalism of National Socialism appears as a challenge to rationality, and science plays an important role in the perceived social and political success of the Soviet Union. In short, the left begins to see science as a source of social and moral values, and even as generating democracy itself. Science is seen as opposed to capitalism, and criticism of science becomes associated with obscurantism, and thus fascism. When the particular political circumstances of the 1930s no longer pertained, the faith in science remained as a general political consensus shared by left and right in France. After 1945, a sort of republican consensus on science was established between the Gaullist right and the communist left. National reconstruction depends upon a state sector that favours technological progress, and economic development offers a general state of well-being for all that is widely felt to be linked to scientific progress (p. 124). This consensus regarding science helps to explain, Petitjean feels, the influence that the PCF managed to preserve within scientific and university institutions, despite the Cold War. The status, content and function of science in France in this post-war period were simply not matters for discussion.

Then, in the late 1960s and the 1970s, the consensus around science, this 'noyau dur' is finally questioned. Science is associated with conservative or even repressive social forces, and the PCF, associated with those who hold a certain degree of power in the domain of science, is challenged by a younger, anti-authoritarian extreme left. However, by the second half of the 1970s, this anti-authoritarian challenge to science begins to be forced out of the public domain. The debate is revived in the 1980s, but this time it is the defenders of science who set out the terms. Petitjean claims that, with the arrival in power of the left in 1981, Jean-Pierre Chevènement gives a new impetus to the struggle against movements that are seen as being 'anti-science'. Chevènement feels at this stage that the economic crisis which takes hold in the early 1980s brings along with it a wave of irrationalism, in the same way that the economic crisis of the 1930s was accompanied by an irrationalism which fed into fascism. The Republic is perceived to be in danger – threatened, bizarrely enough by, amongst other things, the media success of Uri Geller – and Chevènement calls science to the rescue, organising a national symposium on 'Recherche et responsabilité' (pp. 127-8). Although the report provided by the symposium pointed out the twin pitfalls of an irrational rejection *and* 'une vision apologétique' of science, Chevènement still succeeded in re-establishing a republican consensus around science.

In 1992 the United Nations conference in Rio on 'environment and development' was similarly designed to promote the notion that science, technology and industry can resolve all problems. For Petijean, both the Rio conference and *l'affaire Sokal* are couched, as far as public debate is concerned, in terms of 'défense de la science et de la raison contre l'obscurantisme qui mène au fascisme' (p. 130). However, the discussion generated in the 1990s by these two issues also represents the first time, since the 1960s, that the issue of the social function of science and the question of progress have existed as a debate within the public sphere. Petitjean feels that the defenders of the 'scientistic' point of view, which opposes science as rationality to antiscience as obscurantism, are finally on the back foot. Rather than seeing *Impostures intellectuelles* as an arrogant and outdated manifestation of the desire to police thought, to control scientific metaphors, it should be seen as an expression of the difficulties experienced by the left in abandoning the notion that science, social progress and socialism are inextricably linked (p. 133). Petitjean considers Sokal and Bricmont to be involved in a much wider defence of science than would be implied by their careful selection of specific examples of the misuse of scientific metaphors. *Impostures intellectuelles* is an intervention which seeks, consciously or not, to bolster 'la version française du complexe scientifico-militario-industriel américain' (p. 124), associated with the faith in technology and science promoted by the *Trente glorieuses*, and which only now looks to be threatened by voices of opposition and protest.

Les Lumières, les postmodernes et les *poujadistes*

Jean-Luc Gautero considers the political implications of *l'affaire* in the broader context of the legacy of the Enlightenment (Gautero 1998). For Gautero, Sokal and Bricmont are overly attached to a narrow definition of 'reality'. They refuse, to the point of obsession, to acknowledge any approach to reality which does not accord with theirs (p. 72). In short, their belief in 'la pureté inattaquable de leur science' is nothing more than an act of faith, and for this reason they are unable to accept the validity of a constructivist reading of science. As far as Gautero is concerned, Sokal's open invitation to social constructivists to test the conventions of physics by jumping out of his apartment window indicates a sort of fundamentalist refusal of the constructivist position. Such is their *irrational* faith in science, Gautero suggests, they are unable to accommodate any view which challenges their one-dimensional view of reality. Their purist defence of Enlightenment rationality masks feelings of ambivalence with regard to the 'rationality' that they defend so vigorously. In this way, he condemns Sokal and Bricmont as unfaithful to the spirit of Enlightenment:

> Les philosophes des Lumières ont travaillé à dissiper les ténèbres qui obscurcissaient leur siècle; veiller à ce que leurs Lumières restent bien en place là-bas, plus de deux cents ans en arrière, ce n'est pas prolonger leur œuvre, c'est même la trahir si cela doit nous empêcher d'allumer de nouvelles Lumières qui dissipent les zones d'ombre qu'elles laissent ici et maintenant. (p. 74)

Jean-François Revel, on the other hand, writing in *Le Point*, condemns what he sees as postmodern relativism in the strongest terms (Revel 1997). He suggests that 'l'échec de la philosophie' has led 'postmodern' philosophers to exact a sort of childish revenge by showing how science has also failed. Now, there is no truth,

only opinions: but of course, Revel notes with heavy irony, 'les postmodernes' fail
to apply this relativism to their own theories:

> *C'est pourquoi ils ont contre-attaqué en usant d'armes étrangères à l'intelligence,*
> *consistant surtout à traiter Sokal de réactionnaire "poujadiste", et – cela ne saurait*
> *tarder – de sympathisant du Front national et de "révisionniste". Pitoyables égare-*
> *ments! Il est vrai, lorsqu'on a érigé la tricherie en système et qu'on est pris la main*
> *dans le sac, comment riposter, sinon en changeant de terrain avec la plus constante*
> *mauvaise foi? L'honnêteté intellectuelle serait un suicide. De plus, ce sont les post-*
> *modernes qui sont réactionnaires. Car s'il n'y a aucune différence entre le vrai et le*
> *faux, le bien et le mal, le juste et l'injuste, toutes les idées, tous les comportements*
> *deviennent légitimes, y compris le racisme et le totalitarisme. L'enracinement dans*
> *son identité définit la seule vérité et la morale? C'est retomber dans les conceptions*
> *nazies. C'est tourner le dos à toutes les conquêtes de la vraie gauche depuis trois siè-*
> *cles. (1997, p. 121)*

What is striking in this quotation – quite apart from the vehemence and
dismissive tone – is the fact that Revel has reconfigured *l'affaire Sokal* so that it
becomes a lens through which to view a series of well-established debates around
the left and the right in France, and their relationship to the Republic. If 'les
postmodernes' have insisted on equating Sokal with two anti-republican forces,
namely 'poujadism' and Le Front National, then Revel is forced to highlight their
own tendency towards a sort of anti-republican ghettoisation of identity. What is
more, this extreme and dishonest relativism, reveals a complicity with the dark
forces of totalitarianism. In a conventional rhetorical move, Revel, writing in the
right-of-centre *Le Point*, accuses the postmodernists of betraying the 'real' left,
whose achievements are presumably to be grudgingly but sportingly admired.

Chiens de garde et le néo-libéralisme

Jacques Bouveresse is, unlike Revel, firmly on the left politically, but his approval
of Sokal and Bricmont's stance in *Prodiges et vertiges de l'analogie*, equating it with
a broad defence of *rationality* rather than science, also opens up the debate to
questions pertaining to the Republic and democracy. Intellectual 'seduction', such
as Debray's use of Gödel discussed above, has somehow established itself as a
'democratic' way in which to express one's arguments. Confronted with this, a
dismayed Bouveressse proposes a more rational mode of argument. As far as he is
concerned, rational thinking – what Hume calls 'the calm sunshine of the mind' –
is a rare, local and fleeting phenomenon. All the more reason, then, for it to be
nourished and defended, since it is so crucial for democracy:

> *Je ne sais pas jusqu'à quel point les gens sont capables réellement de se servir un peu*
> *plus de leur raison. Mais je comprends mal la répugnance que les intellectuels éprou-*
> *vent aujourd'hui à les y inciter. Si par impossible on réussissait à mettre un peu plus*
> *de raison dans les conduites et dans les affaires humaines, qui n'en comportent sûre-*
> *ment pas beaucoup, cela ne ferait peut-être, comme on dit, pas beaucoup de bien,*
> *mais on ne voit vraiment pas quel mal cela pourrait faire. (p. 151-2)*

Bouveresse's argument must be seen in the context of the move towards a form of 'collective' intellectual engagement that has crystallised around Pierre Bourdieu in the second half of the 1990s, and in particular since the public sector strikes of 1995. The fact that *Prodiges et vertiges de l'analogie* appears in the Liber-Raisons d'Agir collection obviously places Bouveresse squarely within this project. Bouveresse implies that members of a certain French intellectual class have become a sort of unreasonable, out-of-touch and overly sensitive *mandarinat*. What is more, they have entered into a dangerous alliance with the world of journalism and journalistic values:

> *Nos penseurs célèbres n'ont la plupart du temps rien des "généreux guerriers" aux-quels Locke fait allusion. Ils ont plutôt tendance à refuser le combat (ou, plus exact-ement, le débat) et à rechercher de préférence, avec le concours des forces journalistiques, la victoire par forfait. (p. 122)*

In fact, Bouveresse goes further to argue that certain French intellectuals, in alliance with journalists, are in the process of acting as 'chiens de garde' (obviously picking up on Serge Halimi's book for Liber-Raisons d'Agir) for the neo-liberal consensus which some have defined as 'la pensée unique'. This consensus demands a 'positive', 'conciliatory' attitude, frowning upon criticism (p. 147), and these 'chiens de garde' act in extreme bad faith, by refusing the right to criticise in the name of freedom of thought (p. 135). As we have seen already, the 'République des lettres' is corrupt and has apparently abandoned republican ideals, dominated as it is by faults that intellectuals condemn all too readily in political life: 'Le clientélisme, le copinage, le cumul et la corruption, que l'on condamne avec vigueur dans tous les autres cas, sont considérés ici plus ou moins comme la façon normale de faire' (p. 123). Properly philosophical rigour is replaced by a system of judgement governed by belief, convention, admiration and ritual: in short, Bouveresse implies, the values of an isolated mandarin elite. One way in which this hypocrisy might be undermined, he provocatively suggests, would be to apply the market system, which these 'penseurs' accept all too readily within their own field, much more rigorously so that each one has a quantifiable index of the usefulness of what he or she produces (p. 138).

Bouveresse effectively accuses those thinkers who have rejected the criticisms of Sokal and Bricmont out of hand of a contemporary 'trahison des clercs'. We are living, Bouveresse claims, at a point in time when 'il est difficile de ne pas écrire de sociologie' (p. 20). In other words, the political problems associated with global neo-liberalism are much more pressing than the issues addressed by the majority of French intellectuals. Bouveresse finally claims in his epilogue that Sokal and Bricmont might be considered to have uncovered nothing less than a sort of 'pathology' lurking at the heart of the supposedly rude health of thought in French life (p. 149). The pathology identified by Bouveresse is the anti-republican drive to seduce rather than to persuade by rational argument, and the preferred mode of this seduction is nothing more than a form of 'propaganda', which is at odds with the aims of democracy. Rather than seeking to attack the 'dictatorship of reason' (Bouveresse refers here to the so-called *nouveaux philosophes*), intellectuals would do better to introduce some much needed rationality into human affairs. Similarly, rather than creating an elite star-system, intellectuals should concentrate on the collective and democratic project of disseminating and diffusing rationality. This is the democratic impulse that is one of the motivations behind the Liber-Raisons d'Agir publishing project.

Loïc Wacquant, a close associate of Pierre Bourdieu, adopts a very similar position to Bouveresse, saying that he considers that 'Transgressing the Boundaries' provides an exemplary illustration of the elementary operations of 'intellectual alchemy' which have allowed 'postmodernism' to claim a sort of surface radicalism for itself. This postmodernism has seduced a generation of academics, who are nostalgic for the ideals of the 1960s, but who lack the means to express these political ideals other than on paper. They seek to attack empirical knowledge as being complicit with oppressive networks of 'power-knowledge', and to reject the 'meta-narrative' science, and emphasising the 'errors' of Enlightenment thinking. However, all this fancy intellectual footwork is really no more than an abstract and sterile alternative to real political commitment. It also provides a useful excuse for avoiding the laborious but necessary task of archival or empirical work (Wacquant 1997, p. 15).

In fact, Sokal and Bricmont themselves argue along similar lines, detecting a certain political discouragement which stems from a general disorientation on the left. In their epilogue to *Intellectual Impostures*, they suggest that this political discouragement in the face of an increasingly dominant free market capitalist system may be a plausible sociological explanation for the development of postmodern ideas (1998, pp. 189-90). In an era when communist regimes have collapsed, Third World independence movements have all but abandoned the quest for autonomous development, and social-democratic parties have adopted neo-liberal policies, it is not surprising, they suggest, that a form of discouragement is generated in academics. In support of their argument they quote from Noam Chomsky who, writing in the 1990s, expresses his frustration following a trip to Egypt:

> The way it showed up there, in very educated circles with European connections, was to become totally immersed in the latest lunacies of Paris culture and to focus totally on those. For example, when I would give talks about current realities, even in reseach institutes dealing with strategic issues, participants wanted it to be translated into post-modern gibberish. For example, rather than have me talk about the details of what's going on in US policy or the Middle East, where they live, which is too grubby and uninteresting, they would like to know how does modern linguistics provide a new paradigm for discourse about international affairs that will supplant the post-structuralist text. (Chomsky 1994, pp. 163-4; quoted in Sokal and Bricmont 1998, pp. 189-90)

Conclusion: 'une affaire peut en cacher une autre'

One important theme, one 'trivial' aspect of *l'affaire Sokal*, is to provide a way of talking about the Republic. As we have seen, Bouveresse calls for a more democratic and rational approach in intellectual life, whilst Revel accuses 'les postmodernes' of complicity with totalitarianism, as if they were latter-day communists, undermining the Republic from within. Allain Glykos sees in all of this a worrying trend in the mode of intellectual engagement (Glykos 1998). For Glykos, the term *affaire* is highly revealing, and he plays upon the double meaning of 'affaire(s)' in French in order to indicate a nexus of signification which reveals something about the parlous state of cultural and intellectual debate in contemporary France:

> *Il n'y a pas que l'affaire Sokal. Et d'ailleurs, cette fin de siècle est marquée en France par la multiplication des affaires. A tel point qu'il n'est guère convenable de dire que l'on travaille dans les affaires, ou que l'on est dans les affaires. Mieux vaut travailler, enquêter, sur les affaires. Ces doux parfums de scandales qui planent dans la Cité constituent, qui plus est, le fond de commerce de discours qu'on espérait ne plus jamais entendre. La naïveté est toujours un défaut, pas encore un crime. (p. 293)*

'L'affaire Sokal' was preceded in France by what Glykos calls 'l'affaire Jean Clair', a debate which took off in 1991, concerning the aesthetic criteria for choosing works in museums and art galleries. Both 'affaires' are framed in frequently aggressive and bellicose terms, and both form themselves around a rhetorical framework that produces accusations of *imposture* and of *complot*. Glykos is careful to underline the significance of the fact that these terms are borrowed from the business world when he summarises the two accusations, using terms employed by Laurent Mayet and Jean Baudrillard, as those of 'délit de non-initié' (*imposture*) and 'délit d'initié' (*complot*). Pushing the metaphor to its limits, Glykos claims that postmodern relativism is effectively being accused of having inflated its own stock by means of 'insider-trading', and of attempting a 'hostile takeover' of the physical sciences. Glykos tentatively suggests that these accusations, and the rather sterile spectacle of *affaires* is linked with a contemporary climate of moral righteousness, which in turn is linked to the decline of real political options after the collapse of communism. Art and science have become a sphere in which political arguments that have their roots elsewhere can be played out. Even the debates around Bourdieu and the Editions Liber-Raisons d'Agir publications, which explicitly reject and criticise the media's drive to emasculate political debate, have been transformed into an *affaire* in a similar way. The element of 'complot' is certainly present, in the form of Serge Halimi's attack on fellow journalists, whom he provocatively describes as 'les nouveaux chiens de garde', deliberately evoking Paul Nizan's famous pamphlet from the 1930s (Halimi, 1997). For his part, Glykos is dismayed by the polemical turn that cultural/intellectual debate has taken in France:

> *l'heure est bien à débusquer l'intrus, à dénoncer l'imposture, la mainmise ou le complot, bref à sauver. Mais sauver quoi? La science contre les intellectuels, le sérieux contre le bluff? Sauver l'art de ses tentations à ne plus revendiquer les critères esthétiques qui ont fait son histoire? Bourdieu contre la pensée unique politico-médiatique, Thom contre Lacan, Bacon contre Beuys, Descartes contre Feyerabend? (p. 306)*

For one thing, Glykos fears that this commitment to polemics may be hijacked by a political class which is all too willing to seize the chance to use such disputes for its own ends. Pierre Bourdieu's attempt, for example, to reinstate polemics in the form of a 'scientific militantism' does, Glykos admits, have some virtues. However, it should only function as a point of departure for 'une troisième voie': that is to say, discussion (p. 309). The issue of discussion brings Glykos to the crux of the matter; the function of the media in creating a legitimate and normative public space for the circulation of ideas, as defined in part by Habermas. Once again, Glykos acknowledges that Bourdieu and Halimi are right in many ways to highlight the ethical problems associated with a media that is not currently able to fulfil this role, but he thinks that they may end up being trapped within the system they are attempting to criticise. Discussion, however fragile its chances for life, given the inability of the media to undertake this Habermasian role, is essential. Glykos suggests, in this way, that 'l'espace public' needs to be opened up to a new 'éthique de la discussion'.

Bibliography

Bouveresse, J. (1998) 'Qu'appellent-ils "penser"?', Conférence du 17 juin 1998 à l'Université de Genève. Société romande de philosophie.

Bouveresse, J. (1999) *Prodiges et vertiges de l'analogie*, Paris: Raisons d'Agir.

Derrida, J. (1997) 'Sokal et Bricmont ne sont pas au sérieux', *Le Monde* , 20 novembre, p. 17.

Dorra, M. (1997) 'Métaphore et politique', *Le Monde*, 20 novembre, 17.

Halimi, S. (1997) *Les Nouveaux chiens de garde*, Paris: Raisons d'Agir.

Jeanneret, Y. (1998) *L'Affaire Sokal ou la querelle des impostures*, Paris: P.U.F.

Gautero, J.-L. (1998) 'Raisonner sans entraves: les enjeux politiques de l'affaire', in B. Jurdant (ed.) *Impostures scientifiques: les malentendus de l'affaire Sokal*, Paris: La Découverte/Alliage, pp. 59-74.

Glykos, A. (1998) 'Une affaire peut en cacher une autre', in B. Jurdant (ed.) *Impostures scientifiques: les malentendus de l'affaire Sokal*, Paris: La Découverte/Alliage, pp. 293-313.

Kristeva, J. (1997) 'Réponse à Alan Sokal et Jean Bricmont: une désinformation', *Le Nouvel Observateur*, no. 1716, 25 septembre, p. 122.

Lévy-Leblond, J.-M. (1997) 'La Paille des philosophes et la poutre des physiciens', *Recherche*, no. 299, juin, pp. 9-10.

Norris, C. (1997) 'Sexed Equations and Vexed Physicists', *Journal of Cultural Studies*, vol. 2, no. 1, pp. 77-107.

Petitjean, P. (1998) 'La Critique des sciences en France', in B. Jurdant (ed.) *Impostures scientifiques: les malentendus de l'affaire Sokal*, Paris: La Découverte/Alliage, pp. 118-33.

Revel. J.-F. (1997) 'Les faux prophètes', *Le Point*, 11 octobre, pp. 120-1.

Richelle, M. (1998) *Défense des sciences humaines: vers une désokalisation?* Editions Mardaga, Sprimont.

Sokal, A. D. (1996a) 'Transgresing the Boundaries – Toward a Transformative Hermeneutics of Quantum Gravity', *Social Text*, Spring/Summer, pp. 217-52.

Sokal, A. D. (1996b) 'A Physicist Experiments with Cultural Studies, *Lingua Franca*, May/June, pp. 62-4.

Sokal, A. D. and Bricmont, J. (1997) *Impostures intellectuelles*, Paris: Odile Jacob.

Sokal, A. D. and Bricmont, J. (1998) *Intellectual Impostures: Postmodern Philosophers' Abuse of Science*, London: Profile Books.

Wacquant, L. (1997) 'Les dessus de l'"affaire Sokal" II: petit précis d'alchimie postmoderne", *Liber*, no. 31, juin, pp. 14-15.

Transformations of the French Intellectual

Michael Kelly

When philosophy paints its grey in grey, then has a shape of life grown old. By philosophy's grey in grey it cannot be rejuvenated but only understood. The owl of Minerva spreads its wings only with the falling of the dusk. (Hegel 1967, p. 13)

Hegel's familiar perception, that understanding emerges only a short while before the thing understood reaches the end of its time, may be an excessively melancholic view of social life, but there are many signs that it may be uncomfortably apt for the phenomenon of the French intellectual. This chapter will focus on what in retrospect may appear as the high point of the phenomenon, showing how French intellectuals became nationalised in 1945, ushering in a period when they enjoyed unprecedented prominence both at home and internationally. The moment is viewed in the context of a previous period of historical development, and then in the context of more recent attempts to provide a theoretical basis for understanding what happened.

The concept of the intellectual is used to describe a wide range of writers, artists, performers and academics in contemporary France. In many respects, the issues surrounding this designation have clarified, and a broad consensus has emerged. However, in confirmation of Hegel's insight, it has emerged just at the time when social change and shifting paradigms have thrown its usefulness into doubt. Most studies of French intellectuals acknowledge that their precursors can be traced back to the Enlightenment, particularly to the illustrious precedent of Voltaire, who not only offered a dissenting philosophy but also campaigned personally against concrete examples of injustice, in the Calas case and other similar affairs (Voltaire 1963). With a wide enough definition, still earlier writers can be drawn into the tradition, going back to the schoolmen of the Middle Ages (Le Goff 1975). Scholars are agreed that the term 'intellectual', as a noun, was in limited use in the early nineteenth century. Saint-Simon identified intellectuals as the motor of industrialisation in 1821, and their inherent dynamism was noted by Renan twenty or so years later (Julliard and Winock 1996, p. 14).

The consensus has it that the notion of intellectual emerged onto the national stage in France, when it was popularised at the time of the Dreyfus Affair. A motley crew of writers and artists rallied to the cause of the unjustly accused Jewish-Alsatian army captain, and when they were scornfully dismissed as 'intellectuals' by their opponents, they adopted the title as a badge of honour, thus founding a political and cultural tradition. Though initially the intellectuals appeared as a left-wing grouping, in fact they represented a minority of the French intelligentsia. Dreyfusard writers like Emile Zola, Anatole France or Charles

Péguy were opposed by distinguished anti-dreyfusard writers like Maurice Barrès, Ferdinand Brunetière and Charles Maurras. From an early stage, right wing writers and artists were at pains to assert their pre-eminence in the intelligentsia, and gradually came in some circumstances to accept the title of intellectual themselves. At this time, they were more numerous and wielded greater cultural prestige. The mobilisation of intellectuals during the Great War drew the opposing sides into a degree of national consensus, without significantly attenuating their disagreements (Hanna 1996). During the interwar period, France's intellectuals were increasingly polarised between right and left, reflecting the social and political struggles of the time, including the rise of fascism, the Popular Front, and the Spanish Civil War. Even the eclectic group of non-aligned, 'non-conformist' intellectuals who tried to steer a course that was 'neither right nor left' were ultimately obliged to choose (Loubet del Bayle 1969; Soucy 1985; Soucy 1995).

This changed abruptly in 1940, with the Fall of France, the German occupation and the installation of the Vichy regime. The polarisation did not end in any fundamental sense. On the contrary, it intensified (Kelly 1993). But the right wing intellectuals reigned in Paris and Vichy, while the left were denied access to the public media, and mostly took the path of Resistance or internal emigration. Four years later, in a decisive negation of the negation, the right wing intellectuals faced public humiliation, prosecution, and, in the case of Robert Brasillach, execution. The returning left intellectuals, on the other hand, found themselves cast in the role of national heroes. It was at this point that the figure of the intellectual crystallised in the form which subsequently became one of France's key exportable assets, and it is worth examining in more detail how this process occurred.

The post-war nationalisations introduced far-reaching state intervention into key sectors of the economy, including parts of the finance, raw materials, manufacturing and transport industries. At the same time there was a sharp increase in state investment and regulation in the cultural field, accompanied by a massive mobilisation of cultural producers in the work of national reconstruction. In substance culture was also nationalised. As part of this process, leading writers accepted their national mission, and in so doing became more fully conscious of their status as intellectuals, with all that it now implied.[1]

In the aftermath of 1944, and the liberation, France faced the urgent and difficult task of reconstruction. The appalling material circumstances were compounded by a series of political and ideological conflicts, which left the country on the brink of civil war,[2] and facing the post-war era, in Pierre Nora's phrase, 'mi-vainqueur, mi-vaincu' (half victor, half vanquished) (Nora 1989). The chief precondition of national reconstruction was that the internal conflicts of the

---

1. Some of the following material has already been presented in Kelly (2000). See also Godin (2000) in the same issue.
2. The circumstances are well documented in histories of the period, such as Rioux (1987) and Larkin (1988).

past four years should not be allowed to deteriorate into civil war. National unity therefore became an overriding priority. It was largely achieved thanks to the overwhelming desire of the population to secure an independent French government. And it was facilitated by its willingness to subscribe to the founding myth that the French had massively supported the Resistance and the external 'Free French' movement, and that the collaborators in Vichy and Paris were no more than a tiny band of traitors. Unanimity on these points was essential both for binding the nation together at home, and for presenting a credible united image of France to the outside world, especially to the victorious Allies.

In the face of France's economic and social disarray, the creation of national unity placed heavy demands on symbolic resources. The task fell to 'symbol workers', such as writers, artists, broadcasters, performers and directors. Their challenge was to produce the ideas, images and stories which could knit French people together in an imagined community (Anderson 1991), which they could share, and which could be presented to France's international partners. In putting their shoulder to this wheel, cultural producers accepted the constraints and benefits of a much deeper involvement with the state. In the case of the intellectuals, the shift involved a break with the previous traditions, habits of mind, and self-perceptions, which had cast many of them as independent of the obligations to nation and state, if not in active dissent. Once completed, the new 'nationalised' status of the intellectuals became a comfortable background feature, rarely commented upon. But the process of transition was not wholly painless, as can be glimpsed in the writings of 1945.

Jacques Prévert, in his best selling poetry collection *Paroles*, warned that 'Intellectuals should not be allowed to play with matches' ('Il ne faut pas laisser les intellectuels jouer avec les allumettes').[1] Metaphorically, for him, the intellectuals play with matches by entering into an alliance with the state, giving them access to a source of power, which the poet believes they will abuse. As a confirmed libertarian, Prévert was deeply suspicious of state power, and here criticices the intellectuals' pact with it, by highlighting the benefits they will derive. In ostensibly celebrating others in their work, intellectuals covertly promote their own achievement. No doubt, the poem refers to the many writers and artists who were commissioned to write, paint or sculpt on themes of post-war reconstruction, and who used the opportunity to advance their own aesthetic ends and public reputation: erecting a monument to themselves, as Prévert saw it. The poem goes on to criticise the duplicity of intellectuals who abuse power for purposes of self-aggrandisement, and warns of the danger that creativity will be constricted by the obligations of an official role, which requires monuments.

Prévert clearly did not see himself as an intellectual, but his concerns were shared by Jean-Paul Sartre, who in retrospect appears as the exemplar of all intellectuals.[2] In the second issue of his new journal, *Les Temps modernes*, in

---

1. 'Il ne faut pas' in Prévert (1946), reprinted in Prévert (1992, p. 139-40). Translations are my own unless otherwise stated.
2. This argument has been forcefully proposed in Lévy (2000).

November 1945, Sartre published an even sharper warning against playing with fire, in the shape of state power.

> *Jamais péril plus grave n'a menacé la littérature: les pouvoirs officiels et officieux, le gouvernement, les journaux, peut-être même la haute banque et la grosse industrie viennent de découvrir sa force et vont l'utiliser à leur profit. S'ils réussissent, l'écrivain pourra choisir: il se consacrera à la propagande électorale ou il entrera dans une section spéciale du Ministère de l'Information; les critiques ne se soucient plus d'apprécier ses ouvrages mais d'en supporter l'importance nationale et l'efficacité; dès qu'ils sauront utiliser les statistiques, leur discipline fera de rapides progrès. L'auteur devenu fonctionnaire et accablé d'honneurs s'effacera discrètement derrière son oeuvre. (Sartre 1948, p. 50)*

The threat to literature lies in the fact that it is a valuable resource for the state and its agencies, and Sartre fears that it will be harnessed to social and political purposes, at the expense of artistic integrity. Sartre entitled his essay, 'La Nationalisation de la littérature', referring no doubt ironically to the economic nationalisations. But he presents a careful analysis of the political pressures felt by the Paris literary milieu in 1945, and sustains an argument that a significant shift is occurring. Although the essay is rarely discussed, it illuminates the processes at work in the cultural field, and its argument repays closer scrutiny.

The problem, as Sartre sees it, is that literature is being taken very seriously by the political and cultural elites. It is valued for its dignity, its greatness and the duties it performs. New books are judged by their social importance rather than by their literary merit, and writers are being drawn into official functions, almost like civil servants. He recounts that an official said to him of the actor and theatre director, Charles Dullin, that he is a national asset, and comments: 'Cela ne m'a fait point rire: j'ai peur qu'on ne cherche aujourd'hui par une manoeuvre subtile à transformer les écrivains et les artistes en biens nationaux' (Sartre 1948, p. 35). Today, it may seem quaint to bridle at the idea of prominent cultural figures being regarded as national assets, but Sartre's reaction is at the least clear evidence that this was a new and unwelcome development for him in 1945. In similar vein, he objects to the tendency for new book launches to be conducted like official ceremonies, as if they were 'une contribution bénévole aux festivités de la quatrième République' (which had not at that stage been formally inaugurated) (p. 35). He especially objects to books being judged as *important*, 'comme un discours de Poincaré définissant sa politique monétaire à l'occasion de l'inauguration d'un monument aux morts' (p. 35). This comparison is pregnant with meaning, since Poincaré was above all remembered as the man who saved the *franc*, and rescued the nation from economic catastrophe in 1926. By implication, writers are similarly expected to rescue the nation from catastrophe. Poincaré notoriously launched his financial measures at the unveiling of a war memorial, and by an ironic inversion, it is the writers who are in Sartre's view being transformed into monuments, much as Prévert suggests. However, Sartre sees monumentalisation as a curse rather than a benefit. It arises from the need for instant historical judgment, which enables a work's 'importance' to be measured. It exerts pressure on writers to see themselves as others might see them a hundred years hence. And as a result, it introduces a Medusa's gaze, which turns its object to stone. The writer is petrified in the form of a public monument, perhaps also betokening the death of Art. Sartre fears that, surrounded by high public expectation, the writer is becoming socialised and regarded as an ambassador. Young writers are showered with recognition and honours in a rush for instant consecration, to the point of extreme literary inflation, and 'tout se passe comme si la France avait un besoin éperdu de grands hommes' (p. 45). The situation he describes no doubt reflects Sartre's own rapid elevation to celebrity, but he offers enough examples to suggest that the phenomenon is more widespread.

Analysing the apparent causes of the malaise, Sartre points to the difficulties of literary succession. Many senior figures in the literary establishment were discredited by their wartime activities, while others had died or been forgotten. The result of this sudden massacre of the Grand Old Men ('cette brusque hécatombe des doyens', p. 46) was an urgent need to fill the void left behind. In 1945, Sartre suggests, no author could publish without having some link with the Resistance, or at least a cousin in the *maquis*. Consequently, writers tended to be identified with a particular social group or political movement, and to serve as its public representative. An important factor, in Sartre's view, was that France had been humiliated internationally as a result of the war, and that its literature was one of the few things for which it was still admired, especially by the Western Allies.

> *Sur un seul point nous avons surpris l'étranger: il ne cesse d'admirer la vitalité de notre littérature. « Et quoi! nous dit-on. Vous avez été battus, occupés, ruinés et vous avez tant écrit! » Cette admiration s'explique aisément: si les Anglais et les Américains ont produit peu d'oeuvres nouvelles, c'est qu'ils étaient mobilisés et leurs écrivains dispersés aux quatre coins du monde. Nous, au contraire, persécutés, traqués et, dans beaucoup de cas, menacés de mort, du moins étions-nous en France, dans nos foyers; nos écrivains pouvaient écrire, sinon au grand jour, du moins en cachette. (p. 49)*

The widespread international interest in French literature prompted France to take it more seriously than in the past. Sartre observed wryly that many French people would prefer their country to be best known for military leaders like Turenne or Bonaparte, but for the time being they were willing to settle for poets like Rimbaud or Valéry. As a result, young writers were being boosted into great men, who could be dispatched to London, Stockholm or Washington, to the detriment of their literary development.

Sartre's response to this threat was to encourage writers not to try to see themselves through the eyes of posterity and not to be fooled into believing the inflated rhetoric, which presents them as great men and ambassadors. Writers should follow their own independent path, he argued, rather than 's'engager sur les autostrades nationaux' (p. 52), and they should have the courage to cause scandal and express their anger, when their solitary literary explorations called for it. For his part, he pledged that his journal would do its best to assist in the task of literary deflation and to rouse literature from its slumbers.

Sartre's analysis of the situation was lucid, and he was as well placed as anyone to attest to the pressures on French writers to play a representative role in the nation in 1945. He may also have been right in thinking that premature and excessive public recognition was inimical to the development of young writers. However, his proposed remedy falls foul of the duality which he had already enunciated in the concept of committed literature, and which is well summarised in the conclusion to his 'Présentation' of *Les Temps modernes*, published the previous month:

> Je rappelle, en effet, que dans la *"littérature engagée"*, l'engagement *ne doit, en aucun cas, faire oublier la* littérature *et que notre préoccupation doit être de servir la littérature en lui infusant un sang nouveau, tout autant que de servir la collectivité en essayant de lui donner la littérature qui lui convient. (Sartre 1948, p. 30)*

The co-existence of social and literary responsibilities does not easily permit the writer to reject pressing social expectations in the name of literature. It is difficult to argue that, on the one hand, every individual human being is responsible for everything that happens, but on the other, writers should not speak or act on behalf of the country to which they belong. But in any case, the apparent dilemma was already being resolved in practice. Sartre himself was prominent in organisations such as the Comité national des écrivains (CNE, the National Writers' Committee), which was issuing blacklists, and ensuring that writers had the kind of wartime credentials he described. He was also a willing spokesman and literary ambassador on behalf of France.

It is not usual to think of Sartre as a representative of his country, but it was a role he clearly adopted at this time. Some of his most moving essays at the Liberation were written on behalf of France, in the role of spokesman. His short article, 'La République du silence', written for the first non-clandestine issue of the review *Les Lettres françaises*, was very widely circulated in France and America, and his solemn reading of it was broadcast on the new French national radio station (Sartre 1949, pp. 11-14). His evocative description of Paris under the German occupation was published two months later in *La France libre*, the London-based magazine published by the Free French authorities, with the explicit intention of explaining French affairs to an English-speaking audience. He concluded:

> Et, enfin, si ces pages vous ont aidé à mesurer ce que notre pays a souffert, dans la honte, dans l'horreur et dans la colère, vous penserez comme moi, je crois, qu'il a droit au respect jusque dans ses erreurs. (Sartre 1949, p. 42)

Addressing his readers in this way, Sartre was already a spokesman for his country, and it was a role he continued over the following months. In January 1945, he and six other journalists went to the United States as guests of the U.S. Office of War Information. During the five months he stayed there, reporting on America for French newspapers, he also interpreted France to the Americans, and did his best to advance France-American relations.[1] Since in this way Sartre had spent a large part of 1945 abroad as a cultural ambassador, it is difficult not to conclude that by November, the process of nationalisation was too far advanced to be reversed. Sartre's essay of that month appears as a last cry of alarm before the end: he was not waving but drowning. Four months later in April 1946, Sartre was interviewed on French national radio on his return from another visit to the United States. Invited by a deferential journalist, Bernard Montour, to describe his impressions, Sartre enthused about the welcome he had received, and called for more effort to be put into cultural diplomacy, urging that 'Il faut utiliser tous les moyens pour promouvoir la culture française aux États-unis [...] c'est la meilleure propagande' (Montour 1946). [2]

Sartre was by no means the only intellectual to speak on behalf of France. Albert Camus emerged at the same time as a voice of the nation, and most writers with an acceptable wartime record were happy to lend their talents to supporting the national reconstruction. Paul Valéry, perhaps France's most distinguished living writer, offered sonorous support in the last few months of his life. After his death, a state funeral in August 1945 provided the opportunity for de Gaulle and senior political figures to pay their solemn respects in Paris and Sète. Valéry was buried in the cemetery overlooking the Mediterranean coast, the subject of his best known poem ('Cimetière marin'), enabling dignitaries to exhibit the indissoluble link between the restored state and the glories of French literature. At the other end of the political spectrum, Louis Aragon, the most prominent French communist writer of the time, energetically built on the persona of 'poète national' (national poet) that he had developed in clandestinity. His wartime poems were widely circulated after the Liberation, and 'La rose et le réséda' (the rose and the mignonette) in particular, became a symbol of reconciliation between the previously hostile Catholic and socialist traditions, in a new spirit of national unanimity (Aragon 1946, pp. 19-20). If the state looked to writers to provide support for the reconstruction of national culture and identity, writers also looked to the state to provide the material means of expression. The acute shortages and rationing of the period meant that government departments closely controlled publication. While the Ministry of Information granted or withheld permission to publish, the Ministry of Industrial Production became a crucial gatekeeper for editors and publishers, who often had to beg and wheedle for vital allocations. Literary and intellectual life was conducted in close association with the state, as part of the material and cultural reconstruction of the nation.

Accepting Sartre's analysis of the nationalisation of French literature, it may nevertheless appear excessive to extend it to the nationalisation of French intellectuals more broadly. However, Sartre's approach is characteristic of the writers of the period, who made little use of the term intellectual as a noun. This is particularly true of those writers who are most frequently identified as

---

1. See Contat and Rybalka (1970, pp. 117-23).
2. This is taken from my transcription from the tape, consulted at the Inathèque in the Maison de la radio, Paris.

intellectuals themselves. The recent growth in historiography of intellectuals has tended to institutionalise Sartre's own later formulation of intellectuals as being writers, artists, scientists and scholars who get involved in public debate outside their area of specialisation (Sartre 1972b, pp. 375-455). But this notion was not available in 1945, and 'intellectual' was still used as a noun that mainly applied to others, however paradoxical it may seem in a period which, in retrospect, appears rather as the hey-day of the French intellectuals. When Prévert criticised intellectuals for playing with matches, he was echoing the stance of writers across the non-communist left and centre movements who, when speaking about intellectuals, were not implicitly including themselves.

This is particularly visible in three groups of writers who are now generally regarded as archetypal intellectuals. The first group are the existentialists and the wider constituency surrounding the review *Les Temps modernes*. As well as Sartre, Simone de Beauvoir and Maurice Merleau-Ponty, it includes such writers as Albert Camus, Raymond Aron and Boris Vian, among many others. The second group are the left Catholics and their sympathizers around reviews like *Esprit* and *Témoignage chrétien* and the Éditions du Seuil publishers. As well as the directors of these, Emmanuel Mounier, André Mandouze and Paul Flamand, it includes writers such as Jean Lacroix, Claude-Edmonde Magny, Jean-Marie Domenach, Denis de Rougemont, and Paul Ricoeur. The third group are the Christian Democrats, whose spiritual leader Jacques Maritain was more often in New York and Rome than in Paris, but which included philosophers like Pierre Teilhard de Chardin and Gaston Fessard as well as writers and journalists like François Mauriac, Stanislas Fumet and Louis Terrenoire.

The texts written by the members of these groupings make remarkably few references to intellectuals, and when they do so, it is in the same spirit as Sartre, who wrote pityingly that:

> *les intellectuels anglo-saxons qui forment une classe à part, coupée du reste de la nation, sont toujours éblouis quand ils retrouvent en France des hommes de lettres et des artistes étroitement mêlés à la vie et aux affaires du pays. (Sartre 1948, p. 49)*

It is striking that Anglo-Saxon 'intellectuals' are contrasted with French 'men of letters and artists', all the more remarkable since the American and British writers of the period would have been even less likely than the French to describe themselves as intellectuals. The collective noun 'intellectuals' functions as a purely objective description, applied by a commentator to an external group, much as did the concept of 'clerk' or 'cleric' in Julien Benda's celebrated prewar polemic against *La trahison des clercs* (Benda 1927). During the period of strong politicisation of intellectuals in the late 1930s, the protagonists who thought of themselves primarily as writers and artists began signing petitions and joining organisations identifying themselves as intellectuals. Although their most radical members belonged to the Association des Ecrivains et Artistes Révolutionnaires, the broad anti-fascist and anti-Munich groupings took titles which incorporated the term intellectual. These included the Comité de vigilance des intellectuels antifascistes (CVIA) and the Union des intellectuels français (UDIF) (Sirinelli

1990, pp. 132-214). Nonetheless, it was still rare in 1945 for the noun 'intellectual' to be used with a verb in the first or even the second person. Most commonly, the conjugation would run that *I* am an author, *you* are a writer, and *they* are intellectuals. Two main factors contributed to the emergence of intellectuals as a self-conscious group: the importance of the Resistance role and the policies of the French communist party.

The role of intellectuals during the occupation was one of the most prominent themes of the Liberation. Those writers, artists and journalists who had supported Vichy or the Germans had done so recently and visibly in the public arena. Conversely, those who had supported the Resistance now found their clandestine writings republished for a mass readership, which regarded them as custodians of the nation's honour. The trial and execution of the writer Robert Brasillach, for collaboration with the enemy, made the question of the intellectual's responsibility into one of the most hotly debated issues of the year. The galaxy of luminaries from the worlds of culture and science, who petitioned General de Gaulle to exercise clemency, made it clear that they fully accepted the responsibility of intellectuals, and the text of their request identified them as 'les intellectuels soussignés' (Sirinelli 1990, pp. 241-43).

Writers who had joined the Resistance, for their part, looked back nostalgically at what they now saw as their finest hour. Meditating on this in the first issue of *Les Temps modernes*, Merleau-Ponty commented:

> En face de l'armée allemande et du gouvernement de Vichy, où, comme dans tous les appareils d'Etat, la généralité sociale dominait, la résistance offrait ce phénomène si rare d'une action historique qui ne cessait pas d'être personnelle. Les éléments psychologiques et moraux de la politique paraissaient ici presque seuls, et c'est pourquoi on a pu voir dans la résistance les intellectuels les moins enclins à la politique.
> L'expérience de la résistance a été pour eux une expérience unique et ils voulaient en garder l'esprit dans la nouvelle politique française, parce qu'elle échappait enfin au fameux dilemme de l'être et du faire qui est celui de tous les intellectuels devant l'action. De là ce bonheur à travers le danger, où nous avons vu certains de nos camarades, d'ordinaire tourmentés. (Merleau-Ponty 1945, p. 64)

Though he describes intellectuals objectively as a group, Merleau-Ponty comes close to a first person relationship in his reference to 'certains de nos camarades', and it is possible to detect or imagine an acknowledgement of his own experience of the dilemma of intellectuals confronting the question of action. The unique nature of the Resistance experience was a frequent theme for writers, who as Merleau-Ponty suggested, tended to want its spirit to be maintained in the postwar arrangements. In that sense, the identity of 'Resistance intellectual' was in 1945 a positive and valorising one which largely overcame the slightly stigmatising associations that had previously clung to the term intellectual. There were counter-examples, in people like Brasillach, Drieu la Rochelle and the dozens of writers and artists named in lists of collaborators by the CNE (Assouline 1985; Sirinelli 1990). However, for the most part, these were considered as exceptions. Sartre, speaking primarily to an American readership, declared that 'la quasi-totalité des intellectuels, une partie des industriels et des commerçants ont milité contre la puissance occupante' (Sartre 1949, p. 45). This was a point taken up energetically by the communist party. Maurice Thorez's report to the Tenth Party Congress in June 1945 argued that:

> Lorsque les prétendues élites sombraient dans la faillite et la trahison, c'est du peuple qu'ont surgi les forces neuves qui contribuèrent si vaillamment à la libération du pays. Forces de la Résistance, cohortes valeureuses des Forces françaises libres, bataillons intrépides des Forces françaises de l'intérieur, masse obscure et anonyme des ouvriers, des paysans, des intellectuels de France, hommes, femmes, jeunes gens et jeunes filles de chez nous, toutes ces forces neuves, et elles seules, peuvent assurer demain la rénovation et la grandeur de la France. (Thorez 1966, p. 346)

A reader might be surprised to see the intellectuals assimilated categorically into the 'people', let alone into '[la] masse obscure et anonyme des ouvriers, des paysans, des intellectuels'. However, the aim of the passage was to build on the strong mood of national unanimity and to encourage intellectuals to move more strongly towards a degree of social self-awareness. The hope was that they would come to identify themselves as a distinct social group, in a broad social and political alliance with the workers and peasants, who formed the social basis for the party's support.

The communist party played an influential role in highlighting the role of intellectuals in the Resistance, especially those of its own members who had been executed or died in deportation, most prominently Georges Politzer, Jacques Salomon and Jacques Decour (Daniel Decourdemanche), later joined by Danielle Casanova. Initially, the task of mobilising intellectuals was given to the experienced teacher, turned politician, Georges Cogniot, and the young philosopher Roger Garaudy. Their interventions at the Tenth Congress echoed Thorez (Cogniot and Garaudy 1945). They saluted the heroes of the intelligentsia who died for their country (Cogniot and Garaudy 1945, p. 17). They celebrated the great French artistic, literary and scientific traditions. And they called on intellectuals in all branches of culture and education to put their weight behind the work of national reconstruction, led by the party. Their credentials enabled them to speak in the first person as 'intellectuels' (Cogniot and Garaudy 1945, p. 6), though they did so sparingly. Subsequently the same themes were developed with increasing force as the communist party recognised not only the symbolic value of prominent figures, but also the importance of intellectuals as a rapidly growing social and electoral group (Caute 1964; Verdès-Leroux 1983). The party set an agenda in which intellectuals were invited to become more aware of their specificity, and at the same time to extend their political partisanship into their intellectual activity. From the onset of the Cold War, the intellectual became a prominent part of the French political landscape, and a figure who seemed always to have been there (Kelly 1997).

The dissident stance of so many intellectuals during the following decades did not prevent them from being national treasures, however inconvenient they may at times have been for a particular government. General de Gaulle was more aware of this than most, and twenty years or so later, when his advisers approached him about one of Sartre's current skirmishes with the law, he is reported to have commented that 'on n'arrête pas Voltaire' (Atack 1999, p. 74). The comparison with the Enlightenment philosopher is often made of Sartre, and betokens not simply his high cultural prestige, but also his importance as a national figure.

Recent studies of French intellectuals have largely focused on their struggles for political power or cultural capital within the overall social field (Boschetti 1988; Debray 1979; Jennings 1993). They consider the often difficult relations of intellectuals to this or that French institution, organisation, issue or policy. But underpinning all the battles and controversies is a prior commitment to the primacy of the French nation, as incarnated by the State. This now appears too self-evident to mention, following half a century in which the worst taunt that could be flung at an intellectual is that they are lacking in national commitment. Sartre's protest against the incipient nationalisation of literature marks a moment of transition. It may now be difficult to imagine what life was like before that time, but an examination of the situation in 1945 demonstrates that the national commitment of the French intellectuals was constructed in these specific historical circumstances.

The following thirty years, the *Trente glorieuses* of modernisation and economic prosperity, spanning the Cold War, the Algerian War, the May 1968 events and their aftermath, appear now as the zenith of influence of the French intellectuals. They hold an endless fascination, even for those, like Raymond Aron at the time, (Aron 1955) or Tony Judt more recently (Judt 1992), who regard the influence of most of them as misguided or nefarious. Their words and actions were, and still are, scrutinised and hotly debated in France. But their impact has always been amplified by the international attention they have attracted, confirming the French conviction that their intellectual debates articulate issues of universal human concern and ratifying the centrality of universalism in French national identity. In this respect, the postwar intellectual climate in France overcame the dichotomy of the Dreyfus Affair, where conservative nationalists were opposed by cosmopolitan humanists: Army, Church and Nation against Justice, Human Rights and Republic. In the crucible of the occupation and liberation, these conflicting elements were fused, ideologically, into a single national universalism based on a synthesis of the internationalist perspectives of the left with the traditional nationalism of the right. It was in essence a pragmatic, rather than a theoretical construction. And it flourished so long as its premises remained unexamined. Perhaps, as several commentators have suggested, its success was the success of a generation (Sirinelli 1988). It was the first generation born in the twentieth century, too young to fight in the First World War, and reaching their prime with the onset of the Second. Perhaps it was the onset of maturity and retrospection that provoked a more probing self-analysis, and began to unravel the extraordinary intellectual integument of 1945.

Certainly, a key moment in the process of intellectual reappraisal was Sartre's classic plea for the intellectual (Sartre 1972a). Both an analysis and a self-justification, it set the terms of subsequent theories of the intellectual as the transgressive specialist, 'technicien du savoir pratique' who departs from his (or more rarely her) specialism and 'se mêle de ce qui ne le regarde pas'. While offering an intuitively satisfying account of what intellectuals had been for the past thirty (or perhaps eighty) years, it also pointed to a founding contradiction in the identity of the intellectual, who was shown to combine competence (in an area of thought) with incompetence (in the field of action). Applying to the socio-political domain the humanist universalism of their technical knowledge, intellectuals inevitably found themselves exposed and vulnerable. This therefore posed more sharply the problem of power, and whether the intellectual should accept specifically political responsibilities. Sartre's reflection was followed rapidly by the first waves of public self-doubt among intellectuals, and the emergence of a generation of new philosophers anxious to shed, and shred, the intellectual baggage of their elders, together with the challenge of women writers against the latter's 'phallogocentic' conceptions. These developments led to the anguished debate over the 'silence of the intellectuals' in the early Mitterrand years after 1981. An avowedly left-wing government with an intellectual as its leader found that French intellectuals had begun to return to their fields of competence, and were increasingly disinclined to become involved in political issues. It was around the same time that high profile intellectuals began to attenuate their withering critiques of intellectual opponents and focus their critical analysis more on the category of intellectual as such (Flower 1991; Jennings 1993).

Régis Debray was one intellectual who did not shrink from political responsibilities, and became an advisor to President Mitterrand. However, separately from this, he began a detailed analysis of the itinerary of the French intellectuals over the previous century (Debray 1979; Debray 1980). He discerned an evolution in their social basis since the late nineteenth century. Whereas the earliest intellectuals had been teachers, based in the University, he argued, they were overtaken by a group of writers whose power came from the publishing industry. Now, he concluded, the next generation of intellectuals were beginning to base their power in the broadcast media. To a large extent he was talking about the intellectual elites who could inflect public opinion, rather than the growing number of people in the intellectual professions. His analysis was given force by intellectuals such as Bernard-Henri Lévy, so-called 'nouveau philosophe', whose pithy and iconoclastic books and television programmes on the French intellectual tradition entertained and outraged in equal measure (Lévy 1987; Lévy 1991). Lévy embodied the new media-oriented intellectual elite, deftly navigating the slippery interfaces between theoretical innovation, 'edutainment' and self-promotion. Pierre Bourdieu offered a sociology of intellectual capital (Bourdieu 1979; Bourdieu 1982), followed by an unforgiving exegesis of how the intellectual elite was formed (Bourdieu 1989). His account of the pursuit of distinction, and the cultural capital it yields, combines a measure of empirical analysis with an array of powerful concepts (field, habitus, capital, reflexivity) and an ethical concern which does not eschew polemic. His success in the University and in publishing made him the closest thing to an old-style intellectual at the turn of this century.

At the same time as the intellectuals took the path of reflection on their own condition, an impressive cohort of cultural historians also began to deploy their academic power on the social development of intellectuals since the late nineteenth century. There is now an abundance of historical studies, published in France, including, for example, (Chebel d'Appolonia 1991; Ory 1990; Ory and Sirinelli 1986; Rieffel 1993). And a succession of seminars and conferences have taken up the theme, far too many to enumerate. The 1260-page dictionary of French intellectuals, published in 1996, is a valuable work of reference, but serves more symbolically as a monument to the glories of a past era (Julliard and Winock 1996).

No doubt, it is a tautology to suggest that the intervention of the historians confirms that intellectuals are history, but during the mid 1990s, there was a continuous debate in France over whether the intellectuals had had their day. The debate was fuelled by the intervention of figures like Bourdieu, Lévy and Derrida in political and social issues, from domestic strike movements to the armed conflicts in the Gulf, the Balkans, Africa and elsewhere. It was also fuelled by the parallel debates over globalisation and the end of French exceptionalism. To some extent, these debates confirm the continued vitality of the French intellectual tradition, but at the same time they erode the notion of the intellectual as an exceptional social and cultural figure. The social changes in France, as in most advanced industrial countries, have changed the terms of the argument. The most rapidly expanding economic sectors are those which traditionally provided the spawning grounds for intellectuals: education, leisure, culture, and the information industries. And at the same time, public affairs have ceased to be viewed as a specialist field which 'does not concern' the educated workforce. The imperatives of a broad conception of citizenship are high on the agenda of government, and actively promoted through the state education system and a range of government-sponsored initiatives. It may now seem curiously anachronistic to offer Sartre's definition of the intellectual to a new generation of educated professionals who expect to have both an area of recognised expertise and a legitimate duty of involvement in social and political developments. From another viewpoint too, the concept of the French intellectual may appear a little dated to new generations who see their life extending beyond France's borders. The processes of internationalisation, under such headings as European integration, globalisation, environmental protection and world climate change, now cast citizenship in a wider context than the national community, however important that continues to be for culture and identity. More than ever, the aspiration to the universal finds itself unduly constrained by a purely national perspective, which limits both what can be thought and what can be achieved in addressing the issues with which the intellectual or the citizen is now vitally concerned.

In offering a lucid analysis of the French intellectuals of the past, today's writers may be assuming the role of Minerva's Owl, and bringing their understanding at the twilight of the intellectuals. However, Hegel never believed that knowledge was wasted, but rather that it enabled further levels of understanding to be achieved. Even if French intellectuals are no more than a passing moment in 'the long procession of historical cultures and individuals' (Hegel 1977, p. 591), an understanding of them may cast a clearer illumination on the issues of thought and social change with which they were so urgently engaged.

Bibliography

Anderson, B. (1991) *Imagined Communities. Reflections on the Origin and Spread of Nationalism*, 2nd revised ed., London: Verso.

Aragon, L. (1946) *La Diane française*, Paris: Seghers.

Aron, R. (1955) *L'Opium des intellectuels*, Paris: Calmann-Lévy.

Assouline, P. (1985) *L'Epuration des intellectuels: 1944-1945*, Bruxelles: Editions Complexe.

Atack, M. (1999) *May 68 in French Fiction and Film*, Oxford: Oxford University Press.

Benda, J. (1927) *La Trahison des clercs*, Paris: Grasset.

Boschetti, A (1988) *The Intellectual Enterprise: Sartre and 'Les Temps modernes'*, translated by R. C. McCleary, Evanston: Northwestern University Press.

Bourdieu, P. (1979) *La Distinction: critique sociale du jugement*, Paris: Minuit.

Bourdieu, P. (1982) *Ce que parler veut dire: l'économie des échanges linguistiques*, Paris: Fayard.

Bourdieu, P. (1989) *La Noblesse d'état: grandes écoles et esprit de corps*, Paris: Minuit.

Caute, D. (1964) *Communism and the French Intellectuals 1914-1960*, London: Macmillan.

Chebel d'Appolonia, A. (1991) *Histoire politique des intellectuels en France, 1944-1954. 2* vols, Questions au XXe siècle. Paris: Editions Complexe.

Cogniot, G., and Roger G. (1945) *Les Intellectuels et la Renaissance française*, Paris: Editions du PCF.

Contat, M. and Rybalka, M. (1970) *Les Ecrits de Sartre*, Paris: Gallimard.

Debray, R. (1979) *Le Pouvoir intellectuel en France*, Paris: Ramsay.

Debray, R. (1980) *Le Scribe*, Paris: Grasset.

Flower, J. (1991) 'Wherefore the intellectuals?', *French Cultural Studies*, vol. 2, no. 6, October, pp. 275-90.

Godin, E. (2000) 'French Catholic Intellectuals and the Nation in Post-War France', *South Central Review*, vol. 17, no. 4, pp. 45-60.

Hanna, M. (1996) *The Mobilization of Intellect*, Cambridge, Mass: Harvard University Press.

Hegel, G.W.F. (1967) *Hegel's Philosophy of Right*, translated by T.M. Know, Oxford: Oxford University Press.

Hegel, G.W.F. (1977) *Phenomenology of Spirit*, translated by A.V. Miller, Oxford: Oxford University Press.

Jennings, J., (ed.) (1993) *Intellectuals in Twentieth-Century France: Mandarins and Samurais*, London: Macmillan.

Judt, T. (1992) *Past Imperfect. French Intellectuals 1944-1956*, Berkeley & Los Angeles: California University Press.

Julliard, J., and Winock, M., (eds.) (1996) *Dictionnaire des intellectuels français*, Paris: Seuil.

Kelly, M. (2000) 'The Nationalization of French Intellectuals in 1945', *South Central Review*, vol. 17 (4), pp. 14-25.

Kelly, M. (1993) 'French Catholic Intellectuals during the Occupation', *Journal of European Studies*, vol. 23 (1-2), pp. 179-91.

Kelly, M. (1997) 'French intellectuals and Zhdanovism', *French Cultural Studies*, vol. 8, no. 22, February, pp. 17-28.

Larkin, M. (1988) *France since the Popular Front: Government and People, 1936-1986*, Oxford: Oxford University Press.

Le Goff, J. (1975) *Les Intellectuels au Moyen Age*, Paris: Seuil.

Lévy, B.-H. (1987) *Eloge des intellectuels*, Paris: Grasset & Livre de Poche.

Lévy, B.-H. (1991) *Les Aventures de la liberté*, Paris: Grasset.

Lévy, B.-H. (2000) *Le Siècle de Sartre*, Paris: Gallimard.

Loubet del Bayle, J. L. (1969) *Les Non-conformistes des années 30*, Paris: Seuil.

Merleau-Ponty, M. (1945) 'La guerre a eu lieu', *Les Temps modernes*, octobre, pp. 48-66.

Montour, B. (1946) *Jean-Paul Sartre revient des Etats-Unis*, (interview), 1 avril 1946, Paris: Radiodiffusion française.

Nora, P. (1989) 'Mi-vainqueur, mi-vaincu', in A. Simonin and H. Clastres (eds.) *Les Idées en France 1945-1988. Une chronologie*, Paris: Gallimard.

Ory, P. (1990) *Dernières questions aux intellectuels*, Paris: Olivier Orban.

Ory, P., and Sirinelli, J. F. (1986) *Les Intellectuels en France, de l'affaire Dreyfus à nos jours*, Paris: Armand Colin.

Prévert, J. (1946) *Paroles*, Paris: Gallimard.

Prévert, J. (1992) *Oeuvres complètes*, Paris: Pléiade, Gallimard.

Rieffel, R. (1993) *Les Intellectuels sous la Ve République*, 3 vols, Pluriel, Paris: Calmann-Lévy & CNRS Editions.

Sartre, J. P. (1948) *Situations II*, Paris: Gallimard.

Sartre, J. P. (1949) *Situations III*, Paris: Gallimard.

Sartre, J. P. (1972a) *Plaidoyer pour les intellectuels*, Paris: Gallimard.

Sartre, J. P. (1972b) *Situations VIII*, Paris: Gallimard.

Sirinelli, J. F. (1988) *Génération intellectuelle*, Paris: Fayard.

Sirinelli, J. F. (1990) *Intellectuels et passions françaises: manifestes et pétitions au XXe siècle*, Paris: Gallimard.

Soucy, R. (1985) *French Fascism: The First Wave 1924-1933*, New Haven: Yale University Press.

Soucy, R. (1995) *French Fascism: The Second Wave 1933-1939*, New Haven: Yale University Press.

Thorez, M. (1966) *Oeuvres choisies, 1938-1950*, T2, Paris: Editions sociales.

Verdès-Leroux, J. (1983) *Au Service du parti: le parti communiste, les intellectuels et la culture (1944-1956)*, Paris: Fayard/Minuit.

Voltaire. (1963) *L'Affaire Calas*, Paris: Nouvel Office d'Edition.

Naming The Popular: Youth Music, Politics and Nation in Contemporary France[1]

David Looseley

In June 1981, the surprise appearance of Jack Lang, Minister of Culture, at a Stevie Wonder concert in Paris heralded the new Socialist government's ambition to recognise youth music as a legitimate form, and the beginning of a fascinating era of muddled, sometimes torrid debate on the subject. This debate is important to French cultural history for two reasons. First, it is a crucial crossroad in the country's struggle with mass culture and Americanisation. Second, pop music in France (or *le rock* as pop is generically known today) has, like cultural policy itself, been a discursive artefact from the start, as the political scientist Philippe Teillet argues:

> *Terme générique qui recouvre des expressions souvent incohérentes, le rock n'existe qu'au travers d'un discours (histoire, critique, actualités) dont il est l'objet et qui le forme. [. . .]. Entre le discours et les pratiques s'établit un rapport de contemplation, de jugement et de détermination, un système normé qui peut faire référence. (Teillet 1991, pp. 218-20)*

At first, he contends, the rarity and high cost of appropriate musical instruments and the shortage of properly equipped concert venues meant that French fans' passion for the music was to a large extent mediated through the music press, in the form of monthly magazines like *Rock&Folk* and *Best*. To this, one should add that, as a foreign-language form imported from the US and Britain rather than one springing organically from a Francophone community as *la chanson française* did, pop reached France with *ready-made* discursive packaging (including linguistic) and therefore required further mediation. This arguably made its implantation doubly traumatic for the French cultural establishment. It was perceived as transgressive because it projected an 'image excessive, sauvage et immorale'(Teillet 1991, p. 219), and as alien and inauthentic to boot.

Another discursive element in France's relationship with Anglo-American pop is the struggle to name it. As the music settled in, the term *la chanson française* became less and less apt. Throughout the 1960s and early 1970s, the labels *yéyé* and *la pop-music* were successively used, but they too became outmoded and were

1. I am grateful to Philippe Teillet for his extremely generous clarifications and bibliographical assistance. I also wish to thank Patrick Mignon; and Olivier Donnat, and Frédérique Mauduit of the Ministry of Culturé's Département des études et de la prospective.

replaced in the mid-70s by *le rock*. This term only confused matters, however, since, as the sociologist Pierre Mayol points out (1994, p. 9), it is a 'false singular' covering all the styles previously covered by *la pop-music* as well as the harder, group-based sounds equated with the term in English. Then the 1980s term *le rock alternatif* appeared, indicating more experimental rock produced by independent labels, together with *la world music* and, in the 1990s, *le rap*, *la techno* and *les boys bands*. Rap and techno complicate the picture even more because they are often seen as making a generic break from pop as it has generally been understood since the 1960s.[1] At official level, a number of terms have been tried: *chanson* and *variétés*, *rock*, *musiques d'aujourd'hui*, *musiques amplifiées*, and the current one, *musiques actuelles*. None has proved sufficiently flexible to cover pop's variable geometry. Meanwhile, some vociferous intellectuals have objected to the trend in the social sciences and the state administration to describe pop as 'a culture' (as in '*la culture jeune*') or 'cultural'.

What I want to do, therefore, in this chapter is examine debates about policies for popular music and illustrate how the problem of naming pop is at their core. I shall look at three 'case studies', spread over roughly a decade: Alain Finkielkraut's *La Défaite de la pensée* (1987), Marc Fumaroli's *L'Etat culturel* (1991), and a recent report produced for the Ministry of Culture by the Commission nationale des musiques actuelles (1998). But I shall start by summarising the Ministry of Culture's own response to pop, in the light of its evolving definition of culture.

At its creation under Malraux in 1959, the Ministry was allocated the task of promoting, preserving and democratising culture in its most conventional acceptation. What are today known as creative or cultural industries, operating in a market economy which (supposedly) ensures their survival, were not in those days deemed worthy or needful of cultural engineering by the state. Acting against their legitimation was Malraux's humanist conception of culture as great *works* – 'les oeuvres capitales de l'humanité, et d'abord de la France' (1959, quoted in Looseley 1995, p. 37). Such works were held to be spiritually uplifting and immortal, situated somehow outside historical, economic and social specificities and meeting universal 'cultural needs'. They had nothing in common with the manufactured and fashion-led 'products' of mass culture, which only debase the human spirit by pandering to its primitive fascination with sex, blood and death. Malraux's response to this debasement was *action culturelle*, or democratisation: countering the harmful influence of such products and satisfying real cultural needs by widening access to the great works.[2] Once available to all, they can form the basis of a common popular culture and a renewed national identity.

In the course of the 1960s, Malraux's liberal humanism was steadily undermined, especially by the burgeoning social sciences which insisted that cultural needs and practices, far from being universal, were socially and

---

1. Despite the terminological difficulties existing in English as well as French, and to avoid making them worse, I shall use the English term 'pop' generically throughout, as it is still widely used, whereas in French *la pop* and *la pop-music* have largely died out.

2. Malraux's view of mass culture was more complex than this might suggest: see Looseley (1999).

historically constructed. After the events of May 1968 and Malraux's disillusioned resignation, a different policy construction emerged which bore the marks of such influences (Looseley 1999). This became known as 'cultural democracy', intended to signal an alternative to Malraux's 'democratisation'. At its heart was a discursive shift from 'high' or 'classical' culture in the singular, to 'popular' cultures in the plural. Here, the new sociology of Bourdieu, though influential, was considered too pessimistic to be of much practical use in the development of an alternative policy, since he appeared to view popular culture as merely a debased version of high culture. But throughout the 1960s, the sociologist of leisure Joffre Dumazedier (1962) had been working on a more optimistic reading which drew a qualitative distinction between active and passive leisure. Active leisure involves personal or collective creativity in a whole range of forms – sport, recreation and tourism as well as participation in the arts – and is a vehicle of social progress deserving of state encouragement. In the 1970s, the cultural theorist Michel de Certeau helped extend the notion of cultural democracy, particularly in work he undertook on behalf of the Ministry of Culture's research unit, the SER (known today as the DEP). In *La Culture au pluriel* (1974) and *L'Invention du quotidien* (1980), he proposed a more supple conception of culture which included not just creative *works* but the infinite variety of *acts* of creativity in which all human beings engage daily, most of them 'perishable' in that they are not intended to produce enduring artefacts. Concurrently, this perceived need for inclusiveness was being confirmed by the first scientific surveys of cultural practices produced by the SER in 1973 and 1981, which demonstrated the social immobility of demand for high-cultural forms alongside the remarkable spread of mass-cultural tastes, in particular popular music.

This drive to redefine national policy had little impact until 1981, when Mitterrand became President, the Socialist Party (the PS) formed a government, and Jack Lang was made Minister of Culture. Before Lang, such calls as there had been for the state to recognise popular music had focused mostly on French *chanson* and jazz, but pop was a different matter. It was not just that it had Anglo-Saxon roots (so did jazz and the newer forms of *chanson*); but it was possessed of a sound and a sensibility which many found frivolous, alienating and disturbing, on left as well as right. The post-1968 left developed a quasi-Marxist critique of the Americanised entertainment industries. Like Adorno, it dismissed pop as standardising and diversionary, encouraging cheap sentiment and mindless surrender to wild rhythms which distracted from a more rational critique of consumer society. But this grim disapproval started to soften in the late 1970s, as pop became the creative form which French youths identified with most, while left-wing intellectuals made peace with the pleasures of the cultural supermarket (Rigby 1990, pp. 162-3) and local demand persuaded some PS town councils to see the light.

This change of heart at local level inevitably impacted on central government from 1981. Early on, Lang proclaimed that there would no longer be any hierarchy between classical, experimental and popular musics. His Director of Music and Dance, Maurice Fleuret, a well known music critic, similarly cast himself as '"le directeur de toutes les musiques, de l'accordéon jusqu'à l'industrie phonographique"' (quoted in Hunter 1990, p. 144). From the first, however, policies for popular music were diverse not to say incoherent. At first, traditional French *chanson* was the focus, but this proved a non-starter in terms of public support and attention soon shifted to pop (Eling 1999, pp. 131-4). Lang set up a training school for popular music, the Studio des variétés, and, with some setbacks, a purpose-built concert venue in Paris, Le Zénith. The Ministry of Communication meanwhile, separate from Culture at the time, legalised private radio, giving birth to innumerable pop stations and a number of wrangles with record companies over performing rights. Fleuret, on the other hand, wanted to give more of a boost to music *making* and was instrumental in creating the Fête de la musique in 1982, which invited amateurs and professionals of every level of ability to take to the streets to mark the summer solstice by making music. Like the Millennium Dome in Britain, the Fête was emblematic, favouring DIY fun over rigour and training, and pointing the way to a novel experience of nationhood: togetherness achieved through the celebration and shared enjoyment of creativity. In this, it naturally targeted the creative energy of the young.

Beyond such discrete initiatives, much of the early work for popular music and the young was conducted at grass-roots level by a newly created unit within the Ministry, the Direction du développement culturel (DDC). Reflecting Lang's early view that creativity can heal society, the DDC implemented the principle of cultural democracy by encouraging outreach work aimed at 'new publics', including young people from underprivileged backgrounds. This strategy highlighted the social rather than aesthetic nature of pop, in particular its usefulness in tackling problems in the inner cities and suburbs (Teillet 1991). But Lang's statements also hinted at a different though equally functional approach. Culture and the economy, Lang would often claim, are one and the same battle. And as economic crisis began to loom in 1982, support for creative enterprise and the cultural industries was foregrounded (Looseley 1995). During Lang's second term of office from 1988 to 1993, he appointed a special advisor on pop (Bruno Lion), who took the economic slant further by professionalising the sector, aiding record labels, TV programmes, and so on; all at the expense, some felt, of the artistic.

All of these measures were part of a wider shake-up (at least in spirit) of the traditional, aesthetic criteria by which state aid had been distributed and justified since Malraux. Inevitably, the change generated heated debate. Lang was excoriated as the high priest of an anything-goes relativism known as *le tout-culturel*, of which pop became the emblem. Some objected to such crude commercial forms being placed on an equal footing with high-cultural ones. Others welcomed the recognition but challenged Lang's way of going about it, calling for more rather than less state intervention. As so often in French cultural affairs, these controversies exposed conflicting assumptions about the place and purpose of culture in contemporary society. By the late 1980s, youth music thus found itself implicated in an intellectual panic in which France's cultural tradition and republican identity were deemed to be under threat.

Most vocal among those who sprang to their defence were the philosopher and scholar Alain Finkielkraut, in a book gloomily titled *La Défaite de la pensée* (1987), and a respected professor of art history at the Collège de France, Marc Fumaroli, in *L'Etat culturel* (1991). Both were indignant about the anything-goes policy, though Fumaroli went further by denouncing the Ministry's entire history. In their respective arguments, each reveals a disdain for pop, at least in so far as any claims are made for its artistic status. This is where naming becomes a problem. Fumaroli's book is premised on the belief that the term culture can only be applied to the informed appreciation of the arts and heritage in their most traditional senses and that this can only be achieved through education, not democratisation. The Ministry, he argues, has therefore made two serious errors. Since Malraux, it has tried to democratise culture without educating taste, so that today the French have become robotic cultural tourists. And since Lang and his experiments with cultural democracy, it has turned the word culture into 'un énorme conglomérat composé de "cultures" dont chacune est à égalité avec toutes les autres' (Fumaroli 1991, p. 171). Fumaroli is not hostile to popular music as such. He speaks warmly of 'popular arts' like operetta, which has the merit 'de bien servir la langue nationale, et de renforcer sa fonction naturelle de lien commun entre Français' (1991, p. 78), or of Piaf and Chevalier, who are as capable of evoking the great 'lieux communs' of the human condition as Joyce or Proust (1991, p. 76); though it is hard to escape the feeling that this support rests on an essentialism of taste which patronisingly divides high and educated preferences from '[le] goût moyen et populaire qui convenait vraiment au plus grand nombre' (1991, p. 78). What is perfectly clear, though, is that the word 'culture' cannot possibly be applied to such a travesty of the authentically popular as pop:

> La France, avant d'adopter des stéréotypes sociaux et moraux inventés à Greenwich Village, avant de s'habiller en jean et de devenir sourde et muette à force de danser dans le torrent sonore rock, avait été capable de s'habiller à son goût et de chanter en comprenant et en sentant les paroles de ses propres chansons. *(1991, p. 167)*

The emergent French rap scene is similarly described as 'importée des quartiers ensauvagés du Nouveau Monde' and 'l'imitation servile en France d'une des dernières trouvailles du *show-business*' (1991, p. 33).

Fumaroli's position here is based upon the importance of culture to nationhood and the threat of undiscriminating Americanisation. The same is true of Finkielkraut, though he represents a more significant instance of anti-pop discourse because his quarrel is not with cultural policy *per se*. On the contrary, his stance links back to the post-war decentralisation and democratisation movement upon which Malraux drew in order to design France's first cultural policy. As part of a long-standing struggle to elevate the aesthetic experience of working people in the name of republican values, this loose affiliation of artists, intellectuals and cultural workers disapproved of the new mass culture in much the same terms as Adorno: standardisation, passivity, dumbing down. Finkielkraut takes up this critique by deploring the post-modern confusion of 'culture' in the sense of 'la vie avec la pensée' – intellectual, demanding and improving – with the anthropological-cum-consumerist interpretation of the term which embraces any custom or entertainment you care to name, from ballet to football, opera to advertising. Finkielkraut is particularly disturbed by youth culture, which in his view perfectly epitomises the mass-cultural experience: immediate, impersonal, unchallenging, non-verbal:

> la 'culture jeune', cette anti-école, affirme sa force et son autonomie depuis les années soixante, [. . .]. Fondée sur les mots, la culture au sens classique a le double inconvénient de vieillir les individus en les dotant d'une mémoire qui excède celle de leur propre biographie, et de les isoler, en les condamnant à dire "Je", c'est-à-dire à exister en tant que personnes distinctes. Par la destruction du langage, la musique rock conjure cette double malédiction: les guitares abolissent la mémoire; la chaleur fusionnelle remplace la conversation, cette mise en rapport des êtres séparés; extatiquement, le "je" se dissout dans le Jeune. (Finkielkraut 1987, pp. 172-3)

The polarity here between collective frenzy and individual reflection has been standard to indictments of pop since the early days. But Finkielkraut nicely exemplifies the special difficulty which France's literary culture has had with it because of its presumed negation of the eternal virtues of reason, individual responsibility and respect for the past which French culture is deemed to enshrine, in favour of the immediacy of sensation. However, by the time of *La Défaite de la pensée*'s publication in 1987, Finkielkraut was already fighting a losing battle. For, despite the reinforcements brought by Fumaroli and others, pop culture, like mass culture generally, was rapidly acquiring legitimacy, not solely as a result of government recognition but also because a new generation of French social scientists – Antoine Hennion, Patrick Mignon and Paul Yonnet, alongside Mayol and Teillet – had come of age in the era of pop and was now calmly examining it for what it was, opening up a new field of academic enquiry. Ten years after *La Défaite de la pensée*, the traditionalists had been routed. After Lang's departure in 1993 followed by four years of comparative stasis under the right, Catherine Trautmann became the next PS Minister of Culture. But her resolve to continue the Lang line on pop mostly proved uncontroversial, even when she extended official validation to techno, a dance music even more shocking than rock or rap in its frantic pace and rejection of words.

One effect of the intellectual debates of the late 80s and early 90s was to obscure more practical questions about what exactly a policy for pop should look like. Lang's measures had mostly been discrete and symbolic. In 1986, Jacques Renard, once Lang's *directeur de cabinet* and by then virtually his amanuensis, confessed as much: 'L'art a autant besoin de reconnaissance que de subventions. La reconnaissance par l'Etat d'expressions artistiques jusqu'ici négligées est un acte symbolique essentiel auxquels les artistes eux-mêmes sont extrêmement sensibles. En reconnaissant, il confère une dignité nouvelle [. . .]' (Renard 1987, pp. 52-3). This looked suspiciously like a theory of inaction, removing the need for major expenditure. But symbolism could not supplant policy indefinitely. In 1998, Trautmann set up the 'Commission nationale des musiques actuelles' chaired by the director of the Studio des variétés, Alex Dutilh, which submitted a report on the future of popular-music policy in September 1998. Here, a different kind of debate about the social, economic and aesthetic dimensions of pop can be identified.

The report uses the symbolic nature of Lang's recognition of pop as a springboard, giving credit where it is due but recommending that the Ministry now design a much more coherent policy for the sector. Ultimately, the Commission insists, the object of any cultural policy has to be the public (Commission 1998, p. 19). This means combining a raft of measures for the music professions with, among other things, the provision of more systematic aid to amateur practices and community musics; the inclusion of *musiques actuelles* in school syllabuses and exams; and even the requirement that prospective directors of public music schools demonstrate competence in this area. But the real interest of the report for our purposes resides in the ideology underlying such recommendations.

Doubtless with oppositional voices like Fumaroli's and Finkielkraut's in mind, the Commission mounts an assertive defence of *les musiques actuelles*. They are important economically of course, creating jobs, wealth, and so on; but also socially, because they constitute 'la réponse citoyenne à bien des maux qui fracturent notre société'. They are of value culturally because they are of the people – 'des musiques populaires au sens le plus noble du terme' – and are therefore 'democratic' in their 'authenticity'. They are of value developmentally in that, by speaking 'of the world and to the world', they can educate taste and introduce the young to other art-forms. And they have a therapeutic value for an ailing sense of nationhood, in an age when France's cultural exceptionalism is threatened:

> A l'heure où les repères se fluidifient à la vitesse du son, nos musiques sont également porteuses de sens et constitutives d'une mémoire collective et d'un perpétuel mouvement. Et face à la logique d'une mondialisation inéluctable, nombreux sont les artistes français à pouvoir faire résonner au-delà de nos frontières élastiques, le chant bien légitime de notre exception culturelle. (Commission 1998, p. 16)

What is striking about these justifications of pop is the extent to which they reflect the principles by which support for the arts has traditionally been justified in France. Although the Commission is happy to spell out the economic and social benefits of the music industry, it invokes above all the civic values of disinterestedness, patrimonial continuity and national identity that had characterised the Malraux ministry. For this reason, it dislikes the term 'musiques actuelles' it has been saddled with, which conditions the way the music is thought about. The privileging of the present (*actuelles*) serves only to obliterate the musics' past and future, constructing them as rootless commodities in thrall to passing fashions, social trends and market forces and bracketing them off from the arts as a whole. And yet, the report insists, as if replying to Finkielkraut's critique, French popular music is anchored in the national memory by perennial aesthetic values: 'de IAM à Louise Attaque ou Julien Lourau, ce que nous écoutons aujourd'hui procède aussi bien de Jacques Brel et Boris Vian que de Damia ou Emile Vacher' (Commission 1998, p. 9). The report goes on to say 'les musiques actuelles produisent et enrichissent les éléments d'un patrimoine en perpétuel mouvement. Elles fonctionnent à partir d'une mémoire "active". C'est dans l'actualisation permanente de leurs racines et dans le respect de leur différence que se fonde et s'enrichit la notion d'identité culturelle' (Commission 1998, p. 66). With culturally loaded vocabulary and references of this kind, pop is painstakingly winched out of *l'actualité* into the safety of eternal cultural values:

> indépendamment de leurs enjeux économiques et sociaux considérables, les musiques actuelles constituent un secteur artistique à part entière. Les valeurs humanistes en constituent un axe central: développement de la sensibilité, de la créativité, de la mémoire, mise en valeur de la subjectivité, de la différence. (Commission 1998, p. 65)

This salvage operation provides the intellectual justification for a call for parity of treatment.

This is the basic thrust of the *rapport general* which forms the first half of the document, the second half consisting of submissions by the Commission's four sector-specific working parties. Of these, the one which best illuminates the Commission's value-system is by the 'Les Publics' group, drafted by none other than Philippe Teillet. What makes it particularly interesting from our point of view is how unusually well qualified Teillet was to write it. On the one hand, he is a political scientist at the University of Angers with a doctorate in rock policy and several pioneering academic articles on the subject to his credit (Teillet 1991, 1996, and forthcoming). On the other, he has a personal investment in pop in that he is president of Le Chabada, a subsidised popular-music centre in Angers comprising a concert venue, club and rehearsal space. His section provides most of the report's intellectual underpinning and his work as a whole usefully counterbalances the ideas of Fumaroli and Finkielkraut. While they approach pop from a polemical and mostly theoretical perspective drawn from the humanities, in Teillet we glimpse a scholarly sociology being brought to bear on the practicalities of policy-making.

The core of all his writings is the binary divide between cultural democracy and democratisation. In his academic work, he has pointed up the influence of Certeau on the development of pop policy and demonstrated the discursive shift this involves. Pop, particularly in its most innovative moments like rock'n'roll or punk, represents itself as spontaneous, immature, disposable; in Certeau's terminology, it is more about 'perishable' creative acts than definitive 'works'. It is also about those instinctual, irrational impulses which Malraux and Finkielkraut see high culture resisting in the name of the aesthetic, the transcendent and immaterial (Teillet 1991, pp. 235-45). The consequence of this for policy was the DDC's emphasis on 'le social', though as Teillet shrewdly notes (1991), this could and did easily mutate into an emphasis on the economic, the ephemerality of creativity becoming the ephemerality of consumption.

At this juncture, one might conclude that Teillet is fairly sympathetic to the cultural-democracy line. Yet when as a member of the Commission seven years later he is required to draw up a set of concrete proposals, acting as advocate as much as analyst, this turns out not to be so, since he criticises the Lang ministry for concentrating on the social and economic at the expense of the aesthetic and lasting. As in the general report, this criticism would seem to be made in the name of an essentially national imperative. For Teillet's group as for the Commission as a whole, the primary danger posed by the global music industry is not standardisation as Adorno thought but social fragmentation. This is caused by the segmentation of taste, which is itself due to the cultural industries' commodification of the music and their niche marketing, assisted by new domestic technologies like the Internet and the shift in post-industrial societies towards what Gilles Lipovetsky (1983) calls 'personalisation'. For Teillet, the way out is a return to a democratisation strategy akin to Malraux's, in order to counterbalance the post-1968 emphasis on cultural democracy which led the government to recognise pop in the first place. The government, he argues, has simply assumed that pop must be 'popular' and does not therefore require to be democratised. But this is a false assumption, the result of discursive confusion (Teillet, forthcoming). Although 'popular' as a genre in the sense that it is appreciated much more than 'classical' music and by a sociologically more diverse constituency, pop is far from innocent of sociological and cultural determinations.

What Teillet objects to in the 'rhétorique faussement savante de la spontanéité et de l'immédiateté' (Commission 1998, *Les Publics*, pp. 8-9), associated with Certeau (though he is not mentioned here), is the implication, also visible in Fumaroli in a different way, that tastes are natural, rather than socially determined as Bourdieu argues. Teillet points out that the segmentation of taste referred to earlier is in fact especially prevalent in the less advantaged social categories, which are mostly limited to the less challenging products of the global mainstream, and to recorded more than live music. Eclecticism, on the other hand, is more common in the more advantaged (Commission 1998, *Les Publics*, p. 20), while the kind of exclusively high-cultural values associated with the Malraux ministry and the likes of Finkielkraut and Fumaroli, where distinctions are confidently drawn between culture and entertainment, are, for Teillet as for Bourdieu, based upon 'des dominations sociales et des choix esthétiques arbitraires longtemps considérés comme naturels' (Commission 1998, *Les Publics*, p. 11).

Teillet's central demand, then, is the popularisation of the 'popular': that is, for the traditional principles of *action culturelle* laid down by Malraux to be applied to pop. Unlike Malraux, however, Teillet is not blind to the difficulty of achieving this. For Malraux, cultural action mostly meant giving easier access (by decentralisation or keeping prices low) to works which had already been legitimated both by time and the traditional *instances de légitimation*: critics, scholars, museum curators, educators. There was, then, and remains a recognisable (though increasingly challenged) canon to which policy could refer and, in the case of musics other than the popular, a hierarchy of training, qualification and expertise. Pop enjoys none of these advantages. The possibility of legitimation by time, scholarship and training is largely absent (formal music training has never been a condition of entry into the music business), while the judgements of critics don't have the same legitimating weight as in other arts (Commission 1998, *Les Publics*, p. 11). It is therefore only public approval – in other words market forces – which offers any credible yardstick and it is largely to this that policy-makers, aware of their own ignorance of the field, have turned, rather than intervening to influence supply and demand (Teillet, forthcoming). The result is that those artists who don't reach a large audience, because their work is experimental or challenging, are largely ignored and the public is denied access to them. So what is the answer? The same as for high culture under Malraux: state intervention to disseminate such music more widely and to widen people's taste horizons, in the name of republican fraternity:

> *le rôle des pouvoirs publics et des équipements qu'ils soutiennent est [. . .] de favoriser la découverte par les publics de musiques ou d'expressions artistiques qui ne font pas partie de leurs références habituelles. Ainsi, de favoriser des métissages sociaux, l'émergence de solidarités nouvelles et, par la médiation musicale, la reconnaissance de l'Altérité. (Commission 1998, Les Publics, pp. 7-8)*

This means freeing all popular music from the purely commercial imperatives which currently drive it, for example by giving certain types of music venue the means to provide a programme which actively seeks to lead the public 'd'univers esthétiques familiers vers de moins connus', including towards other art-forms (Commission 1998, *Les Publics*, p. 20).

What emerges from the 'case studies' and the ministerial discourse I have examined is that all can be positioned along the axis running between cultural democratisation and cultural democracy, the binary opposition which has characterised policy debate since the beginning. Although the Commission's parameters for culture are much less exclusive than Malraux's or Finkielkraut's, all three are linked (Fumaroli is the exception) to the extent that they are unabashed believers in civic interventionism, convinced that the state's duty is to intervene to alter – that is, improve – national taste. Furthermore, all three (and Fumaroli too in this respect) repudiate the construction of culture as the spontaneous, ephemeral activities and productions of the here and now. Instead, all view culture not simply as a process but as a body of significant, aesthetic works made to last and which connect in some way with similarly significant works from the past. As a result, all make some form of qualitative distinction between culture in this sense and the cruder industrialised products of the market. This discourse sets them apart from the Anglo-American, cultural-studies perspective known as 'cultural populism' (McGuigan 1992), which accepts public taste as a given, to be studied for what it is rather than what it should be.

However, where the Commission – and Teillet's group in particular – differs markedly from Malraux, Finkielkraut and Fumaroli is that it tries to go beyond the dichotomy between democratisation and cultural democracy. Drawing on theorists from the sociology of culture (Passeron, Moulin, Menger), the Publics group stresses that these two are not mutually exclusive at all and that they must actually work hand in hand if the public is really to be placed at the heart of policy. This is because one specificity of the sector is that the highly diverse musics it includes don't emanate only from a limited number of professional institutions but also from a multitude of more or less informal sources and situations: 'Elle doit sa vitalité à l'élargissement considérable du nombre des musiciens, à leurs multiples occasions de confrontations et d'échanges' (Commission 1998, *Les Publics*, p. 3). Being a pop musician doesn't necessarily entail working full-time or being qualified, as there is no clear demarcation between the amateur and the professional. Equally, there is no clear demarcation between spectators and musicians, since the latter make up a comparatively larger number of the former than in other arts (Commission 1998, *Les Publics*, p. 24). Furthermore, the obstacles encountered by amateurs and professionals are broadly the same: access to rehearsal facilities, cost of buying instruments, and so on. What is required, then, in this respect is a cultural-democracy strategy, which would help this rich musical culture to flourish and continue to produce new work. Once produced, however, such work is not equally accessible to all; the cultural-democracy strategy therefore needs to be complemented by traditional democratisation, of a kind common in other arts but so far denied to popular music.

Ultimately, the Dutilh report and the cultural debates which preceded it are important in two ways. First, they shed light on the process of legitimation in France, the strategies naturally (perhaps unconsciously) adopted by pioneers and proselytisers in order to have their favoured form validated by the public body which matters most, the Ministry of Culture. In order to speak up for pop against the likes of Fumaroli and Finkielkraut, the Commission must attempt to bring it into the warm embrace of France's patrimonial, aesthetic and humanist values. This is a standard legitimating rhetoric, which in recent years has been seen at work on French rap. What it in fact shows is the importance of discourse in the legitimation and policy processes. Fumaroli, Finkielkraut and the Dutilh report share an anxious awareness that naming is the battlefield on which culture wars are lost or won; accordingly, the Publics group sets out explicitly to change 'les modalités intellectuelles d'appréhension de ces musiques, modalités qui ont ici, comme dans bien d'autres domaines, des conséquences pratiques incontestables' (Commission 1998, *Les Publics*, p. 9).

Second, they show that, despite changes of regime and cultural values, the focus of debate today remains the civic, republican discourse of democratisation, the mission which Malraux set the Ministry more than forty years ago and which today's policy strategists are still trying to map on to post-1968 notions of cultural democracy. Pop, it would appear, has been adopted as the site where this might best be achieved. After the report was submitted, Trautmann took up only some of its recommendations, wanting more time to consider the others (though in the event she was ousted before this interval had ended). Nevertheless, it was striking that she too, like the Commission, began speaking of *les musiques actuelles* as if they contained a chance of resolving the democratisation/democracy polarity, because they drew no line between 'the most popular practices' involving listeners, spectators and amateurs and 'the most avant-gardist experimentation'

(Trautmann 1998, p. 8). Perhaps, then, today's debates about pop are one of the crucibles in which tomorrow's new policies for French culture as a whole are being forged.

Bibliography

Certeau, M. de (1974) *La Culture au pluriel*, new edition, Paris: Seuil, 1993.

Certeau, M. de (1980) *L'Invention du quotidien*, vol. 1: *Arts de faire*, new edition with introduction and notes by L. Giard, Paris: Gallimard/Folio, 1990; translated as *The Practice of Everyday Life*, Berkeley: University of California Press, 1988.

Commission nationale des musiques actuelles (1998), *Rapport de la Commission nationale des musiques actuelles à Catherine Trautmann, Ministre de la culture et de la communication*, septembre (comprises a number of separate contributions in booklet form, including Teillet's *Les Publics*).

Dumazedier, J. (1962) *Vers une civilisation du loisir?*, Paris: Seuil.

Eling, K. (1999) *The Politics of Cultural Policy in France*, Basingstoke: Macmillan.

Finkielkraut, A. (1987) *La Défaite de la pensée*, Paris: Gallimard.

Fumaroli, M. (1991) *L'Etat culturel: essai sur une religion moderne*, Paris: Fallois.

Hunter, M. (1990) *Les Jours les plus Lang*, Paris: O. Jacob.

Lipovetsky, G. (1983) *L'Ere du vide: essai sur l'individualisme contemporain*, Gallimard.

Looseley, D.L. (1995) *The Politics of Fun: Cultural Policy and Debate in Contemporary France*, Oxford and Washington D.C.: Berg.

Looseley, D. L. (1999) 'The work and the person: discourse and dialogue in the history of the Ministry of Culture', in M.E. Allison and O.N. Heathcote (eds.) *The Fifth Republic: Forty Years On*, Bern: Peter Lang.

Mayol, P. (1994) *La Planète rock: histoire d'une musique métisse, entre contestation et consommation*, 'Dossiers pour un débat' series, no. 29, Fondation pour le Progrès de l'Homme.

McGuigan, J. (1992) *Cultural Populism*, London and New York: Routledge.

Renard, J. (1987) *L'Elan culturel: La France en mouvement*, Paris: Presses universitaires de France.

Rigby, B. (1991) *Popular Culture in Modern France: A Study of Cultural Discourse*, London and New York: Routledge.

Teillet, P. (1991) 'Une Politique culturelle du rock?', in P. Mignon and A. Hennion (eds.), *Rock: de l'histoire au mythe*, Paris: Anthropos, pp. 217-46.

Teillet, P. (1996) 'L'Etat culturel et les musiques d'aujourd'hui', in A. Darré (ed.) *Musique et politique: les répertoires de l'identité*, Rennes: Presses universitaires de Rennes, pp. 111-25.

Teillet, P. (forthcoming) 'Eléments pour une histoire des politiques publiques en faveur des "musiques amplifiées"', Paris: La Documentation Française.

Trautmann, C. (1998) Budget statement reproduced in Ministry of Culture and Communication, *Lettre d'information*, no. 34, 23 septembre.

The New Democracy: Michel Maffesoli and the Analysis of Everyday Life

Max Silverman

A few years ago, the political and cultural commentator Régis Debray posed the crisis of contemporary France in terms of the conflict between the Republic and democracy (Debray 1989). For Debray, as for many others, the battle-lines are drawn up in the following way: the Republic stands for the Enlightenment ideals of universalism, equality, reason, the public sphere of citizenship, high culture and the word, whilst democracy stands for particularism and cultural identity, freedom, emotion, the blurring of the public and private spheres, mass culture and the image. This argument is invariably accompanied by a nostalgic lament for a pure France (the republican community of citizens) which is today at the mercy of American liberalism and multiculturalism (the democratic society of brash individualism and ethnic identities).

A particularly original voice in the analysis of the 'new democracy' (which some call 'post-modernity') is that of the sociologist Michel Maffesoli. In a number of works written over more than twenty years, Maffesoli has provided a fascinating insight into societies in transition.[1] His broad understanding of the transition from a modern to a post-modern age does not differ markedly from that of Debray. However, unlike the partisan analysis of Debray (or, for example, that of Alain Finkielkraut), whose reflections are suffused with deep gloom as to the present state of the human condition, Maffesoli perceives recent developments in terms of a re-enchantment of the world after the collapse of modernity's project of rationalisation and what Max Weber analysed as the disenchantment of the world (TT: 49-50, 56, 128; CM: 66; IE: 85). In this chapter I propose to consider some of the main features of Maffesoli's vision and to evaluate his analysis of the re-enchantment of everyday life.

At the heart of Maffesoli's analysis is his understanding of the dual nature of all political and social processes which one can loosely define as the affective and cognitive aspects of political and social life. The affective is that formless, spontaneous, ambiguous and life-confirming force or passion ('une effervescence' in Durkheim's terminology, TP: 207) which underpins all desire to live with

---

1. I will not be citing all Maffesoli's works but will make reference to the following, using abbreviations for convenience: *La Conquête du Présent* – CP; *Le Temps des Tribus* – TT; *La Transfiguration du Poltique* – TP; *La Contemplation du Monde* – CM; *L'Instant Eternel* – IE. (Full references to these works can be found in the bibliography.)

others. The cognitive is the formal shaping and channelling of this force into projects and institutions. Strictly speaking, they are not two distinct processes at all for one is always present in the other. Historically in the West, the affective has been most apparent at times of popular, political or religious ferment ('révolutions, révoltes, fêtes, commémorations, insurrections', TP: 36) prior to its inevitable recuperation and institutionalisation within more formal structures. The affective exceeds and is unsettling of any cognitive apparatus and formal institutionalisation. It is the 'non-logique' which shadows the order of the 'logique', the heterogeneous and plural nature of things which threatens all attempts at homogeneity and unity, the unconscious tracking of all conscious programmes of power, the unruly and ambivalent site of desire which is profoundly disruptive of plans for coherence, the rusing of a Robin Hood when confronted with official edicts from Nottingham (CP: 61); it is Bakhtin's 'carnival' or Kristeva's 'semiotic' inscribed within sociological enquiry.

But therein lies its novelty and interest. As Maffesoli points out, traditionally, sociology and political science have foregrounded the cognitive side of political and social processes, concentrating on the actions of associations, institutions, political parties, states, nations and so on. Frequently missing from the sociologist's field of vision has been that other area of human activity which is the source of all social and political life. It is this imbalance which Maffesoli seeks to correct, not simply with a view to reappraising the nature of sociological enquiry (of which more later) but also because the contemporary period can best be understood in terms of a new explosion of the affective side of human activity to the detriment of the cognitive project.

Although the tension between these two faces of human activity has been ever-present throughout the history of the West, modernity (and particularly the nineteenth century) witnessed the most profound attempt to eradicate ambivalence and diversity through the imposition of a single, rational and abstract order. Whether by means of the Jacobin concept of the public good or the totalitarian ideologies of fascism and really existing socialism – 'tyrans, bureaucrates, technocrates' (TP: 52) – the quest for unity was the same. The conjunction of rationalism, science and knowledge (TP: 45-6) established the universal principles which would would reduce ambiguous voices to single truths. The 'clerks' of progress provided legitimacy for this monopoly on truth and power (TP: 55). However, the more recent crisis in the structures and institutions of modernity (what Maffesoli terms in one book 'la transfiguration du politique') has ushered in a new paradigm.[1] The failure of state-inspired social engineering as a means to realise utopian visions of humanity has opened up social life once more to ambiguity, ambivalence, contradiction and diversity. Maffesoli's distinctive approach is particularly apparent in his analysis of this de-rationalisation of social life and the nature of 'le quotidien' today.

---

1. For a fuller discussion of French cultural debates around modernity and post-modernity, see Silverman (1999).

The principal victim of 'la transfiguration du politique' is the autonomous and sovereign individual. 'L'individu n'est pas, ou n'est plus, maître de lui', proclaims Maffesoli (TP: 119; see also TP: 165). In *Le Temps des tribus*, Maffesoli outlines the decline of individualism and the rise of diverse networks or groups that he terms 'neo-tribes'. The 'neo-tribe' could be any micro-grouping whose solidarity depends on the visible manifestation of shared characteristics, whether it be 'une chevelure extravagante ou colorée, un tatouage original, la réutilisation de vêtements rétro ou encore le conformisme d'un style "bon chic bon genre"' (TT: 140). New tribalism is that proliferation of sects, cults, networks, sporting and musical communities (any number of which we might belong to at any one time) which has become such a prominent feature of the contemporary 'mégapole' (TP: 207). What is important here is the fragmentation of the contours defining the singular nature of the individual and the flow of feeling linking 'self' and 'other'. The trajectory of the individual, with its emphasis on the demarcation of boundaries, has now been transcended by a 'quasi-animal' or mystical force (TT: 117) which, contrary to the principle underpinning individual autonomy, blurs the boundaries which separate individuals and binds them together in communal or tribal formations. Hence, 'neo-tribes' are guided not by the principles of individuation and separation but by their opposites, namely the loss of individuation and an openness to 'the other'. If separation and the construction of dichotomies were characteristic traits of modernity's rationalism, then the blurring of contours characterises post-modernity (TP: 115). Proximity and empathy, fusion and confusion are the order of the day, not distance, distinction and the patrolling of boundaries (CM: 48). Maffesoli profoundly disagrees, then, with those who see 'un parallèle entre la fin du politique et le repliement sur l'individu, ou ce que l'on appelle le retour du narcissisme' (TT: 100; see also CM: 135). As the sub-title to *Le Temps des tribus* makes apparent, this is, instead, the age of 'le déclin de l'individualisme'. Today's hedonism is a clear sign of this development for we have passed from 'le bonheur égoiste' of modernity to the 'bonheur partagé' of post-modernity (CM: 53).

The 'neo-tribe' is a major sign of the spirit of the age for it is a direct product of the reversal of the hierarchy established under modern conditions between the cognitive and affective sides of social life, that is, between the primacy of the rational individual and that of the community of emotion (IE: 11). The 'being-together' ('être ensemble', CP: 67; TP: 165-180), which is central to the existence of the 'neo-tribe', is precisely that affective and spontaneous process of communion with 'the other' ('se perdre dans l'autre', CP: 18), that 'sensualisme polymorphe' (CP: 67) which institutions (political, economic, religious, cultural etc.) regulate, systematise and appropriate for their own ends. If we fail to recognise the new flourishing of this 'spontaneity' in social life, we will fail to appreciate the profound shift which has taken place in society. Maffesoli puts it in these terms:

> *cette spontanéité peut s'artificialiser, c'est-à-dire se civiliser et produire des oeuvres (politiques, économiques, artistiques) remarquables. Mais il est toujours nécessaire,*

ne serait-ce que pour mieux en apprécier les nouvelles orientations (ou les ré-orien-tations), de revenir à la forme pure qu'est "l'être-ensemble sans emploi". Cela peut en effet servir de toile de fond, de révélateur aux nouveaux modes de vie qui renaissent sous nos yeux. (TT: 125)

'Etre ensemble sans emploi' marks the difference between the proliferation and diversity of micro-groups today and the large collectivities of modernity. Unlike the 'sujets historiques' of the modern era (the bourgeoisie or the proletariat), who were collectivities harnessed to some grand cognitive design, 'neo-tribes' have no mission to accomplish. As Maffesoli observes, 'c'est moins l'objectif à atteindre que le fait d'être ensemble qui va prévaloir' (TT: 132). They exist for the moment, not for some future goal; they gratify their desire in the here-and-now rather than defer their gratification until later: 'ce qui est important c'est l'énergie qui est dépensée pour la constitution du groupe *en tant que tel*' (TT: 149). Not the vehicle of any historical project, their 'raison d'être' (if one can still use such a positivist and utilitarian term) is simply to exist. They are the purest manifestation of the existential subject: 'le tribalisme [...] s'épuise dans l'acte' (TT: 210).

In *Le Temps des tribus*, Maffesoli describes the qualities which abound today (and which find their expression in the 'neo-tribe') through a range of overlapping terms: 'l'affectif' (pp. 135-6, 138), 'la communauté émotionnelle' (pp. 16, 129), 'chaleur' (p. 59), 'effervescence' (following Durkheim, pp. 58, 138), 'vitalisme' (pp. 52-3, 59, 62), 'proxémie' (pp. 42, 58), 'entraide' (p. 44), 'aura' (following Walter Benjamin, pp. 34, 45, 188). These characteristics of post-modernity, which have re-enchanted social life, are all in contra-distinction to the disenchanting principles of rationality, coherence and individuality of modernity. He talks of the polymorphous and subversive nature of 'la puissance' as opposed to the regulating 'pouvoir' of economico-political institutions (pp. 11, 52-3, 75, 77, 99; see also TP: 65; IE: 93-119). He opposes 'la densité de la socialité' (pp. 59, 72) or the 'vouloir vivre sociétal' (p. 52), in which we adopt different roles in social settings, with the modern construction of the 'social', in which the individual has a function to fulfil in society (p. 117). He adopts Nietzsche's distinction between the Gods Apollo and Dionysos to characterise the shift from 'le social' to 'la socialité': today we live under the sign of *Dionysos* just as, a century ago, Apollo was in the ascendancy (TT: 45; CP: 18, 37, 64; CM: 70; IE: 15-6, 59, 141). In other words, the 'logique rationnelle' of the Enlightenment has given way to the 'logique non-rationnelle' (TT: 217), 'logique contradictorielle' (TP: 89; IE: 119) or 'désordre' (CP: 37) of our post-Enlightenment age. And just as the former marked out the boundaries defining a single individuality, the latter blurs the boundaries between 'self' and 'other' and allows for 'la multiplicité de vie' (TP: 89):

Dans le cadre de la thématique du dionysiaque, dont le paroxysme est la confusion, les masses effervescentes (promiscuités sexuelles, festives, sportives) ou les masses courantes (foules banales, consommatrices, suivistes...) outrepassent les caractéris-tiques du principe d'individuation. (TT: 138)

In his most recent book, *L'Instant éternel: le retour du tragique dans les sociétés postmodernes*, Maffesoli draws together a number of the themes which have been present throughout his work, especially those concerning *time* and *ritual*. The linear and mechanical concept of time of modernity ('le temps rationnel et orienté vers un but à atteindre' (IE: 77); 'un temps utile, un temps strictement linéaire, un temps projectif [...] le temps de l'histoire individuelle, [...] celui de l'histoire sociale [...] avec un début et une fin' (IE: 79)), has given way to a discontinuous succession of present moments which are not recuperated within a progressive and linear narrative. We live today the time of a perpetual present ('l'instant éternel' or 'un temps immobile' (IE: 55-92)) in which not linearity but circularity, repetition and myth are the major figures: 'la répétition, le concret, le rituel, en bref toutes choses qui sont la marque de la vie courante et qui s'expriment, au mieux, dans le "calendrier des fêtes de la religion quotidienne"' (IE: 76). Myth and ritual imply repetition of the same in the present ('un non-temps') rather than progression towards a goal in the future (IE: 80; see also CP: 109-132). They imply a cyclical rather than linear concept of time. In the absence of a project or goal for the future, which was the cement for the grand collectivities of modernity, the repetitive nature of ritual binds together the 'neo-tribes' of today: 'le rituel rappelle à la communauté qu'elle "fait corps"' (TT: 32; see also TT: 211-12; IE: 80). Communities are no longer formed according to voluntary contracts entered into by free and rational individuals but by means of myths in which we participate (TT: 21).

Hence also the distinction that Maffesoli makes between the *dramatic* nature of modern collectivities and the *tragic* nature of post-modern 'tribus' (CP: 19; TT: 32, 65, 193-4; TP: 42-3; IE). 'Le drame' implies linearity guided by an *a priori* and programmed vision of the single and unique goal; 'le tragique', on the other hand, implies the cyclical nature of things and is constituted by an indefinite number of 'arabesques' (TP: 43) whose heterogeneity no pre-determined path or ultimate goal can encapsulate. The meaning of 'le drame' is always projected forwards towards an end-point; 'le tragique' is self-sufficient and exhausts its own meaning within itself. The tragic vision is one which accepts the status quo (and ruses with it, as we shall see) rather than one which strives for change and the creation of a new order (TT: 65). The tragic vision appreciates the world 'tel qu'il est' in a suspended or immobilised time (IE: 79, 85; see also TP: 104). This is the vision which underpins post-modernity: we have passed from the 'dramatic' imperatives of modernity ('l'activisme, la production, le travail', CM: 58) to a hedonistic 'vouloir-vivre' of the present day.

The tragic vision is the transformation of rationalised everyday life into spectacle, 'la vie, en son entier, qui devient une oeuvre d'art' (TP: 159; see also CM: 66). It is what we know (following Walter Benjamin) as the aestheticisation of everyday life, or what Maffesoli also calls the 'théâtralisation de la vie quotidienne' (CP: 171-87). It is precisely that transportation 'hors de soi' which shatters the stable ego of the individual, that blurring of the boundaries between self and other in an erotico-mystical communion, that playful adoption of numerous masks in the theatre of life (IE: 142-53), that construction of unforeseen 'correspondances' between the conscious and the unconscious (CP: 20), that 'poétique de la vie quotidienne' (CP: 101) which are all epitomised by Baudelaire's poet/flâneur in the setting of the crowd (IE: 110). It is the imaginative re-enchantment of everyday life central to the Surrealists' wanderings in the city (see for example André Breton's *Nadja* or Louis Aragon's *Le Paysan de Paris*; see also CP: 94, 150).[1] It is the magical dream-world of the cinema which transforms linear time and stable identity, so clearly analysed by Edgar Morin in *Le Cinéma ou l'homme imaginaire* (CP: 89-106).

However, if Maffesoli's 'tragique', 'socialité', 'puissance' and 'tribalisme' all have these qualities in common with modernism's subversion of rationalised modern society, there is one major exception: what was formerly the avant-garde's challenge to 'la logique rationnelle' has now become everyone's everyday reality. It is as if society *as a whole* has divested itself of its rationalising mission, de-colonised itself and rediscovered the playful, affective, mythical and aesthetic side to social life. Maffesoli talks of the predominance of 'le style esthétique' today following 'le style théologique' of the Middle Ages and 'le style économique' of modernity (CM: 15, 45-54). Today we have rediscoverd the *art* of living when formerly we were subjected to the *function* of being. In the process, we have rediscovered the *ethical* response to life – that move towards 'the other' in the act of communion (TT: 31-2; 34) – prior to its colonisation by institutionalised *morality* (cf. Bauman 1993). If modernity's institutionalisation of dramatic time according to the principles of unity and homogeneity entailed the moralisation of everyday life, then post-modernity's tragic vision according to the principles of plurality and heterogeneity reinstates the ethical dimension of everyday life (IE: 225).

As a further refinement of this appraisal of 'la transfiguration du politique', Maffesoli suggests that the break with a single vision projected in linear time towards the future, and the emergence today of an open space which contains the infinite potential of the present moment, denotes the transition from a monotheistic to a polytheistic paradigm in the West. We are witnessing today a rediscovery of the mystico-religious vein of human behaviour (which is essentially pagan) before its colonisation by institutional monotheistic religions (TT: 91-2), a rediscovery of the environment and 'le territoire' before their transformation into economic and political units (IE: 117, 213). This 'religiosité', as Maffesoli calls it (TP: 181-90), is the affective underside of western politics and ideology beyond the 'diverses modulations historiques ou sociales' (TT: 57). It is the pure act of communion (contained within the literal meaning of 'relier' at the heart of 'religion', TT: 119) which springs from the 'vitalisme irrépressible' of the people

---

1. 'La ville, dans sa banalité est potentiellement riche des aventures que sécrètent ses innombrables rues et lieux divers, de même le donné social, dans son aspect le plus courant, par le jeu de la différence, peut susciter des situations, des rencontres et des moments particulièrement intenses' (CP: 41; for a fuller discussion of the ever-present 'socialité' to be found in the city, see CP: 80-7, 150, 201).

(TT: 57). It is more in keeping with the polytheism of eastern religions rather than the monotheism of western religions founded on 'le fantasme d'Unité' (CP: 39). Maffesoli thus observes:

> *curieux retour des choses, qui fait qu'après la domination exclusive du mode de*
> *penser et d'être occidental, sous-tendu par la conception du temps linéaire, ce soient*
> *maintenant les "Orients mythiques" qui prennent leur revanche et imposent, par*
> *l'accentuation du présent, une présence au monde, à ses plaisirs, à ses joies, mais*
> *aussi à ses cruautés et à ses peines. (IE: 75)*

Detecting numerous parallels between everyday life today in the West and the principles of Zen Buddhism or Tao, he asks 'la vie ordinaire s'orientalise-t-elle?' (IE: 75; see also TT: 191).

The picture of everyday life which then emerges from Maffesoli's distinctive analysis is one of a new flowering of passions and desires formerly repressed (or 'tranquillisés', TP: 96) by instrumental rationality. Stripped of the rationalising and policing tactics of 'la raison objective' (TT: 90), everyday life is now guided by non-conscious forces. Like the black economy, whose very nature it is to escape the logic of the official economy, the 'socialité au noir' ever-present beneath the surface of historical events has today emerged into the light of day. Now 'la quotidienneté se fonde sur une série de libertés interstitielles et relatives' (TT: 39). Stripped of these same rationalising tactics, the masses appear not as a homogeneous entity with a common purpose and goal but rather as ambiguous, contradictory and versatile (TT: 97). Contemporary tribalism is an expression of the playfulness, duplicity and creativity of the masses. Their ostentatious displays of communal bonding, which constitute what Maffesoli terms 'une structure anthropologique' (TT: 79), are ways of rusing with official structures of power (TT: 79-83). But they are just as likely to do this through silence, abstention, irony and laughter (TT: 144).[1] The 'esthétisation de la vie courante' (TT: 133), practised by the Surrealists and the Situationists to subvert the power structures of 'la raison objective', is now our everyday reality: 'Tout se passe comme si "l'amour fou" et le "hasard objectif" du Surréalisme, la rencontre et la "dérive" du Situationnisme s'étaient progressivement capillarisés dans l'ensemble du corps social' (TT: 131-2; see also CP: 150; TT: 218; IE: 100).

Rather than view the crisis of conventional political and social structures as a fragmentation of social life, Maffesoli suggests that the flowering of the duplicity and creative rusing of the masses through their everyday pursuits constitutes an enhancement of social cohesion. For throughout history it has always been through secret and illicit channels that people have circumvented the alienating tactics of established power and maintained solidarities. Whether it be the history of Jews, who have taken on numerous official guises or masks whilst maintaining their real communal ties unofficially (TP: 90-2), or 'le travail au noir', which

---

1. In the light of this approach to the creativity of the masses, it is perhaps surprising that Maffesoli does not engage more often with the work of Henri Lefebvre and Michel de Certeau.

performs a similar unofficial function in relation to the official economy, this 'double jeu' (CP: 155-65) allows groups to reappropriate their lives from the abstract and alienating structures to which they have been subjected. To ignore the ways in which these playful and duplicitous practices fulfil an important function within social life (as many sociologists have been guilty of doing) is to misunderstand a fundamental aspect of the constitution, endurance and continuation ('la perdurance') of social groups which furnishes the very cement of society:

> Cette duplicité anthropologique présente les caractères de ce que j'ai appelé la "centralité souterraine", qui, au-delà ou en-deçà de l'aspect institué, officiel canonique de la chose publique, garantit aux sociétés une assurance infrangible [...]. La duplicité dit mystiquement et vit pratiquement une forme d'éternité, ne serait-ce que parce que grâce à elle, il est possible à la grande masse de résister, au nom de diverses constructions imaginales, à l'idéologie triomphante du moment. (TP: 92; see also CP: 91; TT: 185; IE: 81)

Society persists not through homogeneity imposed from above but from diversity practised from below. Maffesoli proposes the notion of unity in diversity: the heterogeneous nature of the social order establishes an overall social balance, 'harmonie conflictuelle en quelque sorte' (TT: 186) or 'union en pointillé' (TT: 190), which are, in effect, other ways of defining Durkheim's 'divin social' ('un ensemble complexe, où tous les éléments de l'environnement social et de l'environnement naturel entrent en intéraction permanente' (TP: 181; see also CM: 23-4)).

Maffesoli's reflections on the nature of everyday life are therefore profoundly grounded in a reappraisal of forms of social cohesion. Everyday life is 'le lieu à partir duquel se fonde le lien social' (CP: 12), for social cohesion is to be found in the banal rather than the affairs of state, in those 'trajets, discussions, bricolages, cuisine, promenades, recherches vestimentaires, attitudes par lesquelles un groupe d'individus se reconnaît comme tel' (CP: 13; see also CP: 81). We should recognise 'la nécessité de l'inutile pour fortifier le corps social' (TP: 140; see also CM: 12). But the banal or 'l'inutile' is also a sign of the 'style' of the times: 'l'air du temps, la vie sans qualité, se reconnaisssent dans le concret, et c'est parce que ce concret se vit comme totalité' (CM: 55). Maffesoli's concept of culture is therefore one that challenges the classic Enlightenment distinction between culture and everday life: culture is that which is lived in a concrete way, the 'habitus' of society (CM: 56; IE: 66). (Richard Hoggart is a constant source of inspiration to Maffesoli.) Culture is that which 'permet, fonde et conforte l'être ensemble social' (CM: 114). Hence the importance of everyday life for sociological analysis.

And just as Maffesoli's analysis focuses on the ordinary events of everyday life which lie beyond the order of 'la simple raison instrumentale de l'utilitarisme' (CM: 57), so does he attempt to write a sociology which refuses the dominant norms of modern sociological method. If 'la raison objective' has had its day as the organising principle of modern societies, then so should positivism have had its day as the organising principle of sociological method. Not that political and economic analysis reveals little about how societies work; simply that they are 'impuissantes à exprimer les minuscules situations de tous les jours qui constituent une part essentielle de la trame sociale' (CP: 24). Similarly, if our analytical tools have largely been shaped according to the modern imperatives of democratic individualism (CM: 65), then post-modern 'communautarisme' should dictate a new way of looking at social life.

There is also a pressing need to find a different way of understanding 'les masses' or 'le peuple' which refuses to recuperate them within the broad and homogenising categories ('sujets historiques') of modernity. This is a form of policing and domesticating the masses within 'les a priori dogmatiques' (TT: 88, 95). Hence, Maffesoli's own non-positivist vocabulary and discourse attempt to circumvent 'les gestionnaires du savoir' just as 'tout ce qui est de l'ordre de l'hétérogène et de la compléxité [...] inquiète les gestionnaires du pouvoir' (TT: 88). As part of this subversion of traditional sociological method, Maffesoli frequently deconstructs the founders of modern sociology, Emile Durkheim and Max Weber, to reveal the currents of their thought which escape the order of the very positivism which is at the heart of their own analyses of society and human behaviour (see for example TT: 74, 88, 90, 94, 101, 121-2, 125-6, 134-5). To this extent, one could say that Maffesoli is to the sociology of everyday life what Jacques Derrida is to the philosophy of discourse: they both set out to reveal the polysemic and contradictory nature of their object of study beyond the imposed coherence of rationalist analysis.

If we consider Maffesoli's body of work as a whole, it is clear that it constitutes a significant contribution to the analysis of contemporary social life. However, there are aspects of his 'oeuvre' which are also a possible cause for concern. What strikes the reader of Maffesoli's works most forcefully is the celebratory tone with which he greets 'la transfiguration du politique' of recent years. If certain commentators have welcomed the new freedoms on offer today in the wake of modernity's demise, they have often highlighted, as well, the new dangers inherent in our de-regulated age. This more balanced assessment of recent developments seems to be missing in Maffesoli's vision. He deliberately opposes those who talk only of crisis today. Instead, he celebrates post-modernity in terms of a liberation of the masses from the shackles of the imposed cognitive and institutional order of the modern era, and welcomes a localisation and spiritualisation of life after the abstract and rationalised order of modernity (CP: 16). The release of this 'puissance' from the straitjacket of 'pouvoir' is essentially an escape from alienating official structures and an imaginative reappropriation of life by the people. However, it might be said that Maffesoli seems to equate unthinkingly the rusing, playful and imaginative tactics of the Surrealists with those of the masses today. For might it not be the case that techniques which were subversive in an age of rationalisation when practised by an avant-garde minority might no longer be subversive in an age of de-rationalisation when brought into the mainstream? Yesterday's rusing with power might be today's conforming to new structures of power.[1]

However, it would be wrong to suggest that Maffesoli is unaware of the potential for new dangers in a post-modern age. For example, as regards today's 'neo-tribes', he acknowledges that if they have strong powers of inclusion and solidarity, they also (according to the same logic of group formation) have equally strong powers of exclusion which might account for new forms of ethnic and religious discrimination and violence (CM: 65, 139). It is simply that Maffesoli wishes to shift sociological focus away from negative forms of exclusion to the positive reinvention or 'affirmation' of living together.

Maffesoli prefers to view the new 'socialité' and 'esthétisation de la vie courante' not in terms of their possible political outcomes but in terms of a reinscription of ethics at the heart of social and political life (IE: 83). He therefore pays scant attention to the potential dangers of these developments. We know, for example, that Walter Benjamin located the aestheticisation of politics (politics as theatre) as the essence of fascism. The sort of emotional, visceral and vitalist response to politics which Maffesoli views as a form of people's liberation from totalitarian forms of rationalised oppression might itself be appropriated to fuel new totalitarianisms. Maffesoli is aware of the potential for the harnessing of a polyvalent 'puissance' to the aims of a monovalent 'pouvoir'. Yet his concern is with the plural and ephemeral nature of the former, not the singularity and fixity of the latter. Indeed, the 'polythéisme' of the former, with its openness to 'le tiers' and 'l'étranger', is the surest guarantee of a '"non-racisme" populaire' and safeguard against any political exploitation of the process of 'being together': 'Quoi de plus contraire à la logique du politique [...] à féconder ce soi-même par l'étranger' (TT: 166).

Similarly, his focus on the link between new technologies (especially those which drive the all-pervasive nature of the image) and the expression of dionysian urges is intended to highlight not the 'dumbing down' of rational political debate but rather the flowering of an infinite number of channels for the circulation of unfettered communication and 'des mouvements d'effervescence témoignant avant tout d'un vitalisme indéniable' (TP: 169; see also TP: 173). As Maffesoli observes, 'il est dans la logique des médias de n'être qu'un *simple prétexte* à communication' (TT: 47; see also CM: 74-5). This promotes 'la viscosité groupale' to the detriment of 'l'individualisme' (TP: 169) and reinserts myth and archetype into a rational order. The image and the imaginary are fundamental components

---

1. Zygmunt Bauman defines the difference between the function of carnival in the past, which was indeed a way of rusing with the established order, and the commodification of carnival today as follows: 'Carnival was the same city transformed, more exactly a time interlude during which the city was transformed before falling back into its routine quotidianity. For a strictly defined stretch of time, but a time cyclically returning, the carnival uncovered the "other side" of daily reality, a side which stayed constantly within reach but was normally concealed from view and barred from touching (...). A trip to the temple of consumption is quite another matter. To go for such a trip is like being transported to another world, rather than witnessing the wondrous transubstantiation of the familiar one' (Bauman 2000: 98).

of the 'désir communautaire' (CM: 9) of contemporary social life (see especially CM: 79-126).[1] One only has to look at the way in which the television brings together huge numbers of people to participate emotionally in sporting, musical and other events, allowing us to '"vibrer" en commun' (CM: 67). Hence, under post-modern conditions, 'c'est la technologie qui favorise un réel *réenchantement du monde*' (CP: 20). Maffesoli embraces 'la publicité [...] les clips vidéo [...] le "zapping" télévisuel' (TP: 159; see also CM: 36-7) as so many signs of the ludic, imaginative and communal reinvention of social life today. They are the means by which we enter into a sort of organic or mystical union with others which shatters the confines of the sovereign individual of modernity (CM: 65-75). The dangers of new populisms, propelled by crude emotion channelled through sophisticated technology, do not figure highly in Maffesoli's vision.

The same could be said of his approach to the galloping commodification of affective life today, which is of great concern to those who believe that the freedom of the consumer and the market should not be confused with genuine democracy. It is not that he is blind to the accelerated commodification of desire under late capitalism ('qui donnent aux grandes mégapoles l'allure d'un souk perpétuel où se célèbre une dépense ostentatoire sans précédent' (CM: 14)), just as we noted above that he is not blind to the dangers of ethnic and other forms of exclusion in an age of neo-tribalism. It is simply that his main concern is not with the colonisation of minds and bodies for the purpose of selling products or fundamentalist identities but rather with the de-colonisation and liberation of those minds and bodies to form a new 'socialité'. The de-rationalisation and de-institutionalisation of post-modern society is therefore viewed primarily in terms of freedom from the constraints of the past (cf. Lipovetsky 1983).

Of course, it would be an easy task to manipulate Maffesoli's analysis for one ideological stance or another. For example, it could certainly suit a liberal, free-market (even libertarian) approach, given that Maffesoli seems to equate uncritically the end of ideology with liberation and democracy. It could also suit a New Right perspective in which the attack on the monotheistic, assimilationist and universalist paradigm of the West and the advocacy of pluralism and the right to difference are exploited for neo-racist ends (see for example Benoist 1986). The notion of an affective neo-tribalism suits exclusive as well as inclusive cultural

---

1. Maffesoli's concept of the image is one that sees it as the very antithesis of 'le mécanisme de la raison' (CM: 123). It is the locus of imagination, dream and desire, the spatialisation of time, the aestheticisation of life in its most condensed form and the loss of self within the possibility of communion with 'the other'. As such, it subverts the order of institutional power and the sovereign individual (CM: 122-3; IE: 83-4). This celebration of the imaginative power of the image is a far cry from the demonisation of the image that we see in works such as Simone de Beauvoir's *Les Belles images* (1966) or, more recently, in Debray's *Vie et mort de l'image* (1992). These works bemoan the fact that an image-based society objectifies the world according to crude criteria and thereby reduces its three-dimensional complexity to a two-dimensional superficiality.

differentialism.[1] Yet to read Maffesoli's open-ended work in terms of the political and ideological messages to which it can be made to conform would be (in Maffesoli's own terms) to reduce the plurality of potential meaning to the singularity of fixed meaning, to overlay polymorphous 'socialité' with a utilitarian sense of 'le social'.

In any number of ways, it is easy to see why Maffesoli's approach is anathema to republican diehards. It sees the social value of 'le banal' and 'le quotidien' rather than viewing them as stages which we must surpass in order to elevate humanity to a higher plane. It sees culture as our everyday acts rather than as great works of the spirit. It welcomes the demise of the Enlightenment version of the rational and sovereign individual and celebrates the emotional vitality of new forms of communitarianism. It welcomes mixing, diversity and ambivalence. It is not a brave new world for the future but a celebration of the present. It welcomes the spectacle rather than the rationalisation of life. In other words, it undermines the fundamental principles of republicanism.

Yet herein lies the interest of Michel Maffesoli's work, for French intellectual life is still, to a large extent, dominated by republican dogma. Despite French post-war anti-humanist philosophy, the assault on unitary systems of thought and the challenge to logocentrism and patriarchy, the defenders of the French republican canon have mounted a more robust rearguard action against the forces of fragmentation and pluralism than their counterparts in 'le monde anglo-saxon' (even though, ironically, many of the ideas which have championed the voice of 'the other' in intellectual circles outside France have their roots in French post-modern philosophy). Maffesoli bucks the republican trend of a sense of crisis and a fear of the demise of 'Man'. He welcomes new freedoms and embraces the mutli-faceted, contradictory and inter-connected patterns of contemporary life. He offers us not the republican vision of bovine masses responding like robots to unremitting doses of meaningless stimulation (which is now known as 'culture'). Instead, he proclaims the advent of a colourful new democracy beyond republicanism and modernity. One would like to believe that this democracy, founded on the aestheticisation and re-enchantment of everyday life, brings with it a new ethical dimension to social life, as Maffesoli suggests. One would have to say, however, that the jury is still out on this matter.

---

1.   It is perhaps not too surprising that a chapter by Maffesoli (1986) should have appeared in a collection entitled *Racismes, Antiracismes*, whose politics were highly questionable. However, one should not assume that Maffesoli is in any way connected with the culturalist New Right any more than the well-known writer on racism and anti-racism Pierre-André Taguieff, who also contributed a chapter to this volume. It probably says more about the French debate on these issues than about Maffesoli and Taguieff themselves, for the assimilationist republican tradition is one which immediately associates the concept of difference with the racist politics of the extreme Right rather than views it is a fundamental part of any genuinely pluralist society today.

Bibliography

Aragon, L. (1975, first published 1926) *Le Paysan de Paris*, Paris: Gallimard/Folio.

Bauman, Z. (1993) *Postmodern Ethics*, Oxford: Blackwell.

Bauman, Z. (2000) *Liquid Modernity*, Cambridge: Polity.

Beauvoir, S. de (1966) *Les Belles images*, Paris: Gallimard/Folio.

Benoist, Alain de (1986) *Europe, tiers monde, même combat*, Paris: Laffont.

Breton, A. (1964, first published 1928) *Nadja*, Paris: Gallimard/Folio.

Debray, R. (1989) 'Etes-vous républicain ou démocrate?', *Le Nouvel Observateur*, 30 novembre – 6 décembre, pp. 115-21.

Debray. R. (1992) *Vie et mort de l'image: une histoire du regard en Occident*, Paris: Gallimard/Folio.

Lipovetsky, G. (1983) *L'Ere du vide: essai sur l'individualisme contemporain*, Paris: Gallimard/Folio.

Maffesoli, M. (1986) 'Le Polyculturalisme: petite apologie de la confusion' in A. Béjin and J. Freund (eds.), *Racismes, antiracismes*, Paris: Meridiens Klincksieck.

Maffesoli, M. (1988) *Le Temps des tribus: le déclin de l'individualisme dans les sociétés de masse*, Paris: Meridiens Klincksieck/Livre de Poche.

Maffesoli, M. (1992) *La Transfiguration du politique: la tribalisation du monde*, Paris: Grasset et Fasquelle/Livre de Poche.

Maffesoli, M. (1993) *La Contemplation du monde: figures du style communautaire*, Paris: Grasset et Fasquelle/Livre de Poche.

Maffesoli, M. (1998, first published 1979) *La Conquête du présent: pour une sociologie de la vie quotidienne*, Paris: Desclée de Brouwer.

Maffesoli, M. (2000) *L'Instant éternel: le retour du tragique dans les sociétés postmodernes*, Paris: Denoël.

Silverman, M. (1999) *Facing Postmodernity: Contemporary French Thought on Culture and Society*, London and New York: Routledge.

Intellectuals and Popular Culture in Contemporary France: the Writings of Paul Yonnet

Brian Rigby

The recent publication of Paul Yonnet's *Travail, loisir: temps libre et lien social* (1999) offers an opportunity to look at the current state of the French debate on intellectuals and popular culture, a debate to which Yonnet made such a notable contribution in 1985 with his book *Jeux, modes et masses: la société française et le moderne 1945-1985* (1985a). In the eyes of certain defenders of high culture, the publication of this book positioned Yonnet as one of the main representatives of 'populism'. Indeed, Alain Finkielkraut, whose *La Défaite de la pensée* (1987) has, of course, become the most high-profile critique of contemporary popular culture, even went so far as to rank Yonnet alongside Bourdieu as the principal spokesman for the populist point of view – a coupling which is somewhat ironic, given the obvious disparity of intellectual status between the two, and also given Yonnet's stated disapproval of Bourdieu's whole manner of approaching and analysing popular culture. According to Finkielkraut, Yonnet and Bourdieu were:

> *Deux avatars d'une très longue tradition populiste* [...] *deux exemples de "l'aberration à laquelle sont enclins les intellectuels une fois qu'ils ont réussi à se persuader que la solidarité avec les classes opprimées, exige qu'ils admirent et non qu'ils corrigent ce qui a été la plus grande infortune de ces classes: leur incapacité à participer au développement de la culture spirituelle".* (Kolakowski 1987, p. 178)

From the early 1980s up to the present day, Yonnet has been a regular contributor to *Le Débat*[1] – that quintessential journal of modernising liberal Republicanism, dedicated to fostering a new open spirit in French intellectual, cultural and political life and committed to acknowledging and responding to the rapid cultural changes that France was undergoing in the 1980s and 1990s:

> Le Débat *s'est fondé en mai 1980, sur la conviction qu'une véritable métamorphose du modèle intellectuel était en train de s'opérer. Qu'elle affectait aussi bien les objets et les institutions de pensée que les modes de travail et les formes d'intervention. Et que c'était notre raison d'être de la comprendre et de contribuer à la nourrir, de l'épouser en même temps que de l'infléchir.* (Yonnet 1988, p. 1)

---

1. See, for instance, Yonnet (1983), (1984), (1985a), (1985b), (1985c), (1986), (1990), (1992), (1995), (1996).

However, just as important as this desire to be positive participants and agents in the complex process of change, has been the determination of the journal and its contributors to retain the essence of what they considered to be French republican traditions and values (while accepting that these needed to be adapted and reinterpreted in the light of modern realities). This concern for republican traditions and values was, of course, best exemplified in the publication of Pierre Nora's celebrated multi-volume *Les Lieux de mémoire* (1984-92). This work, edited by the 'Directeur' of *Le Débat*, stands as the single most significant attempt of the contemporary intellectual and academic community to define modern French identity in relation to France's republican past. This crucial desire of the liberal republican intelligentsia to prove its modernity while also rooting itself in an evolved form of traditional Republicanism is a prominent feature of the writings of the contributors to *Le Débat*, although the nature of each writer's compromise solution is, of course, ever likely to differ in emphasis.

Paul Yonnet's contributions are noted for his determination to bring France into the international mainstream of mass and popular culture, principally through his passionate involvement with rock 'n' roll and sport, and so perhaps his interests and attitudes are too idiosyncratic for him to be regarded as an absolutely typical example of a contributor to *Le Débat*. What is more, in his *Voyage au centre du malaise français: l'antiracisme et le roman national* (1993), he produced a volume which threatened to be an embarrassment to his right-thinking associates on the journal. In this much contested and heavily criticised work, Yonnet set out to salvage central aspects of French identity and the French political past from what he considered to be the relentlessly negative and destructive critique of France by the politically correct representatives of anti-racist politics in post-war France.[1] Yonnet adopted the high-risk strategy of rehabilitating Frenchness by attacking anti-racist thinking and by defending the French war record, thereby putting forward ideas which would be bound to be suspected of being, on the one hand, hostile to France's immigrants and ethnic communities, and on the other hand, sympathetic to Vichy and collaboration.[2] Both of these charges are ones which Yonnet would, of course, fiercely reject. In

---

1. For the broader contexts within which to understand Yonnet's critique of anti-racism, see Silverman (2000). Silverman also points out that Yonnet provoked a critical response to his ideas on anti-racism, both within the pages of *Le Débat* and beyond (see Karpik (1993); Wieviorka (1993) and Todorov (1996)).

2. 'La formidable dépréciation du roman national sur laquelle l'idéal antiraciste immigrationniste va ultérieurement fructifier prend la forme d'une révision historique – qui est la véritable révision historique de notre temps, car elle a réussi. Ce révisionnisme historique concerne principalement le régime de Vichy et l'attitude des Français durant la Seconde Guerre mondiale. Il s'étend de manière récurrente à la mémoire du siècle. A l'image d'une France souffrante et héroïque intensément résistante, y compris au travers des tactiques dilatoires et des oppositions passives de l'administration de Vichy, d'une France qui n'a pas à rougir des exactions de poignées de traîtres épurés à la Libération, succède l'image d'une France intensément collaboratrice, initiatrice de législations antisémites, d'une France fasciste, participant à la "solution finale", allant au-devant des voeux des Allemands en déportant les enfants, d'une France raciste et xénophobe, massivement pétainiste jusqu'au bout, sur laquelle pèse une culpabilité collective.' (Yonnet 1993, p. 252).

my view, Yonnet's strategy is, in fact, best understood as part of his ongoing project of identifying with the experience of ordinary French people whom he continues to see as the victims of hegemonic intellectual discourses (in this case, anti-racist and anti-nationalist discourses) (Yonnet 1993, pp. 16-17). Yonnet is keen to stress that his critique of anti-racist and anti-nationalist discourses is intended as a way of wresting the initiative from the extreme right and he insists that it is nothing short of a tragedy that it has thus far been the exclusive preserve of the extreme right to speak up for the nation in the face of the hegemonic anti-racist and anti-nationalist discourses (Yonnet 1993, p. 296).

In *Voyage au centre du malaise français*, Yonnet tries to understand and give validity to the views of ordinary French people who have come to feel that their own identity and way of life have been undermined by the counter-productive politics of anti-racism, which, paradoxically, are themselves responsible, in Yonnet's eyes, for the creation of a 'xénophobie de défense' within the French population. However, Yonnet is not only at odds with the contemporary proponents of anti-racism, but he is also deeply critical of his own generation of 1968, which he considers to have been principally responsible for laying the foundations for anti-patriotic and anti-nationalist feelings in France: 'L'antiracisme des années 1980 est directement issu du ressac de mai 1968' (Yonnet 1993, p. 235). For Yonnet, May '68 is at the heart of the story of the growth of national self-disgust and of the blossoming of the industry of national self-accusation and denigration (Yonnet 1993, pp. 232-53), the chief products of which he lists, more than provocatively, as *Le Chagrin et la pitié*, *Les Boulevards de la ceinture*, Robert Paxton's *La France de Vichy* and *Lacombe Lucien*.[1] In this flourishing anti-French industry, Yonnet reserves a special place for Bernard-Henri Lévy's *L'Idéologie française* (1981) – a book also heavily criticised by Pierre Nora (Nora 1981) – for he sees it as the text which demonstrates how the anti-French feelings of 1968 fed into and fuelled the anti-racist discourse of more recent years:

> L'Idéologie française [...] est [...] un texte historique, car un texte-charnière dans le dépérissement des idéologies soixante-huitardes sur la route de l'antiracisme [...]. L'Idéologie française suinte à toutes les lignes d'une peur maladive de l'identité française, une francophobie parfois délirante [...]. L'Idéologie française est le texte qui pose que l'identité française est par nature tueuse de Juifs, de Noirs, d'Arabes, d'étrangers ou considérés comme tels, et qui exige, en voie de conséquence, son évaporation, sa dissipation, son extinction dans l'universalité [...]. (Yonnet 1993, pp. 280-1)

According to Yonnet, the members of the generation of 1968 were the 'futurs producteurs d'idées dominantes' (Yonnet 1993, p. 252) and, indeed, whether it be in politics, higher education or the media, he believes that this generation came to achieve ideological dominance in French society and were instrumental in forming a consensus of anti-nationalist and anti-racist values (Yonnet 1993, pp.

---

1. For this line of interpretation, Yonnet admits his debt to Ory (1981).

278-9). At the core of *Voyage au centre du malaise français* is, therefore, an assault on the new intellectual elites of French society, who, in Yonnet's view, have conspired in the perpetuation of an anti-French ideology, who have failed to engage sympathetically and knowledgeably with the experience of the mass of ordinary French people and who have seriously damaged the fabric of the nation: 'la cohésion du groupe-Nation'(p. 195); 'les solidarités culturelles de base [...] la sociabilité des groupes élémentaires' (p. 307).

At the heart of Yonnet's writings, as it is at the heart of the writings of all modern French liberal Republicans, is the dilemma of how to create a modern French nation which respects all individuals but which also nurtures a sense of French national identity founded in the French republican past and in the collective culture of its people. Despite expressing some reservations on the French republican model of assimilation, Yonnet is nonetheless convinced that it remains without question the best means of guaranteeing individual freedoms and of nurturing the indigenous national culture:

> Loin d'engendrer la xénophobie et le racisme, l'assimilationnisme individualiste républicain repousse les seuils d'intolérance, précisément parce qu'en stipulant que l'Hexagone accueille des étrangers, non des communautés, que la France naturalise des personnes pour renforcer la nation, non des individus venant gonfler les ethnies internes, il modère les craintes de perte de cohésion du groupe-nation. (Yonnet 1993, p. 295)

In his subsequent works (*Systèmes des sports* (1998) and *Travail, loisir: temps libre et lien social* (1999)), it becomes clear that Yonnet himself tries hard to square the circle by offering his own utopian vision of a modern French society which is made up of individuals who are autonomous, separate and free, but who are also deeply embedded in the cultural fabric of the French nation, and who have a positive and shared sense of French identity. So, for instance, in his treatment of the nature and importance of sport in modern France, his sympathy is obviously with such events as mass marathons which seem precisely to allow for the expression of individual difference, while at the same time exemplifying a spirit of benevolent community. He calls such a sport as mass marathon running 'le sport à la queue leu leu' ('sport in single file') because, although in such a sport one witnesses 'une longue chaîne de différences' (p. 122), one also sees how difference is included, incorporated and celebrated and, indeed, how it becomes in itself a 'facteur de sociabilité' (p. 123). In recent years one has become very accustomed to feel-good accounts which celebrate France as a country where national success is attributed to harmony in diversity – the understandably euphoric accounts which have followed on France's outstanding football victories mark the high-point of the genre. Such accounts usually give expression to the widely-shared desire to show that the French nation has successfully modernised itself (created the conditions for freedom, individualism, efficiency, tolerance, diversity etc.), while also remaining true to its traditional notions of identity and community.

A typical and striking example of this can be seen in a recent publication by Christian Bromberger, an anthropologist who specialises in the analysis of sport (particularly football) and other everyday cultural practices.[1] In his edited volume *Passions ordinaires: du match de football au concours de dictée* (1998), Bromberger celebrates the diversity and vitality of those cultural practices beloved by 'ordinary' French people and puts together the studies of some twenty different academics and writers on topics such as domestic pets, gardening, do-it-yourself, family history, spelling competitions, football, rock music, gambling, sailing, motor-cycling etc. These and the many other activities covered in the volume are clearly meant to add up to a portrait of the diverse lives of 'la France profonde', of ordinary French people. However, the title *Passions ordinaires* encapsulates not only the idea of ordinariness, but also that of dynamism, enthusiasm and optimism – all of which are the very qualities prized in contemporary France as manifestations of a buoyant modern spirit. Like Yonnet, Bromberger is keen to acknowledge and value the actual everyday lives of ordinary French people as well as to highlight their enterprise and their concern for national identity, as is evident, for instance, in the chapters 'La Généalogie: de l'enquête à la quête' (pp. 119-38) and 'Chercheurs de patrimoine en Haute-Provence: une passion et ses enjeux' (pp. 139-62). In his introduction to the volume (pp. 5-38), Bromberger presents himself as sitting one Sunday morning in his customary place under a plane tree at the centre of a village in Provence. From this vantage-point he observes the spectacle of activity and diversity which plays itself out before his fond, admiring eyes:

> *L'idée de ce livre est née à l'ombre d'un platane, sur la place d'un village provençal que je fréquente depuis une trentaine d'années. En ce dimanche de septembre j'assistais à un étonnant chassé-croisé de groupes d'individus dont les tenues (des shorts blancs de tennismen aux combinaisons sombres des motards en passant par les ensembles kaki ou léopard des chasseurs) dessinaient autour de la fontaine un curieux patchwork. Tous les engouements contemporains semblaient s'être donné un fugitif rendez-vous à ce carrefour [...]. Trois joggers, en bloomer et brassière en lycra, traversaient la place, l'air tendu, soucieux de la régularité de leur foulée. Ils furent d'abord gênés par les arabesques de jeunes garçons qui effectuaient des figures sur leurs vélos "free-style" puis par un attroupement de randonneurs, sérieusement chaussées, qui remplissaient leurs gourdes aux canons de la fontaine. Juste revenus de la battue au sanglier, des chasseurs en tenue observaient la scène d'un oeil goguenard. La quiétude de la place fut brusquement troublée par un groupe de motards arborant des jackets en jean sur leurs blousons noirs; leur leader paradait sur une Kawasaki 750H2 aux chromes resplendissants [...]. Les parieurs, qui faisaient la queue pour accéder au 'Point courses' de La civette de la mairie, se retournèrent comme un seul homme pour protester contre cette bruyante intrusion. Au même moment retentit le carillon de l'église paroissiale, indiquant la fin de la messe; bientôt des familles endimanchées traversèrent la place ou s'y attardèrent quelques minutes pour échanger des nouvelles. Près de la fontaine se forme un petit groupe autour de Madame L., une institutrice parisienne à la retraite, qui anime l'association des amis*

---

1. On Bromberger, see Rigby (1998).

du patrimoine: on devait profiter de cette journée ensoleillée pour continuer le chant- ier bénévole de restauration de la chapelle Notre-Dame... (Bromberger 1998, pp. 5-6)

In his spat with Finkielkraut in the 1987 issue of *Le Débat*, Yonnet had expressed his sense of exasperation at the eternal contempt shown by sections of the French intellectual elite towards the everyday leisure and cultural activities of ordinary French people: 'Je me demande parfois d'où la société française tire sa force de résistance aux divagations méprisantes de certains de ses intellectuels' (Yonnet 1987, p. 179). Sympathetic and even celebratory accounts of the leisure and cultural practices of ordinary French people, such as the one quoted from Bromberger's volume, are designed to present a benign and optimistic image of the state of the French nation and to show France as a place where difference, dissent and disharmony are tolerated and absorbed; where there is continuity with an older world, where there is a respect for history and where the civic spirit is still alive and healthy. Indeed, it is from this basis of stability and continuity that France is shown as drawing the energy to renew itself and become a fully participating member of the modern world. Bromberger's utopian vision is obviously to be understood as an act of affirmation and confidence in ordinary French life in the face of the prevailing pessimism and scorn which he clearly still expects from certain key intellectual quarters, although he seldom makes explicit this underlying critique of the way in which France's educational and intellectual life works to repress and stigmatise the leisure and cultural practices of ordinary French people.

In Yonnet's most recent book, *Travail, loisir: temps libre et lien social* (1999), one encounters the same determination that one finds in Bromberger's volume to put forward a positive image of the current state of France and to defend its popular culture and leisure. In Yonnet's book, however, there is a totally explicit attack on the intellectual, political and media classes who, in his view, undermine France's sense of its own identity and worth and who express contempt for the lives and pleasures of its people. In fact, Yonnet's book shows him to have lost none of the anger against the intellectual elites which he had voiced so colourfully and provocatively back in 1987, in direct response to Finkielkraut's *La Défaite de la pensée*.[1] *Travail, loisir...* still has Yonnet arguing with Finkielkraut and others on the nature of popular culture but he clearly feels that the gap between intellectuals and ordinary people has since grown much wider than it was in the 1980s, now that television and the mass media have taken on an even greater importance in

---

1. 'Nous, barbares, allons déferler sur le quartier Latin, remplacer l'eau de la fontaine Saint-Michel par de la bière, et transformer les environs de la Sorbonne en un gigantesque Zénith, armé d'une sono de 250,000 watts et baptisé: "Polygone des zombis." Là, en prélude à nos fêtes dionysiaques, et par revanche tardive sur nos échecs scolaires de cancres, nous brûlerons Chateaubriand, Corneille (oui! oui!), et Jules Barbant d'Aurévilly en un immense auto-dafé (qui rappellera à quelques-uns le bon temps de la rue Guy-Lussac), sous le logo teutonique de Motörhead que nous aurons dressé sur la façade de la Sorbonne, tandis que, pour la énième fois, Keith Richards nous resservira le plus grand solo de guitare de l'histoire du rock'n roll, celui de *Sympathy for the Devil* (Stones), celui qui tue.' (Yonnet 1987, pp. 178-9).

French society. In Yonnet's opinion, France's intellectual classes are even more out
of step and even more incapable of understanding the nature of contemporary
popular culture than they ever were:

> *Une nouvelle fois, c'est la question de l'aptitude des intellectuels à rendre compte
> d'un monde qui n'est plus le leur, qui a relégué leurs rares interventions au-delà du
> prime-time, d'un monde qui les a abandonnés, sur lequel ils n'ont plus de prise et
> dont le fonctionnement leur échappe, qui est posée. (Yonnet 1999, pp. 198-9)*

According to Yonnet, nothing demonstrates this yawning gap between the
intelligentsia and the mass of ordinary people more than the continuing failure of
the intellectuals to understand how French people lead their lives and take their
pleasures. In *Travail, loisir …* Yonnet takes issue, for instance, with Gilles
Lipovetsky, author of several prominent studies of the postmodern condition of
French society,[1] whom he castigates for his analyses of postmodern humour.
According to Lipovetsky, laughter has disappeared from contemporary French
society and has been replaced by a thinner, more knowing, more cynical
'humorous code'. Yonnet picks out some of Lipovetsky's key generalisations in
order to expose them to his withering criticism:

> *Avec la société humoristique commence véritablement la phase de liquidation du rire:
> pour la première fois un dispositif fonctionne qui réussit à dissoudre progressivement
> la propension à rire [...] le rire s'éteint [...] nous sommes entrés dans une phase de
> paupérisation du rire [...]. C'est véritablement la capacité de rire qui désormais se
> trouve entamée, exactement comme l'hédonisme a entraîné un aplatissement de la
> volonté. (Yonnet 1999, p. 192)*

The fact that Lipovetsky can claim that modern French society has witnessed a
loss of 'will' leaves Yonnet completely flabbergasted:

> *La dernière assertion est tellement contraire à ce que nous savons du formidable
> déploiement des travaux volontaires et des activités personnelles en vue de satisfaire
> des fins hédoniques et de loisir, de la propension des agents sociaux à mobiliser à cet
> effet argent et énergie (songeons à l'entraînement sportif, à la préparation des voy-
> ages, des randonnées, au bricolage, au jardinage, aux collectionneurs, etc.), l'asser-
> tion est en un mot tellement étrange que nous serions fondés à nous demander tout
> d'abord à quelles conditions cela peut avoir un sens. (Yonnet 1999, p. 192)*

Yonnet's response is obviously to ask of Lipovetsky and other like-minded
intellectuals where they have been living all these years – and the answer is clearly
not in the modern France that Yonnet himself recognises, a France of which he
himself feels so much a part and from which he believes intellectuals such as
Lipovetsky still feel so remote. When he turns from energy to laughter, Yonnet is
equally astounded. Since, according to Yonnet, 'la fonction sociale du rire est de
célébrer un "être ensemble"'(Yonnet 1999, p. 203), it becomes obvious that
intellectuals such as Lipovetsky must occupy a position outside the national circle

---

1. See Lipovetsky (1983), (1987), (1992).

of sociability ('l'on peut sans grand risque supposer que Gilles Lipovetsky, en l'espèce, ne partageait pas les pratiques populaires du rire'), for only this can explain the failure of intellectuals to see the jokes and hear the laughter, which, contrary to Lipovetsky, Yonnet proclaims as loud and pervasive in modern French society:[1]

> A cerner le contemporain, à dresser un tableau général, à peser les faits de rire, à observer ce qui génère les effets de rire, on réalise: que la recherche du rire (le besoin d'en rire) est un fait majeur au moins de la société française; que la palette des genres de rires représentés est très ouverte; que le burlesque, le loufoque, le baroque, la farce, la satire, la pantomime, le calembour, la contrepèterie, la mascarade se côtoient, parfois s'assemblent et se combinent; qu'il existe une demande permanente et à peu près insatiable du mode de production du rire par l'imitation mode nouveau en tant qu'il est typique de l'ère audiovisuelle; que le rire s'en prend avec virulence aux personnages en place, aux moeurs politiques et médiatiques, voire aux fondements de la cité (le travail, l'argent, la famille, la compétition); qu'il est instrument de récréation, de connaissance, de libération, de protestation, de combat, voire de violence et d'intimidation [...] qu'il a des victimes (les maladroits, les Belges, les gros, les handicapés, les fonctionnaires, les homosexuels, les féministes, les flics, le clergé, les racistes, les alcooliques, les automobilistes, les chefs d'État d'Afrique noire, etc.) et des têtes de Turc (hommes et femmes de pouvoir...); que le sexe est une moquerie et une préoccupation centrale du rire; bref, qu'il y a une vraie politique contemporaine du rire développée autour du pôle dionysiaque du tohu-bohu. (Yonnet 1999, pp. 202-3)

Yonnet uses Bergson's definition of the mechanism and function of laughter in order to show its applicability to those of France's intellectuals who adopt a remote and judgemental stance towards the collective life of the French people. According to Bergson:

> Le rire [...] vise à "plier" les individus, à combattre la distance qu'ils pourraient prendre par rapport au groupe, à annihiler les tendances à la désocialisation. Il est "le châtiment d'une certaine raideur du corps, de l'esprit et du caractère, que la société voudrait encore éliminer pour obtenir de ses membres la plus grande élasticité et la plus haute sociabilité possibles." (Yonnet 1999, p. 205)

In Yonnet's view, comedy on television is now one of the major forces of social cohesion and the social experience of laughter is nurtured and reinforced by the constant repetition and replaying of comedy on television.

1. 'Thierry Le Luron, Coluche, Guy Bedos, Laurent Gerra, Bernard Haller, Michel Boujenah, Alex Métayer, Zouc, Sylvie Joly, Les Trois Jeanne, Smaïn, Didier Gustin, Bigard, Font et Val, Roland Magdane, Guy Montagné, Les Vamps, Bernard Mabille, Patrick Sébastien, Muriel Robin, Pierre Palmade, André Lamy, Laurent Ruquier, Chevallier et Laspales, Les Inconnus, Pierre Desproges, Raymond Devos, Popeck, Élie et Dieudonné, Yves Lecoq, Patrick Timsit [...], jamais les shows des comiques n'auront connu un tel succès au théâtre, dans les music-halls et les cabarets.' (Yonnet 1999, p. 207).

A la télévision, *le rire tapisse les programmes des créneaux horaires de grande écoute, quand près des deux tiers des Français ont toute chance de s'installer pour plus ou moins longtemps devant leur petit écran*, grosso modo *entre 19h.30 et 22h.30. (Yonnet 1999, p. 209)*

If the national community is the one that is forged every evening as people watch comedy in front of the television set, then, of course, intellectuals will for the most part not be members of it, nor will they understand what this community thinks and feels. Yonnet repeats his amazement at the gaps between intellectual tastes and the tastes of the French public – demonstrated time and again, for example, in the constant disparagement by television critics of two comic films which always attract massive audiences when they are shown on television *La Grande Vadrouille* and *La 7e Compagnie* (Yonnet 1999, p. 230). If, however, intellectuals were actually to tune in to TV comedy programmes, they would, according to Yonnet, become aware of the extent to which the mass of French people, when they are watching these programmes, are in fact participating in a mass act of resistance to the new 'moral order' imposed on them elsewhere in their lives.

Thus, when French people watched *Les Grosses Têtes* in their millions, they were glorying in the carnivalesque spectacle of the holding up to ridicule of the whole range of politically correct values:

Les Grosses Têtes est la seule émission, dans les années 1980, avec celle d'André Lang, où l'on peut se ficher directement de l'abbé Pierre et rire ouvertement de cette moquerie: c'est-à-dire son caractère libératoire et oxygénant. Les Grosses Têtes est une émission où l'on dit ce que la norme sociale, mais plus particulièrement médiatique, interdit de dire ou voudrait dissuader de penser, où prend forme et perce une réalité résistante de la société à l'ordre moral médiatique. C'est le décalage avec le discours de cet ordre moral qui provoque le rire, un rire de résistance populaire, un rire de défense, de dévoilement, de retour au réel des pratiques. Ce rire manifeste une résistance à la chape de plomb de la culture de la charité, une opposition à la culture jeune et plus précisément à celle de la "génération morale", à la culture "Monsieur Propre" du bon genre moderne (nouvelle cuisine, minceur, entretien physique, proféminisme, droits de l'homme et antiracisme), et l'attachement à des systèmes de différenciation menacés (par exemple, différenciation par le sexe ou l'alimentation). (Yonnet 1999, p. 221)

If, in Yonnet's view, French academics and intellectuals are the supporters of a new politically correct moral order in the areas of politics and popular culture, then foreign scholars of modern and contemporary France would appear to be running an even greater risk of fulfilling this role and they might, therefore, do well to heed the criticisms which Yonnet intended for internal consumption. There are, indeed, plentiful signs that British and American scholars of modern and contemporary France could be thought to be working in a sub-branch of the miserabilist and pessimistic industries of production of anti-racist and anti-nationalist discourses which Yonnet attacks in his books and articles. Foreign scholars of France are, of course, doubly disadvantaged (one might say doubly alienated) in that it is far more difficult, if not impossible, for them to be the kind of participant observers of contemporary French society whose testimony Yonnet solely respects. Neither embedded in French daily life, nor woven into the fabric of France's contemporary popular culture (or, even more significantly, its popular culture of the recent past), foreign scholars are in particular danger of having an abstract and distant relationship to everyday French cultural experience and of sharing the French intelligentsia's narrow political and cultural focus.

Bibliography

Bromberger, C. (1998) *Passions ordinaires: du match de football au concours de dictée*, Paris: Editions Bayard.

Finkielkraut, A. (1987) *La Défaite de la pensée*, Paris: Gallimard.

Karpik, L. (1993) 'Au centre du malaise', *Le Débat*, no. 75, mai-août, pp. 117-25.

Kolakowski, L. (1987) 'Le Débat du débat', *Le Débat*, no. 45, mai-septembre, p. 178.

Lipovetsky, G. (1983) *L'Ere du vide: essai sur l'individualisme contemporain*, Paris: Gallimard.

Lipovetsky, G. (1987) *L'Empire de l'éphémère: la mode et son destin dans les sociétés modernes*, Paris: Gallimard.

Lipovetsky, G. (1992) *Le Crépuscule du devoir: l'éthique indolore des nouveaux temps démocratiques*, Paris: Gallimard.

Ory, P. (1981) 'Comme de l'an quarante, dix années de retro Satanus', *Le Débat*, no.16, novembre, pp. 109ff.

Nora, P. (1984-92) *Les Lieux de mémoire*, Paris: Gallimard.

Nora, P. (1981) 'Un idéologue bien de chez nous', *Le Débat*, no. 13, juin, pp. 102ff.

Rigby, B. (1991) *Popular Culture in Modern France: a Study of Cultural Discourse*, London and New York: Routledge.

Rigby, B. (1998) 'Ethnology and Popular Culture: Christian Bromberger's *Le match de football*', *Australian Journal of French Studies*, vol. xxxv, no. 1, pp. 32-40.

Silverman, M. (2000) *Facing Postmodernity: Contemporary French Thought on Culture and Society*, London and New York: Routledge.

Todorov, T. (1996) *L'Homme dépaysé*, Paris: Seuil.

Wieviorka, M. (1993) 'Penser le malaise', *Le Débat*, no. 75, mai-août, pp. 126-31.

Yonnet, P. (1999) *Travail, loisir: temps libre et lien social*, Paris: Gallimard, 'Bibliothèque des sciences humaines'.

Yonnet, P. (1998) *Système des sports*, Paris: Gallimard, 'Bibliothèque des sciences humaines'.

Yonnet, P. (1996) 'Le Gréviste et le gouvernant: notes sur un mouvement', *Le Débat*, no. 89, mai-avril, pp. 56-70.

Yonnet, P. (1995) 'L'Entrée en désillusion', *Le Débat*, no. 83, janvier-février, pp. 121-30.

Yonnet, P. (1993) *Voyage au centre du malaise français: l'antiracisme et le roman national*, Paris: Gallimard.

Yonnet, P. (1992) 'La Conjonction des épuisements', *Le Débat*, no. 70, mai-août, pp. 205-8.

Yonnet, P. (1990) 'De la réversibilité dans les années 80', *Le Débat*, no. 60, mai-août, pp. 81-6.

Yonnet, P. (1988) 'Notre histoire', *Le Débat*, no. 50, mai-août, p. 1.

Yonnet, P. (1987) 'Sympathy for the débils', *Le Débat*, no. 45, mai-septembre, pp. 178-79.

Yonnet, P. (1986) 'L'Esthéthique rock', *Le Débat*, no. 40, mai-septembre, pp. 62-71.

Yonnet, P. (1985a) *Jeux, modes et masses: la société française et le moderne 1945-1985*, Paris: Gallimard, 'Bibliothèque des sciences humaines'.

Yonnet, P. (1985b) 'Des modes et des looks: le temps, le paraître et l'être', *Le Débat*, no. 34, mars, pp. 113-29.

Yonnet, P. (1985c) 'Mères porteuses, père écarté', *Le Débat*, no. 36, septembre, pp. 33-7.

Yonnet, P. (1984) 'La Société automobile', *Le Débat*, no. 31, septembre, pp. 128-48.

Yonnet, P. (1983) 'L'Homme aux chats: zoophilie et déshumanisation', *Le Débat*, no. 27, novembre, pp. 111-26.

Contributors

Gill Allwood is Senior Lecturer in French at Nottingham Trent University and author of *French Feminisms* (UCL 1998) and *Women and Politics in France* (Routledge 2000 with Khursheed Wadia). She is currently writing a book on gender and policy in France and articles on various aspects of gender and power relations.

Michael Kelly is Professor of French at Southampton University, UK. He is Associate Editor of the journal, *French Cultural Studies*, co-editor of the journal *Language and Intercultural Communication*, and joint editor of books *French Cultural Studies: an Introduction* (OUP, 1995) and *Pierre Bourdieu: Language, Culture and Education* (Bern, Peter Lang, 1999). He has published widely on French intellectual history, including books on Catholic, Marxist and Hegelian thought. He is currently completing a glossary of French culture and society for Arnold and a monograph on French intellectuals in 1945.

David Looseley is Senior Lecturer in French at the University of Leeds. He has published extensively on French cultural policy, institutions and discourses, including a major study entitled *The Politics of Fun: Cultural Policy and Debate in Contemporary France* (Berg, 1995). He is currently completing a book on French popular music and the music industry since 1945.

Enda McCaffrey is Senior Lecturer in French at Nottingham Trent University. His research interests cover nineteenth and twentieth-century French literature, and French cultural studies. He has written widely on the work of Octave Mirbeau and is the author of *Octave Mirbeau's Literary and Intellectual Evolution as a French Writer 1880-1914* (Mellen, 2000). He is currently working on a book on civil liberties in France, looking at the impact of the recent PaCS legislation.

John Marks is Reader in French at Nottingham Trent University. He has written widely on French thought, and is the author of *Gilles Deleuze: Vitalism and Multiplicity* (Pluto, 1998). He is also the co-editor of *Deleuze and Literature* (EUP, 2000). He is now working on a study of the notion of the event in post-war French thought.

Martin O'Shaughnessy is Principal lecturer in French at Nottingham Trent University. He has written widely on French cinema and is the author of *Jean Renoir* (Manchester University Press, 2000)

Brian Rigby is currently Professor of French at the University of Hull and Managing Editor of the journal *French Cultural Studies*. He is the author of *Popular Culture in Modern France: a Study of Cultural Discourse* (1991), editor of *French Literature, Thought and Culture in the 19th Century* (1993) and joint editor (with N. Hewitt) of *France and the Mass Media* (1991). He has published widely in the area of late 18th and early 19th century literary and cultural history, as well as in the field of modern cultural studies. He is now working on a study of English autobiography and autobiographical fiction.

Georges Salemohamed is Lecturer in French Studies at Loughborough University. He has published on French theory (including Derrida and Levinas), organisation culture, and is currently working on a study of the work of Léon Chestov.

Max Silverman is Professor of Modern French Studies at the University of Leeds. He is a specialist in the areas of immigration, race, nation and citizenship; the city; cultural theory and debates; and colonial and post-colonial theory and cultures. He has written two monographs, *Deconstructing the Nation: Immigration, Racism and Citizenship in Modern France* (Routledge, 1992) and *Facing Postmodernity: Contemporary French Thought on Culture and Society* (Routledge, 1999). He has also edited a collection of essays under the title *Race, Discourse and Power in France* (Avebury, 1991) and has published numerous chapters in books and journal articles on the above topics. At present he is editing a new collection of essays on Frantz Fanon's *Peau noire, masques blancs* for Manchester University Press.

Ben Taylor is Lecturer in Media and Cultural Studies in the Department of English and Media Studies at Nottingham Trent University. He has published elsewhere on the topic of food, and is currently completing a book with three colleagues on food and cultural studies.